JAMES WOOD is a staff writer at *The New Yorker* and a visiting lecturer at Harvard University. He is the author of *How Fiction Works,* as well as two essay collections, *The Broken Estate* and *The Irresponsible Self,* and a novel, *The Book Against God.*

Additional Praise for *The Fun Stuff*

"A more careful reader of sentences than any other reviewer now working . . . What Wood says of Tolstoy—he is 'masterful at the apprehension that forces a sudden reappraisal of reality'—could be said of Wood himself, if we substitute 'fiction' for 'reality.' Which is what we do, as he knows, all the time."   —*Chicago Tribune*

"Engaging . . . measured and assured . . . These essays [convey] the enthusiasm of a critic who is continually learning. Whether he is describing the delight of reading novels by Joseph O'Neill and Aleksandar Hemon, or the thrill of drumming in a rock band, there is a playfulness in Mr. Wood's writing that manages to be risky and reliable at once. . . . It is a pleasure to follow his education, and to learn something in turn."   —*The Economist*

"Wood has become an iconic figure. . . . [His essays] invariably model verbal richness and showcase the depth and breadth of his reading."
—*The Boston Globe*

"Wood's willingness to speak in the accent of literature brings his subjects wondrously alive and close to us."
—*Los Angeles Review of Books*

"The gift of the great critic is to be able to explain complex concepts to the reader in a manner that is neither bamboozling nor patronizing. . . . This is a book that's impossible to read without gaining a greater appreciation of what it means to write well, both in the case of the work under review and, just as pleasurably, the reviews themselves."   —*The Observer* (London)

"Wood's literary criticism recalls an era before academia and imported theory dominated, when men and women of letters held sway. . . . One of the finest critics around."
—*The Independent* (London)

"These essays are shot through with his characteristic light humor and moral seriousness, each expertly constructed paragraph rich with metaphorical insight. . . . *The Fun Stuff* is further evidence that when the telescope is perfectly calibrated, the rest of us, by comparison, are merely squinting in the dark."

—*The Telegraph* (London)

"A superb collection . . . [Wood is] a writer people need to read."

—*The Buffalo News* (Editors' Choice)

THE FUN STUFF

AND OTHER ESSAYS

JAMES WOOD

PICADOR   FARRAR, STRAUS AND GIROUX   NEW YORK

www.picadorusa.com
www.twitter.com/picadorusa • www.facebook.com/picadorusa
picadorbookroom.tumblr.com

Picador® is a U.S. registered trademark and is used by Farrar, Straus and Giroux under license from Pan Books Limited.

For book club information, please visit www.facebook.com/picadorbookclub or e-mail marketing@picadorusa.com.

These essays originally appeared, in slightly different form, in *The New Yorker*, the *London Review of Books*, and *The New Republic*.

Grateful acknowledgment is made for permission to reprint lyrics from the song "Sea and Sand," by Pete Townshend. Copyright © 1973 ABKCO Music, Inc. (BMI), Songs of Windswept Tunes, Inc. (BMI), SUOLUBAF Music (BMI), Towser Tunes, Inc. (BMI). All rights reserved. Used by permission of Universal Music Publishing Group.

Designed by Jonathan D. Lippincott

The Library of Congress has cataloged the Farrar, Straus and Giroux edition as follows:

Wood, James, 1965–
   The fun stuff, and other essays / James Wood. — 1st ed.
     p.   cm.
   ISBN 978-0-374-15956-6
   I. Title.
  AC8 .W8155 2012
  824'.92—dc23

                    2011052184

Picador ISBN 978-1-250-03783-1

Picador books may be purchased for educational, business, or promotional use. For information on bulk purchases, please contact Macmillan Corporate and Premium Sales Department at 1-800-221-7945, extension 5442, or write specialmarkets@macmillan.com.

First published in the United States by Farrar, Straus and Giroux

First Picador Edition: November 2013

10 9 8 7 6 5 4 3 2 1

For Susanna Kaysen and John Daniels
and, as ever, for C.D.M.

CONTENTS

The Fun Stuff: Homage to Keith Moon   3
W. G. Sebald's *Austerlitz*   18
Kazuo Ishiguro's *Never Let Me Go*   30
Thinking: Norman Rush   39
Cormac McCarthy's *The Road*   52
Edmund Wilson   66
Aleksandar Hemon   91
Beyond a Boundary: *Netherland* as Postcolonial Novel   102
Wounder and Wounded   117
Robert Alter and the King James Bible   130
Tolstoy's *War and Peace*   145
Marilynne Robinson   162
Lydia Davis   171
Containment: Trauma and Manipulation in Ian McEwan   182
Richard Yates   194
George Orwell's Very English Revolution   206
"Unfathomable!" (Mikhail Lermontov)   229
Thomas Hardy   243
Geoff Dyer   258
Paul Auster's Shallowness   267

"Reality Examined to the Point of Madness": László
    Krasznahorkai   279
Ismail Kadare   292
English Muddle: Alan Hollinghurst   309
Life's White Machine: Ben Lerner   322
Packing My Father-in-Law's Library   329

Acknowledgments   341

THE FUN STUFF

THE FUN STUFF: HOMAGE TO KEITH MOON

I had a traditional musical education, in a provincial English cathedral town. I was sent off to an ancient piano teacher with the requisite halitosis, who lashed with a ruler at my knuckles as if they were wasps; I added the trumpet a few years later and had lessons with a younger, cheerier man, who told me that the best way to make the instrument "sound" was to imagine spitting paper pellets down the mouthpiece at the school bully. I sang daily in the cathedral choir, an excellent grounding in sight-reading and performance. I still play the piano and the trumpet.

But what I really wanted to do, as a little boy, was play the drums, and of those different ways of making music, only playing the drums still makes me feel like a little boy. A friend's older brother had a drum kit, and as a twelve-year-old I gawped at the spangled shells of wood and skin, and plotted how I might get to hit them, and make a lot of noise. It wouldn't be easy. My parents had no time for "all that thumping about," and the prim world of ecclesiastical and classical music, which meant so much to me, detested rock. But I waited until the drums' owner was off at school and sneaked into the attic, where they gleamed, fabulously inert, and over the next few years I taught myself how to play them. Sitting behind the drums was also like a fantasy of driving (the other great prepubescent ambition), with my feet established on two pedals, bass drum and hi-hat, and the willing dials staring back at me like a blank dashboard . . .

Noise, speed, rebellion: everyone secretly wants to play the drums, because hitting things, like yelling, returns us to the innocent violence of childhood. Music makes us want to dance, to register rhythm on and with our bodies. So the drummer and the conductor are the luckiest of all musicians, because they are closest to dancing. And in drumming, how childishly close the connection is between the dancer and the dance! When you blow down an oboe, say, or pull a bow across a string, an infinitesimal, barely perceptible hesitation—the hesitation of vibration—separates the act and the sound; for trumpeters, the simple voicing of a quiet middle C is more fraught than very complex passages, because that brass tube can be sluggish in its obedience. But when a drummer needs to make a drum sound, he just . . . hits it. The stick or hand comes down, and the skin bellows. The narrator of Thomas Bernhard's novel *The Loser*, a pianist crazed with dreams of genius and obsessed with Glenn Gould, expresses the impossible longing to *become* the piano, to be at one with it. When you play the drums, you *are* the drums. "Le tom-tom, c'est moi," as Wallace Stevens put it.

The drummer who *was* the drums, when I was a boy, was the Who's Keith Moon, though he was already dead by the time I first heard him. He *was* the drums not because he was the most technically accomplished of drummers, but because his many-armed, joyous, semaphoring lunacy suggested a man possessed by the antic spirit of drumming. He was pure, irresponsible, restless childishness. At the end of early Who concerts, as Pete Townshend smashed his guitar, Moon would kick his drums and stand on them and hurl them around the stage, and this seems a logical extension not only of the basic premise of drumming, which is to hit things, but an inevitable extension of Moon's drumming, which was to hit things exuberantly. In the band's very early days, the managers of clubs would complain to Townshend about his drummer. We like you guys, they would say, but get rid of that madman on the drums, he's too loud. To which Moon succinctly replied: "I can't play quiet, I'm a rock drummer."

The Who had extraordinary rhythmic vitality, and it died when Keith Moon died, on September 7, 1978. I had hardly ever heard any rock music when I first listened to albums like *Quadrophenia* and *Who's Next*. My notion of musical volume and power was inevitably circumscribed by my fairly sheltered, austerely Christian upbringing—I got off on classical or churchy things like the brassy last bars of William Walton's First Symphony, or the chromatic last movement of the *Hammerklavier* Sonata, or the way the choir bursts in at the start of Handel's anthem *Zadok the Priest*, or the thundering thirty-two-foot bass pipes of Durham Cathedral's organ, and the way the echo, at the end of a piece, took seven seconds to dissolve in that huge building. Those are not to be despised, but nothing had prepared me for the ferocious energy of the Who. The music enacted the Mod rebellion of its lyrics: "Hope I die before I get old"; "Meet the new boss, same as the old boss"; "Dressed right, for a beach fight"; "There's a millionaire above you, / And you're under his suspicion." Pete Townshend's hard, tense suspended chords seem to scour the air around them; Roger Daltrey's singing was a young man's fighting swagger, an incitement to some kind of crime; John Entwistle's incessantly mobile bass playing was like someone running away from the scene of the crime; and Keith Moon's drumming, in its inspired vandalism, was the crime itself.

Most rock drummers, even very good and inventive ones, are timekeepers. There is a space for a fill or a roll at the end of a musical phrase, but the beat has primacy over the curlicues. In a regular 4/4 bar, the bass drum sounds the first beat, the snare the second, the bass drum again hits the third (often with two eighth notes at this point), and then the snare hits the bar's final beat. This results in the familiar "boom-DA, boom-boom-DA" sound of most rock drumming. A standard-issue drummer, playing along, say, to the Beatles' "Carry That Weight," would keep his 4/4 beat steady through the line "Boy, you're gonna carry that weight, carry that weight, a long time," until the natural break, which comes at the end of the phrase, where, just after the word "time," a wordless, two-beat half-bar readies itself for the repeated chorus. In that half-bar, there might be space for a quick roll, or a roll and a triplet, or something fancy with snare and hi-hat—really, any variety of filler. The filler is *the fun stuff,* and it could be said, without much exaggeration, that nearly all the fun stuff in drumming takes place in those two empty beats between the end of a phrase and the start of another. Ringo Starr, who interpreted his role fairly modestly, does nothing much in that two-beat space: mostly, he just provides eight even, straightforward sixteenth notes (da-da-da-da / da-da-da-da). In a good cover version of the song, Phil Collins, an extremely sophisticated drummer who was never a modest performer with Genesis, does a tight roll that begins with featherlight delicacy on a tom-tom and ends more firmly on his snare, before going back to the beat. But whatever their stylistic differences, the modest and the sophisticated drummer share an understanding that there is a proper space for keeping the beat, and a much smaller space for departing from it, like a time-out area in a classroom. The difference is just that the sophisticated drummer is much more often in time-out, and is always busily showing off to the rest of the class while he is there.

Keith Moon ripped all this up. There is no time-out in his drumming, because there is no time-in. It is *all fun stuff.* The first principle of Moon's drumming was that drummers do not exist to keep the beat. He did keep the beat, of course, and very well, but he did it by every method except the traditional one. Drumming is repetition, as is rock music generally, and Moon clearly found repetition dull. So he played the drums like no one else—and not even like himself. I mean that no two bars of Moon's playing ever sound the same; he is in revolt against consistency, he is always vandalizing repetition. Everyone else in the band gets to improvise, so why should the drummer be nothing more than a condemned metronome? He saw himself as a soloist playing with an ensemble of other soloists. It follows from this that the drummer will be playing a line of music, just as, say, the guitarist does, with undulations and crescendos and leaps. It further follows that the snare drum and the bass drum, traditionally the ball and chain of rhythmic imprisonment, are no more interesting than any of the other drums in the kit;

and that you will need lots of those other drums. Lots and lots. By the mid-1970s, when Moon's kit was said to be "the biggest in the world"—and what a deliciously absurd conceit, anyway!—he had two bass drums and at least twelve tom-toms, arrayed in stacks like squadrons of spotlights; he looked like a cheerful boy who had built elaborate fortifications for the sole purpose of destroying them. But he needed all those drums, as a flute needs all its stops or a harp its strings, so that his tremendous bubbling cascades, his liquid journeys, could be voiced: he needed not to run out of drums as he ran around them.

Average musical performance, like athletic prowess and viticulture—and perhaps novel writing?—has probably improved in the last century. Nowadays, more and more pianists can brilliantly run off some Chopin or Rachmaninoff in a concert hall, and the guy at the local drum shop is probably technically more adept than Keith Moon was. YouTube, which is a kind of permanent Special Olympics for show-offs, is full of young men wreaking double-jointed virtuosity on fabulously complex drum kits rigged up like artillery ranges. But so what? They can also backflip into their jeans from great heights and parkour across Paris. Moon disliked drum solos and did not perform them; the only one I have seen is pretty bad, a piece of anti–performance art—Moon sloppy and mindless, apparently drunk or stoned or both, and almost collapsing into the drums while he pounds them like pillows. He may have lacked the control necessary to sustain a long, complex solo; more likely, he needed the kinetic adventures of the Who to provoke him into his own. His cheerful way of conceding this was his celebrated remark that "I'm the best Keith Moon–style drummer in the world." Which was also a way of saying, "I'm the best Who-style drummer in the world."

Keith Moon–style drumming is a lucky combination of the artful and artless. To begin at the beginning: his drums always sounded good. He hit them nice and hard, and tuned the bigger tom-toms low (not for him the little eunuch toms of Kenney Jones, who palely succeeded him in the Who, after Moon's death). He kept his snare pretty "dry." This isn't a small thing. The talentless three-piece jazz combo at your local hotel ballroom—dinner-jacketed old-timers hacking through the old favorites—almost certainly features a so-called drummer whose sticks are used so lightly that they barely embarrass the skins, and whose snare—wet, buzzy, loose—sounds like a repeated sneeze. A good dry snare, properly struck, is a bark, a crack, a report. How a drummer hits the snare, and how it sounds, can determine a band's entire dynamic. Groups like Supertramp and the Eagles seem soft, in large part, because the snare is so drippy and mildly used (and not just because elves are apparently squeezing the singers' testicles).

There are three great albums by the Who, and these are also the three greatest Moon records: *Live at Leeds* (1970), a recording of an explosive concert at Leeds University on February 14, 1970, generally considered one of the greatest live albums in rock; *Who's Next* (1971), the most famous Who album; and *Quadrophenia* (1973), a kind of successor to *Tommy*, a "rock opera" that nostalgically celebrates the 1960s Mod culture that had provoked and nourished the band in its earlier days. On these are such songs as "Substitute," "My Generation," "See Me, Feel Me/Listening to You," "Won't Get Fooled Again," "Baba O'Riley," "Bargain," "The Song Is Over," "The Real Me," "5.15," "Sea and Sand," and "Love, Reign o'er Me." There is no great difference between the live concert recordings and the studio songs—all of them are full of improvisation and structured anarchy, fluffs and misses; all of them seem to have the rushed gratitude of something achieved only once. From which emerges the second great principle of Moon's drumming: namely, that one is always performing, not recording, and that making mistakes is simply part of the locomotion of vitality. (In the wonderful song "The Dirty Jobs," on *Quadrophenia*, you can hear Moon accidentally knock his sticks together three separate times while traveling around the kit. Most drummers would be horrified to be caught out on tape like this.)

For Moon, this vitality meant trying to shape oneself to the changing dynamics of the music, listening as much to the percussive deviations of the bass line as to the steady, obvious line of the lead singer. As a result, it is impossible to separate him from the music the Who made. The story goes that, in 1968, Jimmy Page wanted John Entwistle on bass and Keith Moon on drums for his new band; and, as sensational as this group might have been, it would not have sounded either like Led Zeppelin or the Who. If Led Zeppelin's drummer, John Bonham, were substituted for Moon on "Won't Get Fooled Again," the song would lose half its passionate propulsion, half its wild excess; if Moon sat in for Bonham on "Good Times, Bad Times," the tight stability of that piece would instantly evaporate.

Bonham's drumming sounds as if he has thought about phrasing; he never overreaches himself, because he seems to have so perfectly measured the relationship between rhythmic order and rhythmic deviation: his superb but tightly limited breaks on the snare, and his famously rapid double strokes on the bass drum, are constantly played against the unvarying solidity of his hi-hat, which keeps a steady single beat throughout the bars. (In a standard 4/4 bar, the hi-hat sounds the four whole beats, or perhaps sounds eight beats in eighth notes.) That is the "Bonham sound," heard in the celebrated long solo—one of devilish complexity—in "Moby Dick," on the live album *The Song Remains the Same*. Everything is judged, and rightly placed: astonishing order. Moon's drumming, by contrast, is about putting things in the wrong place: the appearance of astonishing disorder. You can copy Bonham exactly; but to copy Moon would be to bottle his spilling energy, which is much harder.

The third great Moon principle, of packing as much as possible into a single bar of music, produces the extraordinary variety of his playing. He seems to be hungrily reaching for everything at once. Take, for instance, the bass drum and the cymbal. Generally speaking, drummers strike these with respectable monotony. You hit the crash cymbal at the end of a drum roll, as a flourish, but also as a kind of announcement that time-out has, boringly enough, ended, and that the beat must go back to work. Moon does something strange with both instruments. He tends to "ride" his bass drum: he keeps his foot hovering over the bass drum pedal as a nervous driver might keep a foot on a brake, and strikes the drum often, sometimes continuously throughout a bar. When he breaks to do a roll around the toms, he will keep the bass drum going simultaneously, so that the effect is of two drummers playing together. Meanwhile, he delights in hitting his cymbals as often as humanly possible, and off the beat—just before or after the logical moment— rather as jazz and big-band drummers do. The effect of all these cymbals being struck is of someone shouting out at unexpected moments while waiting in line—a yammer of exclamation marks. (Whereas his habit of entering a song by first crashing a cymbal and then ripping around the kit is like someone bursting into a quiet room and shouting: "I'm here!")

So alive and free is this drumming that one tends to emphasize its exuberance at the expense of its complexity. But the playing on songs like "Won't Get Fooled Again" or "Bargain" or "Love, Reign o'er Me" or "The Song Is Over" is extremely complex: in addition to the intricate cymbal work, Moon is constantly flicking off little triplets (sometimes on the toms, but sometimes with his feet, by playing the two bass drums together); using a technique known as the paradiddle to play one tom against another; and doing press rolls and double-stroke rolls (methods by which, essentially, you bounce the sticks on the drum to get them to strike faster notes), and irregular flams on the snare drum (a flam involves hitting the drum with the two sticks not simultaneously but slightly staggered, and results in a sound more like "blat" than "that"). New technology allows listeners to isolate a song's individual players, and the astonishing isolated drum tracks from "Won't Get Fooled Again" and "Behind Blue Eyes" can be found on YouTube. On "Won't Get Fooled Again," the drumming is staggeringly vital, with Moon at once rhythmically tight and massively spontaneous. On both that song and "Behind Blue Eyes," you can hear him do something that was instinctive, probably, but which is hardly ever attempted in ordinary rock drumming: breaking for a fill, Moon fails to stop at the obvious end of the musical phrase and continues with his rolling break, over the line and into the start of the next phrase. In poetry, this failure to stop at the end of the line, this challenge to metrical closure, this desire *to get more in*, is called enjambment. Moon is the drummer of enjambment.

For me, this playing is like an ideal sentence of prose, a sentence I have always wanted to write and never quite had the confidence to: a long, passionate onrush, formally controlled and joyously messy, propulsive but digressively self-interrupted, attired but disheveled, careful and lawless, right and wrong. (You can encounter such sentences in Lawrence's prose, in Bellow's, sometimes in David Foster Wallace's.) Such a sentence would be a breaking out, an escape. And drumming has always represented for me that dream of escape, when the body forgets itself, surrenders its awful self-consciousness. I taught myself the drums, but for years I was so busy being a good boy that I lacked the courage to own any drums. One could timidly admit to playing them, only if that meant that one never actually played them. At school, I did play in a rock band, but I kept the fact very quiet. The kids I played rock music with did not overlap with the world of classical music. Drumming was a notional add-on, a supplement to the playing of "proper" instruments, a merely licensed rebellion. At school, the classical music path was the scholastic path. Choir school was like being at conservatory— daily rehearsal and performance. And then, later, as a teenager, to work hard at the piano, to sing in the choir, to play the trumpet in a youth orchestra, to pass exams in music theory, to study sonata form in Beethoven, to sit for a music scholarship, to talk to one's parents about Bach (or even, daringly, the Beatles!), to see the London Symphony Orchestra at the Albert Hall, even just to fall asleep during *Aida*—all this was *approved*, was part of being a good student. Nowadays, I see schoolkids bustling along the sidewalk, their large instrument cases strapped to them like diligent coffins, and I know their weight of obedience. Happy obedience, too: that cello or French horn brings lasting joy, and a repertoire more demanding and subtle than rock music's. But fuck the laudable ideologies, as Roth's Mickey Sabbath puts it: subtlety is not rebellion, and subtlety is not freedom, and sometimes it is rebellious freedom that one wants, and only rock music can deliver it. And sometimes one despises oneself, in near middle age, for still being such a merely good student.

Georges Bataille has some haunting words (in *Erotism*) about how the workplace is the scene of our domestication and repression: it is where we are forced to put away our Dionysianism. The crazy sex from the night before is as if forgotten; the drunken marital argument of the weekend is erased; the antic children have disappeared; all the writhing, passionate music of life is turned off; and the excremental body is fraudulently clothed—a false bourgeois order dresses you, and the sack and quick penury await you if you don't obey. But Bataille might also have mentioned school, for school is work, too, work before the adult workplace, and school tutors the adolescent in repression and the rectitude of the bourgeois order, at the very moment in life when, temperamentally and biologically, one is most Dionysiac and most enraged by the hypocritical ordinances of the parental league.

So adolescents quickly get split in two, with an inner and outer self, a lawless sprite inside and a lawful ambassador outside: rock music, or your first sexual relationship, or reading, or writing poetry, or probably all four at once—why not?—represent the possibilities for inward escape. And playing rock is different again from playing classical music, or from writing poetry or painting. In all these other arts, though there may be trancelike moments and even stages of wildness and excess, the pressure of creating lasting forms demands discipline and silence, a charged, concentrated precision; mindful of Pascal's severe aphorism about the importance of staying quietly in a room, one does just that—one *did* just that, even at the age of sixteen—and stares at the sheet of paper, even if the words are not coming. Writing and reading, beautiful as they are, still carry with them the faintest odor of the exam room. (It is exam-silent in the room where I write these words, and how terrible, in a way, is this disjunction between literary expression and the violence of its content!) Rock music, though, is noise, improvisation, collaboration, theater, exuberance, showing off, truancy, pantomime, aggression, bliss, tranced collectivity. It is not concentration so much as fission.

Imagine, then, the allure of the Who, whose vandalizing velocity was such an incitement to the adolescent's demon sprite: "I'm wet and I'm cold, / But thank God I ain't old," sang young Roger Daltrey on *Quadrophenia*, in a song about a "Mod" teenager (named Jimmy, no less) who gets thrown out of his home:

> Here by the sea and sand
> Nothing ever goes as planned
> I just couldn't face going home.
> It was such a drag on my own.
> They finally threw me out.
> My mum got drunk on stout.
> My dad couldn't stand on two feet
> As he lectured about morality.

It is no accident that punk got a fair amount of its inspiration from the Who (the Sex Pistols often performed "Substitute"), or that, a generation later, a band like Pearl Jam would devotedly cover "Love, Reign o'er Me." (Or that Chad Smith, the volcanic drummer of the Red Hot Chili Peppers, has cited Moon as an influence.) Here was a band that, in one obvious way, embodied success, but that, in a less obvious way, dared failure—I mean the large amount of improvisation in their songs, the risky, sometimes loose, excess of their concert performances, the violent earnestness of so many of the lyrics. And the epicenter of this successful failure, this man who wanted to pack as much of *the fun stuff* into his playing as humanly possible, was Keith Moon.

The Who were a kind of performance-art band: there was plenty of calculation amid the carelessness. Pete Townshend was a graduate of the Ealing art school (whose other musical alumni from the 1960s were Freddie Mercury and Ronnie Wood) and has sometimes claimed that the idea of smashing his guitar onstage was partly inspired by Gustav Metzger's "auto-destructive art" movement. That high tone is quite Townshendian. But in one way, it is hard not to think of Keith Moon's life as a perpetual "happening"; a gaudy, precarious, self-destructing art installation, whose gallery placard simply reads: "The Rock-and-Roll Life, Late Twentieth Century." In a manner that is also true of his drumming, he seemed to live at once naively and self-consciously: utterly spontaneous in his scandalous misbehavior, and yet also aware that this is how one *should* live if one is a famous and rich rock musician. His parody is very hard to separate from his originality; his parody *is* his originality. This is one of the most charming elements of his posture behind the drum kit: he is always clowning around—standing up sometimes, at other times puffing out his cheeks like Dizzy Gillespie, grimacing and grinning like a fool in some opera buffa, twirling his sticks, doing silly phantom rolls just above the skins of the drums. A child might think that Moon was a circus performer. His drumming, like his life, was a serious joke.

Nowadays, Moon would probably be classed as having both ADHD and bipolar disorder; fortunately for the rest of us, he grew up in postwar, nontherapeutic Britain and medicated himself with booze, illegal drugs, and illegal drumming. Born into a modest, working-class household in north London in 1946, Moon had a paltry education. He was restless, hyperactive, and often played to the gallery. An art teacher described him as "retarded artistically, idiotic in other respects," and the authorities were doubtless relieved when he left school at the age of fifteen. "You never felt, 'One day he is going to be famous,'" a friend told Tony Fletcher, Moon's biographer. "You felt more likely that he was going to end up in prison."

He had little formal training on the drums. As Gogol's brilliant prose, or Richard Burton's swaggering acting, embodies the temperamental exhibitionism of its creator, so Moon's playing is an extension of his theatrical hyperactivity. His mother noticed that he got bored easily and quickly lost interest in his train set or Meccano. Throughout his short life, he was seemingly addicted to practical jokes: he set off cherry bombs in hotels, dressed up as Adolf Hitler or Noël Coward, rode a wheelchair down an airport staircase, smashed up hotel rooms, drove a car into a swimming pool, and got arrested for breaching the peace. On planes, Moon might do his "chicken soup" routine, which involved carrying a can of Campbell's chicken soup on board, emptying it, unseen, into a sick bag, and then pretending to retch violently. At which point he "would raise it, and pour the sicklike soup back into his mouth, offering up a hearty sigh of relief while innocently inquiring of fellow passengers what they found so disgusting." There was a relentlessness, a curious, drunken patience, to this theatricalism, which often needed preparation and forethought, and certainly demanded a kind of addicted commitment. "Keith wore the Nazi uniform like something of a second skin, donning it intermittently for the next six or seven years," writes Tony Fletcher. *Six or seven years*. His alcoholism and coke snorting were certainly addictions, but perhaps they were merely the solvents needed to maintain the larger, primal addiction to joking and playacting.

Performance is a way of sublimely losing oneself, and there is a sense in which Moon as drummer was another role alongside Moon as Hitler, Moon as Noël Coward, Moon as arsonist, Moon as sick-bag buffoon, and Moon as crazy "rock star." ("I don't give a damn about a Holiday Inn room," he grandly said after some act of vandalism. "There's ten million of them exactly the same.") But "role" suggests choice, freedom, calculation, whereas these roles don't seem to have been chosen so much as depended on. Or to put it another way: despite all the gaiety and partying, the only performance that seems to have truly liberated Moon was the one he enacted behind the drum kit. I often think of Moon and Glenn Gould together, despite their great differences. Both started performing as very young men (Moon was seventeen when he began playing with the Who, Gould twenty-two when he made his first great recording of *The Goldberg Variations*); both were idiosyncratic, revolutionary performers for whom spontaneity and eccentricity were important elements (for instance, both enjoyed singing and shouting while playing); both men had exuberant, pantomimic fantasy lives—Gould wrote about Petula Clark's "Downtown," and appeared on Canadian television and radio in the guise of invented comic personae such as Karlheinz Klopweisser and Sir Nigel Twitt-Thornwaite,

"the Dean of British conductors"; both were gregarious and essentially solitary; neither man practiced very much (at least, Gould
claimed not to practice, and it is impossible to imagine Moon having the patience or sobriety to practice); and with both men, all the
other performing (Gould's hand washing and coat wearing and
melodramatic, pill-popping hypochondria) has the slightly desperate
quality of mania—except the performance behind the instrument,
which has the joyous freedom of true escape and self-dissolution:
Gould *becomes* the piano, Moon *becomes* the drums.

For both Moon and Gould, the performer's life was very
short—Gould abandoned concert performance at the age of thirty-
one; Moon was dead by the age of thirty-two and had not played
well for years. He had perhaps eight really great drumming years,
between 1968 and 1976. Throughout this period, he was ingesting
ludicrous volumes of drink and drugs. There are stories of him
swallowing twenty or thirty pills at once. In San Francisco, in 1973,
he had taken so many depressants (perhaps to come down from a
high, or to deal with preconcert nerves) that, after slopping his way
through several songs, he collapsed and had to be taken to the hospital. When his stomach was pumped, it was found to contain quantities of PCP, a drug described by Fletcher as "used to put agitated
monkeys and gorillas to sleep." What magically happened onstage,
while Moon was being carted away, was incised, years ago, on my
teenage cerebellum. Pete Townshend asked the crowd whether anyone could come up and play the drums. Scott Halprin, a nineteen-
year-old, and presumably soon to be the most envied teenager in
America, got onto the stage and played with the Who. "Everything
was locked into place," Halprin later said of the gargantuan drum
kit; "anyplace you could hit there would be something there. All the
cymbals overlapped."

Both Moon and Gould were rather delicate, even handsome
young men who coarsened with age and developed a thickness of
feature, an almost simian rind. At twenty, Moon was slight and sweet,
with a bowl of black hair upended on his head, and dark, dopey
eyes, and the arched eyebrows of a clown. By the end of his life, he

looked ten years older than he was—puffy, heavy, his features no longer sweetly clownish but slightly villainous—Bill Sykes, played by Moon's old drinking friend Oliver Reed, the arched eyebrows now thicker and darker, seemingly painted on, as if he had become a caricature of himself. Friends were shocked by his appearance. He was slower and less inventive, less vital, on the drums; the album *Who Are You*, his last record, attests to the decline. Perhaps no one was very surprised when he died, from a massive overdose of the drug Heminevrin, a sedative prescribed for alcohol withdrawal symptoms. "He's gone and done it," Townshend told Roger Daltrey. Thirty-two pills were found in his stomach, and the equivalent of a pint of beer in his blood. His girlfriend, who found him, told a coroner's court that she had often seen him pushing pills down his throat, without liquid. Almost exactly two years later, John Bonham died from asphyxiation, after hours of drinking vodka. He was less than a year older than Moon.

There are two famous Glenn Gould recordings of *The Goldberg Variations*: the one he made at the age of twenty-two, and the one he made at the age of fifty-one, just before he died. The opening aria of that piece, the lucid, ornate melody that Gould made his own, sounds very different in each recording. In the young man's version, the aria is fast, sweet, running clear like water. In the middle-aged man's recording, the aria is half as fast, the notes so magnetically separated that they seem almost unrelated to one another. The first aria is cocky, exuberant, optimistic, vital, fun, sound-filled; the second aria is reflective, seasoned, wintry, grieving, silence-haunted. These two arias stand facing each other, separated by almost thirty years, as the gates of a life. I prefer the second version; but when I listen to the second, how I want to *be* the first!

W. G. SEBALD'S *AUSTERLITZ*

In the summer of 1967, a man who remains unnamed but who resembles the author W. G. Sebald, is visiting Belgium. At the Centraal Station in Antwerp, he sees a fellow traveler, with fair, curiously wavy hair, who is wearing heavy walking boots, workman's trousers made of blue calico, and a well-made but antiquated jacket. He is intently studying the room and taking notes. This is Jacques Austerlitz. The two men fall into conversation, have dinner at the station restaurant, and continue to talk into the night. Austerlitz is a voluble scholar—he explicates the slightly grotesque display of colonial confidence represented by Antwerp's Centraal Station, and talks generally about the history of fortification. It is often our mightiest projects, he suggests, that most obviously betray the degree of our insecurity.

Austerlitz and the Sebald-like narrator meet again—a few months later, in Brussels; then, later still, on the promenade at Zeebrugge. It emerges that Jacques Austerlitz is a lecturer at an institute of art history in London, and that his scholarship is unconventional. He is obsessed with monumental public buildings, like law courts and prisons, railway stations and lunatic asylums, and his investigations have swollen beyond any reasonable raison d'être, "proliferating in his hands into endless preliminary sketches for a study, based entirely on his own views, of the family likeness between all these buildings." For a while, the narrator visits Austerlitz regularly in London, but they fall out of touch until 1996, when he happens to meet Austerlitz again, this time at Liverpool Street Station. Austerlitz explains that only recently has he learned the story of his life, and he needs the kind of listener that the narrator had been in Belgium, thirty years before.

And so Austerlitz begins the story that will gradually occupy the rest of the book: how he was brought up in a small town in Wales, with foster parents; how he discovered, as a teenager, that his true name was not Dafydd Elias but Jacques Austerlitz; how he went to Oxford, and then into academic life. Though clearly a refugee, for many years Austerlitz was unable to discover the precise nature and contour of his exile until experiencing a visionary moment, in the late 1980s, in the Ladies' Waiting Room of Liverpool Street Station. Standing transfixed for perhaps hours, in a room hitherto unknown to him (and about to be demolished, to enable an expansion of the Victorian station), he feels as if the space contains "all the hours of my past life, all the suppressed and extinguished fears and wishes I had ever entertained." He suddenly sees, in his mind's eye, his foster parents, "but also the boy they had come to meet," and he realizes that he must have arrived at this station a half century ago.

It is not until the spring of 1993, and having suffered a nervous breakdown in the meantime, that Austerlitz has another visionary experience, this time in a Bloomsbury bookshop. The bookseller is listening to the radio, which features two women discussing the summer of 1939, when, as children, they had come on the ferry *Prague* to England, as part of the Kindertransport: "Only then did I know beyond any doubt that these fragments of memory were part of my own life as well," Austerlitz tells the narrator. The mere mention of the name "Prague" impels Austerlitz to the Czech capital, where he eventually discovers his old nanny, Vera Ryšanová, and uncovers the stories of his parents' abbreviated lives. His father, Maximilian Aychenwald, escaped the Nazis in Prague, by leaving for Paris; but, we learn at the end of the book, he was eventually captured and interned in late 1942, in the French camp of Gurs, in the foothills of the Pyrenees. His mother, Agáta Austerlitz, stayed on in Prague, insouciantly confident of her prospects, but was rounded up and sent to the Terezín ghetto (better known by its German name of Theresienstadt) in December 1942. Of the final destination of Maximilian and Agáta we are not told, but can easily infer the worst: Vera tells us only that Agáta was "sent east" from Terezín, in September 1944.

This short recital, poignant though its content is, represents a kind of vandalism to Sebald's beautiful novel, and I offer it only in the spirit of orientation. It leaves out, most important, all the ways in which Sebald contrives *not* to offer an ordinary, straightforward recital. For what is delicate is how Sebald makes Austerlitz's story a broken, recessed enigma, whose meaning the reader must impossibly rescue. Though Austerlitz, and hence the reader, too, is involved in a journey of detection, the book really represents the deliberate frustration of detection, the perpetuation of an enigma. By the end of the novel, we certainly know a great deal about Jacques Austerlitz—about the tragic turns of his life, his family background, about his obsessions and anxieties and breakdowns—but it can't be said that we really know him. A life has been filled in for us, but not a self. He remains as unknowable at the end as he was at the beginning, and indeed seems to quit the book as randomly and as unexpectedly as he entered it.

Sebald deliberately layers his narrative, so that Austerlitz is difficult to get close to. Jacques tells his story to the narrator, who then tells his story to us, thus producing the book's distinctive repetitive tagging, a kind of parody of the source attribution we encounter in a newspaper: almost every page has a "said Austerlitz" on it, and sometimes the filters of narration are thicker still, as in the following phrase, which reports a story of Maximilian's, via Vera Ryšanová, via Austerlitz, and collapses the three names: "From time to time, so Vera recollected, said Austerlitz, Maximilian would tell the tale of how once, after a trade union meeting in Treplitz in the early summer of 1933 . . ." Sebald borrowed this habit of repetitive attribution from the Austrian writer Thomas Bernhard, who also influ-

enced Sebald's diction of extremism. Almost every sentence in this
book is a cunning combination of the quiet and the loud: "As usual
when I go down to London on my own," the narrator tells us in a
fairly typical passage, "a kind of dull despair stirred within me in
that December morning." Or, for instance, when Austerlitz describes
how moths die, he says that they will stay where they are, clinging
to a wall, never moving "until the last breath is out of their bodies,
and indeed they will remain in the place where they came to grief
even after death." In Thomas Bernhard's work, extremity of expression is indistinguishable from the Austrian author's comic, ranting
rage, and his tendency to circle obsessively around madness and suicide. Sebald takes some of Bernhard's wildness and estranges it—
first, by muffling it in an exquisitely courteous syntax: "Had I realized
at the time that for Austerlitz certain moments had no beginning or
end, while on the other hand his whole life had sometimes seemed
to him a blank point without duration, I would probably have waited
more patiently." Second, Sebald makes his diction mysterious by a
process of deliberate antiquarianism. Notice the slightly quaint, Romantic sound of those phrases about the moths: "until the last breath
is out of their bodies . . . the place where they came to grief."

In all his fiction, Sebald works this archaic strain (often reminiscent of the nineteenth-century Austrian writer Adalbert Stifter) into
a new, strange, and seemingly impossible composite: a kind of mildly
agitated, pensive contemporary Gothic. His characters and narrators
are forever finding themselves, like travelers of old, in gloomy, in-
imical places (East London, Norfolk) where "not a living soul stirred."
Wherever they go, they are accompanied by apprehensions of uneasiness, dread, and menace. In *Austerlitz*, this uneasiness amounts
to a Gothicism of the past; the text is constantly in communion with
the ghosts of the dead. At Liverpool Street Station, Jacques Austerlitz feels dread at the thought that the station is built on the founda-
tions of Bedlam, the famous insane asylum: "I felt at this time," he
tells the narrator, "as if the dead were returning from their exile and
filling the twilight around me with their strangely slow but incessant
to-ing and fro-ing." In Wales, the young Jacques had occasionally

felt the presence of the dead, and Evan the cobbler had told the boy of those dead who had been "struck down by fate untimely, who knew they had been cheated of what was due to them and tried to return to life." These ghostly returnees, Evan said, could be seen in the street: "At first glance they seemed to be normal people, but when you looked more closely their faces would blur or flicker slightly at the edges." In the tellingly empty town of Terezín, not far from Prague, Austerlitz seems to see the old Jewish ghetto, as if the dead were still alive, "crammed into those buildings and basements and attics, as if they were incessantly going up and down the stairs, looking out of the windows, moving in vast numbers through the streets and alleys, and even, a silent assembly, filling the entire space occupied by the air, hatched with gray as if it was by the fine rain."

This is both a dream of survival and a dread of it, a haunting. To bring back the dead, those "struck down by fate untimely"— Jacques's parents, say, or the imprisoned victims of Theresienstadt— would be a miraculous resurrection, a reversal of history; yet, since this is impossible, the dead can "return" only as mute witnesses, judging us for our failure to save them. Those resurrected dead at Terezín, standing in "silent assembly," sound very much like a large court, standing in judgment against us. Perhaps, then, the guilt of survival arises not just from the solitude of success (the "success" of having been lucky, of having outlived the Nazis) or the irrational horror that one's survival involved someone else's death (an irrationality that Primo Levi explores in his work). There is also guilt at the idea that the dead are at our mercy, that we can choose to remember or forget them. This is finely caught in a stray passage by Theodor Adorno, in an essay on Mahler, written in 1936: "So the memory is the only help that is left to them [the dead]. They pass away into it, and if every deceased person is like someone who was murdered by the living, so he is also like someone whose life they must save, without knowing whether the effort will succeed."

Saving the dead—that is the paradoxically impossible project of *Austerlitz*, and it is both Jacques Austerlitz's quest, and W. G. Sebald's, too. This book is like the antiques shop seen by Jacques in Terezín; it is full of old things, many of them reproduced in the photographs in the text: buildings, an old rucksack, books and paper records, a desk, a staircase, a messy office, a porcelain statue, gravestones, the roots of trees, a stamp, the drawing of a fortification. The photographs of these old things are *themselves* old things—the kind of shabby, discarded picture-postcards you might find at a weekend flea market, and which Sebald greatly enjoyed collecting. If the photograph is itself an old, dead thing, then what of the people caught—frozen—by the photograph? (Flickering slightly at the edges, as Evan the cobbler describes the dead.) Aren't they also old, dead things? That is why Sebald forces together animate and inanimate objects in his books, and it is why the inanimate objects greatly overwhelm the animate ones in *Austerlitz*. Amid the photographs of buildings and gravestones, it is a shock to come upon a close-up of Wittgenstein's eyes, or a photograph of the rugby team at Jacques's school. The human seems to have been reified by time, and Sebald knowingly reserves an entire page for his shocking photograph of skulls in mud (supposedly, skeletons found near Broad Street Station in 1984, during excavations). Toward becoming these old things, these old headstones in mud, we are all traveling. (In the north of England, a cemetery used to be called a "boneyard," the phrase somehow conveying the sense of our bones as mere lumber or junk.)

Yet some are traveling faster than others, and with more doomed inevitability, and there is surely a distinction between, on the one hand, the photograph of Jacques's rugby team, and on the other, the photograph of Jacques's mother or the photograph (itself a still from a film) of the imprisoned inhabitants of Theresienstadt. As Roland Barthes rightly says in his *Camera Lucida*, a book with which *Austerlitz* is in deep dialogue, photographs shock us because they so finally represent *what has been*. We look at most old photographs, and we think: "That person is going to die, and is in fact now dead." Barthes calls photographers "agents of death," because they freeze the subject and the moment into finitude. Over photographs, he writes, we shudder as over a catastrophe that has already occurred: "Whether or not the subject is already dead, every photograph is this catastrophe." This effect is surely heightened when we look at photographs of victims of the Nazis—whether being rounded up, or just walking along a street in a ghetto. In such cases, we think: "They *know* they are going to die, and they are certainly already dead, and there is nothing we can do about it." As the stolid rugby players do not, these victims seem to be looking at us (even when they are not directly looking at the camera) and asking us to *do* something. This is what gives the photograph of young Jacques a particular intensity. The boy in his party cape, with the wedge of unruly fair hair, looks out at the camera not imploringly but confidently, if a little skeptically. Yet understandably, Jacques Austerlitz, looking at this photograph of himself, from a time when he was still in Prague and still had parents and had not yet been put on the train to London, tells the narrator that he feels "the piercing, inquiring gaze of the page boy who had come to demand his dues, who was waiting in the gray light of dawn on the empty field for me to accept the challenge and avert the misfortune lying ahead of him." Jacques Austerlitz was rescued by the Kindertransport, and thus did indeed avert the misfortune lying ahead of him. But he could not avert the misfortune lying ahead of his parents, and so, even in middle age, he is forever frozen in the attitude of that picture, always waiting to avert misfortune. So he resembles the little porcelain horseman that he saw in the window of the antiques shop in Terezín, a small statue of a man rescuing a young girl, arrested in a "moment of rescue, perpetuated but forever just occurring." Is Jacques Austerlitz the rescuer, or the one awaiting rescue? Both, surely.

There is, of course, a further dimension to Sebald's use of photographs: they are fictional. In the very area of historical writing and historical memory most pledged to the sanctity of accuracy, of testimony and fatal fact, Sebald launches his audacious campaign: his use of photographs relies on, and plays off, the tradition of verity and reportage. On the one hand, these photographs sear us with the promise of their accuracy—as Barthes says, photographs are astonishing because they "attest that what I see has existed . . . in Photography, the presence of the thing (at a certain past moment) is never metaphoric." We are lulled into staring at these photographs, and saying to ourselves: "There is Jacques Austerlitz, dressed in his cape. And there is his mother!" We say this, in part because photographs make us want to say this, but also because Sebald mixes these photographs of people with his undeniably accurate and veridical photographs of buildings (for instance, the photograph of the Breendonk prison, in Belgium, where Jean Améry was tortured by the Nazis, and which the narrator visits, *is* a photograph of the actual building). On the other hand, we know, in our heart of hearts (and perhaps unwillingly?) that Jacques Austerlitz is a fictional character, and that therefore the photograph of the little boy cannot be a photograph of him.

In fact, in this book, Sebald's photographs of humans can be said to be fictional twice over: they are photographs of invented characters; and they are often photographs of actual people who once lived but who are now lost to history. Take the photograph of the rugby team, with Jacques Austerlitz supposedly sitting in the front row, at the far right. Who are these young men? Where did Sebald get ahold of this faded group portrait? And is it likely that any of them are still alive? What is certain is that they have passed into obscurity: we don't look at the portrait and say to ourselves, "There's the young Winston Churchill, in the middle row." The faces are unknown, forgotten. They are, precisely, not Wittgenstein's famous eyes. The photograph of the little boy in his cape is even more acute in its poignancy. I have read reviews of this book that suggest it is a photograph of the young Sebald—such is our natural desire, I suppose, not to let the little boy pass into orphaned anonymity. But the photograph is not of the young Sebald; I came across it in Sebald's literary archive at Marbach, outside Stuttgart, and discovered just an ordinary photographic postcard, with, on the reverse side, "Stockport: 30p," written in ink.* The boy's identity has disappeared (as has

---

* Deutsches Literaturarchiv, Marbach am Neckar. Sebald once confided, in an interview, that about 30 percent of the photographs in *The Emigrants* had an entirely fictitious relationship to their supposed subjects. Sebald, for instance, wrote the farewell note that Ambros Adelwarth writes to his family, and then took the photograph himself.

the woman whose photograph is shown as Agáta, the boy's mother),
and has disappeared—it might be said—even more thoroughly than
Hitler's victims, since they at least belong to blessed memory, and
their murders cry out for public memorial, while the boy has van-
ished into the private obscurity and ordinary silence that will befall
most of us. In Sebald's work, then, and in this book especially, we
experience a vertiginous relationship to a select number of photographs of humans—these pictures are explicitly part of the story
that we are reading, which is about saving the dead (the story of
Jacques Austerlitz); and they are also part of a larger story that is
not found in the book (or only by implication), which is also about
saving the dead. These people stare at us, as if imploring us to rescue them from the banal amnesia of existence. But if Jacques Austerlitz certainly cannot save his dead parents, then we certainly
cannot save the little boy. To "save" him would mean saving every
person who dies, would mean saving everyone who has ever died in
obscurity. *This*, I think, is the double meaning of Sebald's words
about the boy: it is Jacques Austerlitz, but it is also the boy from
Stockport (as it were), who stares out at us asking us to "avert the
misfortune" of his demise, which of course we cannot do.

If the little boy is lost to us, so is Jacques Austerlitz. Like his
photograph, he has also become a thing, and this is surely part of
the enigma of his curious last name. He has a Jewish last name,
which can indeed be found in Czech and Austrian records; as
Jacques correctly tells us, Fred Astaire's father was born with the last
name of Austerlitz ("Fritz" Austerlitz was born in Austria, and had
converted from Judaism to Catholicism). But Austerlitz is primarily
not the name of a person but of a famous battle, and a well-known
Parisian train station. The name is unfortunate for Jacques, because its historical resonance continually pulls us away from his
Jewishness (from his individuality), and toward a world-historical
reference that has nothing much to do with him. Imagine a novel in
which almost every page featured the phrase "Waterloo said" or
"Agincourt said." Sebald plays with this oddity most obviously in

the passage when the young Austerlitz first finds out his true surname, at school. "What does it mean?" asks Jacques, and the headmaster tells him that it is a small place in Moravia, site of a famous battle. During the next school year, the battle of Austerlitz is indeed discussed, and it turns out to be one of the set pieces of Mr. Hilary, the romantic history teacher who makes such an impression on the young Jacques. "Hilary told us, said Austerlitz, how at seven in the morning the peaks of the highest hills emerged from the mist . . . The Russian and Austrian troops had come down from the mountainsides like a slow avalanche." At this moment, when we encounter the familiar "said Austerlitz," we are briefly unsure whether the character or the battle itself is speaking.

Go back, for a minute, to the headmaster's reply, because it is one of the most quietly breathtaking moments in the novel, and can stand as an emblem of Sebald's powers of reticence and understatement. The headmaster, Mr. Penrith-Smith (a nice joke, because Penrith-Smith combines both an English place-name, and the most anonymous, least curious surname in English), has told Jacques that he is not called Dafydd Elias but Jacques Austerlitz. Jacques asks, with the enforced politeness of the English schoolboy, "Excuse me, sir, but what does it mean?" To which Mr. Penrith-Smith replies: "I think you will find it is a small place in Moravia, site of a famous battle, you know." And that is all! And it is 1949. Jacques asks the question that could be said to be the question of the entire novel, and the headmaster refers him only to the famous battle of 1805 between the French and the Austrians. Consider everything that is omitted, or repressed, from this reply. The headmaster might have said that Austerlitz is a Jewish name, and that Jacques is a refugee from the Nazis. He might, with the help of Mr. Hilary's expertise, have added that Austerlitz, near Brno in what was then Czechoslovakia, once had a thriving Jewish population, and that perhaps Jacques's name derived from that community. He might have mentioned that in 1941, the Germans established the ghetto of Theresienstadt, north of Prague (named after Queen Maria Theresa, who, in 1745, issued an edict limiting the number of Jewish families in Moravia), and that the remaining Jews of Austerlitz almost certainly perished there, or later in Auschwitz, to which place most of the inmates of Theresienstadt were eventually taken. He might have added that Jacques's parents were unlikely to be alive.

But Mr. Penrith-Smith says none of this, and Jacques Austerlitz will spend the rest of the novel trying to find his own answer to his own question. Instead, the headmaster's bland reply turns Jacques into the public past, into a date. What does it mean? The answer Jacques receives is, in effect: "1805, that's what it means." Of all the rescues that the novel poses, the most difficult may be this one: to restore to Jacques Austerlitz the individuality of his name and experience, to rescue the living privacy of the surname "Austerlitz" from the dead, irrelevant publicity of the place-name "Austerlitz." Jacques should not be a battle, nor a railway station, nor a thing. Ultimately, we cannot perform this rescue, and the novel does not let us. The private and the public names keep on intertwining, and herein lies the power of the novel's closing pages. We helplessly return to the Gare d'Austerlitz, from where Jacques's father may have left Paris. In the new Bibliothèque Nationale, Jacques learns that the very building rests on the ruins of a huge wartime warehouse, where the Germans "brought all the loot they had taken from the homes of the Jews of Paris." It was known as the Austerlitz-Tolbiac storage depot. Everything our civilization produced was brought here, says the library official, and often pilfered by German officers—ending up in, say, a "Grunewald villa" in Berlin. This knowledge is like a literalization of the well-known dictum of Walter Benjamin's, that there is no document of civilization that is not at the same time a document of barbarism. Standing on the ruins of history, standing both in and on top of history's depository, Jacques Austerlitz is joined by his name to these ruins; and again, at the end of the book, as at the beginning, he threatens to become simply part of the rubble of history, a thing, a depository of facts and dates, not a human being. And throughout the novel, present but never spoken, never written—it is the most beautiful act of Sebald's withholding—is the other historical name that shadows the name Austerlitz, the name that begins and ends with the same letters, the name that we sometimes misread Austerlitz as, the place that Agáta Austerlitz was almost certainly "sent east" to in 1944, and the place that Maximilian Aychenwald was almost certainly sent to from the French camp in Gurs, in 1942: Auschwitz.

KAZUO ISHIGURO'S
NEVER LET ME GO

Works of fantasy or science fiction that also succeed in literary terms are hard to find, and are rightly to be treasured—Hawthorne's story "The Birthmark" comes to mind, and H. G. Wells's *The Time Machine*, and some of Karel Čapek's stories. And just as one is triumphantly sizing up this thin elite, one thinks correctively of that great fantasist Kafka, or even of Beckett, two writers whose impress can be felt, perhaps surprisingly, on Kazuo Ishiguro's novel *Never Let Me Go*. And how about Borges, who so admired Wells? Or Gogol's "The Nose"? Or *The Double*? Or *Lord of the Flies*? A genre that must make room for Kafka and Beckett and Dostoevsky is perhaps no longer a genre but merely a definition of writing successfully; in particular, a way of combining the fantastic and the realistic so that we can no longer separate them, and of making allegory earn its keep by becoming indistinguishable from narration itself.

Never Let Me Go is a fantasy so mundanely told, so excruciatingly ordinary in transit, its fantastic elements so smothered in the loam of the banal and so deliberately grounded, that the effect is not just of fantasy made credible or lifelike, but of the real invading fantasy, bursting into its eccentricity and claiming it as normal. Given that Ishiguro's novel is explicitly about cloning, that it is, in effect, a science fiction set in the present day, and that the odds against success in this mode are bullyingly stacked, his success in writing a book that is at once speculative, experimental, and humanly moving is almost miraculous.

Never Let Me Go is narrated, with punitive blandness, by a woman called Kathy. It begins: "My name is Kathy H. I'm thirty-one years old, and I've been a carer now for eleven years." It maintains this tone of pristine ingenuity for almost three hundred pages. Kathy's story is about a private boarding school she attended, called Hailsham, in the English countryside, and in particular about two close friends, Ruth and Tommy. It becomes clear enough that although the novel is set in the late 1990s, it inhabits a world somewhat adjacent to the one we know. Kathy refers to "donors" (her present job as a carer seems to involve looking after these donors); the school she is reminiscing about does not seem to have had teachers but "guardians." These guardians appear to be human beings like you and me—they are referred to by the pupils as "normals." But the children they look after are not normal: the girls, for instance, will never be able to have babies, and all the pupils appear to be destined not to join ordinary life when they graduate, but to become "donors," and to lead abbreviated, highly controlled adult lives.

Reviews of this singular novel have tended to stress the first-stage detection involved in reading it; whereas Ishiguro, as ever, is interested in far foggier hermeneutics. That is to say, in this novel of exquisite occlusions, the question of who these children are and what their function is in modern society is never very deeply withheld. By the hundredth page or so, even if we had not divined it much earlier, we realize that Hailsham is a school of cloned children, created in order to provide top-notch organs for donation to normal, uncloned British citizens. At the age of sixteen, the children will leave Hailsham, spend some time in an intermediate establishment, and then get "called up." All will first be chosen to be carers, their task to look after an assigned donor; some, like Ruth and Tommy, will be swiftly requested for donation: perhaps a kidney or a lung will be removed. In the course of their fourth donation they will "complete"; they will die.

To be sure, Ishiguro wants to ration the pace at which we receive this terrible information, but that is because his real interest is not in what we discover but in what his characters discover, and how it will affect them. He wants us to inhabit their ignorance, not ours. The children at Hailsham live in a protected environment. They know that they are different, but their guardians are cryptic about this difference. Gradually, through tiny leaks on the part of these guardians, the children gather a burgeoningly complete picture of their fate. By the time they leave school, they know the essential facts. So what might it mean to learn, as a child, that one will never bear children, or hold a meaningful job, or sail into adulthood? How will these children interpret the implications of their abbreviation, the meaning of their mutilated scripts?

Much of the success of the book has to do with the way Ishiguro renders the normality, even tedium, of the world of Hailsham, and then inserts into it icy slivers of menace. Hailsham is like any other school, and if the children feel different, then they are merely like the privileged students of any happy, self-regarding private establishment. The first third of the book chronicles the squabbles and jockeying and jealousies of ordinary schoolchildren. Kathy is clearly in love with Tommy, who seems to be a troubled boy; but Tommy chooses Ruth, who is dismayingly mercurial in her feelings toward Kathy, supposedly her closest friend. There is much rivalrous power play, of a kind familiar from books and films about school days, between Ruth and Kathy.

Kathy's pale narration represents a calculated risk on Ishiguro's part, since it means that his novel is almost entirely written in what Nabokov once called "weak blond prose." Kathy's diction is relaxed into colloquialism and cliché. A teacher "loses her marbles"; a rainy day is "bucketing down"; students about to get into trouble are "for it"; students who have sex are "doing it." She is fond of the supremely English word "daft," and uses woolly intensifiers—"I don't know how it was where you were, but at Hailsham the guardians were really strict about smoking." Ishiguro has always enjoyed ventriloquizing drab English voices: the upholstered butler in *The Remains of the Day*; the narrator of *The Unconsoled*, who sounds like those hysterically calm captions on Glen Baxter cartoons; the narrator of *When We Were Orphans*, whose fiddly, precise English resembles a parody of Anthony Powell. Kathy's voice is like an expository writing paper by a not very bright freshman; it pushes to new extremes Ishiguro's interest in the studied husbanding of affect:

> We were in Room 5 on the ground floor at the back of the house, waiting for a class to start. Room 5 was the smallest room, and especially on a winter morning like that one, when the big radiators came on and steamed up the windows, it would get really stuffy. Maybe I'm exaggerating it, but my memory is that for a whole class to fit into that room, students literally had to pile on top of each other.

So bland is this voice, so banal its daily disclosures, that the reader has a kind of amazed admiration for Ishiguro's freakish courage: one imagines him coming downstairs from a day of writing and triumphantly exclaiming to his wife: "I've done it! I've nailed the scene about the lost geometry set! Tomorrow, I'll write up the class quiz scene."

But Kathy is somewhat anxiously, and interestingly, ingratiating, and her habit of addressing the reader as if the reader were the same as her—"I don't know how it was where you were, but at Hailsham . . ."—has a fragile pathos to it. She wants to be one of us, and in some way she assumes she is. The very dullness of these children, their lack of rebelliousness, even incuriousness, is what grounds the book's fantasy. They seem never to want to run away from their school, to throw over the commanded lives they must eventually lead. Full comprehension of who they are and why they were created makes them sad, but only resignedly so. This is the only reality they have ever known, and they are indeed creatures of habit. Ishiguro shakes this banality every so often, as the terribleness of what has been done emerges. For example, the children's artworks are collected every month by a woman known only as Madame, and taken out of the school to a gallery. (We later learn that this is an

attempt to see whether the children have souls.) Ruth senses that
Madame is frightened by the children, even repelled, and they de-
cide to test their surmise one day by rushing her as a group and
watching her response. They are right:

> I can still see it now, the shudder she seemed to be sup-
> pressing, the real dread that one of us would accidentally
> brush against her. And though we just kept on walking, we
> all felt it; it was like we'd walked from the sun right into
> chilly shade. Ruth had been right: Madame *was* afraid of
> us. But she was afraid of us in the same way someone might
> be afraid of spiders. We hadn't been ready for that. It had
> never occurred to us to wonder how *we* would feel, being
> seen like that, being the spiders.

Kathy goes on to say that "the first time you glimpse yourself through
the eyes of a person like that, it's a cold moment. It's like walking
past a mirror you've walked past every day of your life, and suddenly
it shows you something else, something troubling and strange." In
another episode, which lends the book its title, Kathy remembers
becoming obsessed with a song called "Never Let Me Go." She
would play this song again and again:

> I just waited for that bit that went: "Baby, baby, never let me
> go . . ." And what I'd imagined was a woman who'd been
> told she couldn't have babies, who'd really, really wanted
> them all her life. Then there's a sort of miracle and she has
> a baby, and she holds this baby very close to her and walks
> around singing: "Baby, never let me go . . ." partly because
> she's so happy, but also because she's so afraid something
> will happen, that the baby will get ill or be taken away from
> her. Even at the time, I realised this couldn't be right, that
> this interpretation didn't fit with the rest of the lyrics. But
> that wasn't an issue with me.

This is an acute rendition of how any young girl might misread the lyrics of a song; and it is shadowed, of course, by the actual facts of this girl's life. One day, Kathy is dancing by herself, holding a pillow in her arms and crooning along to the song, "Oh baby, baby, never let me go." She looks up and in the doorway Madame is watching her: "And the odd thing was she was crying . . . she just went on standing out there, sobbing and sobbing . . ."

Kathy, Tommy, and Ruth eventually leave Hailsham and are billeted at a place called the Cottages, where they have much more freedom, and join a group of older teenagers. But it is a freedom they barely exercise. They borrow a car and drive through Norfolk. On one such outing, to the coastal town of Cromer, friends of the trio are sure that they have seen what they call "a possible" for Ruth:

> Since each of us was copied at some point from a normal person, there must be, for each of us, somewhere out there, a model getting on with his or her life. This meant, at least in theory, you'd be able to find the person you were modelled from. That's why, when you were out there yourself— in the towns, shopping centres, transport cafés—you kept an eye out for "possibles"—the people who might have been the models for you and your friends.

The friends follow the woman whom they consider Ruth's possible, or original. But the longer they watch her, the less like Ruth she seems, and the excitement of the surveillance fizzles. Only then does it become apparent that Ruth is terribly disappointed. She bursts out, bitterly:

> "They don't ever, *ever*, use people like that woman . . . We all know it. We're modelled from *trash*. Junkies, prostitutes, winos, tramps. Convicts, maybe, just so long as they aren't psychos. That's what we come from . . . A woman like that? Come on . . . If you want to look for possibles, if you

want to do it properly, then you look in the gutter. You look in rubbish bins. Look down the toilet, that's where you'll find where we all come from."

The entire episode testifies to what is strangely successful in this book: the way it rubs its science fictional narrative from the rib of the real, making it breathe with horrid plausibility, and then the way it converts that science fiction back into the human, managing to be at once sinister and ordinarily affecting.

Ruth and Tommy break up, and Kathy becomes a carer and Tommy a donor, and Kathy takes Ruth's place as Tommy's lover, as she had to, and the novel's title begins to vibrate with premonition, for we know that Tommy has made three donations, and is thus only one operation away from death. The novel is weakened by a didactic ending, in which the spirit of Wells or Huxley bests the spirit of Borges. Kathy and Tommy manage to track down a former guardian, Miss Emily, and Madame, and these now-aged ladies apologize to the cloned couple for what they have done to them, and attempt to exonerate themselves by claiming that they always had the best interests of the children at heart. Madame admits to Kathy that when she saw, all those years ago, the little girl crooning to the song, she cried because she saw "a new world coming rapidly. More scientific, efficient, yes. More cures for the old sicknesses. Very good. But a harsh, cruel world. And I saw a little girl, her eyes tightly closed, holding to her breast the old kind world, one that she knew in her heart could not remain, and she was holding it and pleading, never to let her go."

The novel hardly needed this preaching, partly because it has already so effectively dramatized the horror of what has been brought about, and partly because of course the cloning of human beings hardly needs denunciation. The book wobbles into treatise here. But *Never Let Me Go*, while certainly a dramatized attack on cloning, could probably not give much final consolation to those conservatives or religionists who talk about protecting "a culture of life." For it is most powerful when most allegorical, and its allegorical power has to do with its picture of ordinary human life as in fact a culture of death. That is to say, Ishiguro's book is at its best when, by asking us to consider the futility of cloned lives, it forces us to consider the futility of our own. This is the moment at which Kathy's appeal to us—"I don't know how it was where you were, but at Hailsham . . ."—becomes double-edged. For what if we are more like Tommy and Kathy than we at first imagined? The cloned children are being educated at school for lives of perfect pointlessness, pointless because they will die before they can grasp their adulthood. Everything they do is dipped in futility, because the great pool of death awaits them. They possess individuality, and seem to enjoy it (they fall in love, they have sex, they read George Eliot), but that individuality is a mirage, a parody of liberty. Their lives have been written in advance, they are *prevented and followed*, in the words of *The Book of Common Prayer*. Their freedom is a tiny hemmed thing, their lives a vast stitch-up.

We begin the novel horrified by their difference from us and end it thoughtful about their similarity to us. After all, heredity writes a great deal of our destiny for us; and death soon enough makes us orphans, even if we were fortunate enough, unlike the children of Hailsham, not to start life in such deprivation. Without a belief in God, without metaphysical pattern and leaning, why should our lives not indeed be sentences of a kind, death sentences? Even with God? Well, God hath numbered thy kingdom and finished it: the writing may well be on the wall anyway. To be assured of death at twenty-five or so, as the Hailsham children are, seems to rob life of all its savor and purpose. But why do we persist in the idea that to be assured of death at seventy or eighty or ninety returns to life all its savor and purpose? Why is sheer longevity, if it most certainly ends in the same way as sheer brevity, accorded meaning, while sheer brevity is thought to lack it? The culture of life is not such a grand thing when seen through these narrow windows.

Ishiguro's novel has no need to be didactic about cloning, because it is allegorical about it instead. At its best, the book is seamlessly allegorical, generating meaning without strain. It is here that it becomes reminiscent of Kafka (a clear influence on *The Uncon-soled*), and Beckett, whose Hamm, in *Endgame*, yells: "Use your head, can't you, use your head, you're on earth, there's no cure for that," an earth that Tess, in Hardy's novel, calls a blighted star, and which Hardy again calls blighted in his poem "When Dead":

> This fleeting life-brief blight
> Will have gone past
> When I resume my old and right
> Place in the Vast.

So this curious, surprisingly suggestive and tender novel forces us, finally, to send Kathy's apparently naive appeal back to her, in a spirit of horrified allegiance: "I don't know how it was where you were, but here in this fleeting life . . ."

THINKING: NORMAN RUSH

Joseph Conrad has had relatively little influence on the contemporary American novel. Naipaul, Greene, and Céline (in *Journey to the End of the Night*), all keen absorbers of Conrad, were partly prodded abroad by the disintegration of empires, British and French, which offered rich and seedy locales for the observation of politics and motive. But America is its own vast imperium, reducing its satellites to mere moons, and in general American novelists have found quite enough at home to interest them. Philip Roth famously wrote in the early 1960s that perhaps the novel could not keep up with the wild fictionality of American reality. Those American writers interested in non-American worlds, and drawn to the examination of alien politics, such as Robert Stone and Joan Didion, have tended to labor under Graham Greene's easier shadow, rather than risk Conrad's more taxing presence.

Norman Rush is the great exception. Surely the only considerable American novelist who has never yet written about America (though he is very interested in Americans), he has set his three books in Botswana, a country in which he lived between 1978 and 1983. The books, like eclipses, arrive rarely, but tend to impose themselves massively. *Mating*, Rush's first novel (his first book was a fine collection of stories called *Whites*), appeared in 1991; *Mortals*, larger still than the intricate and dense *Mating*, is only his second novel, and has been at least a decade in the making. It might be said that both these remarkable books have as their theme the clash of American desire and African politics, and that both are about the eruption into American lives of charismatic seducers. In *Mating*, the female narrator, an American anthropologist, becomes enamored of Nelson Denoon, a showy intellectual who has founded a utopian community in the Kalahari Desert; and the central story of Rush's new novel concerns an American woman's affair with an African-American therapist named Davis Morel, who has arrived in Botswana from Cambridge, Massachusetts, ready to go native and to preach a curious blend of militant atheism and self-help healing.

Rush recalls Conrad not only in theme but also in language, even if he does not precisely resemble him. The Conrad of whom Ford Madox Ford wrote that he practiced a "ferocious avoidance" of the ordinary sentence, who would go to great lengths to disrupt and to ornament the standard literary vernacular, must be an example to Rush. One reason that Rush has so excited literary readers—and excited them on the strength, until now, of only one novel—has to do with his extraordinary prose, which could only be American, and which, like Bellow's language, combines high and low registers in greatly unstable compounds. He is very interested in speech, in the slightly barbaric twisting of language that we commit when we speak, or speak to ourselves.

In addition, his American characters are proficient, perhaps slightly glib intellectuals, who enjoy showing off their mastery of the latest technical argot. This argot has thoroughly contaminated their ordinary speech. The narrator of *Mating* spoke—and thus the whole novel sounded—like this: "This jeu maintained its facetious character, but there came a time when I began to resent it as a concealed way of short-circuiting my episode of depression, because he preferred me to be merry, naturally." (That little rhythmic hiccup at the end of the sentence, closed by the literally feminine ending of the adverb, which seems to stick out over the end of the sentence, is a favorite device of Rush's when he wants to capture the hobbled but speedy pace of talk.) Or: "Undressed he became very laissez-faire. He was fundamentally sexually secure." Or: "I was manic and global. Everything was a last straw. I went up the hill on passivity and down again."

In the way of all powerfully narrated first-person monologues, *Mating* occasionally breeds in the reader the desire to escape the constant intensity and interest of the language, as houseguests sometimes want to escape their overvivid hosts. It is the price that the writer pays for the immediacy of first-person access. *Mortals* is told in the conventional third person, so that it distributes its effects more spaciously and calmly, as is proper for such a massive work. But Rush has not lost his interest in spoken language; indeed, he has intensified his study, at once funny and brilliant, of what happens to language when brainy Americans get mixed up with it. *Mortals* is many things, and does many things beautifully, but one of its great achievements has to be the fidelity with which it represents consciousness, the way in which it tracks the mind's language.

The book's consciousness—we inhabit only his, despite the many other characters—belongs to Ray Finch, a minor (that is to say, unpublished) Milton scholar, who is teaching at a school in Gaborone, the capital of Botswana, and also doing contract work for the CIA. (The book is set in 1992.) Ray is a liberal meliorist, with no great affection for the agency—the type of man who thinks that Americans do good, that communism was well vanquished, but that Guatemala was a sorry example of American overreaching. He reports to the station chief, named Boyle, whom he loathes. Ray is an involving presence (fortunately enough, given the book's length). He is highly intelligent, a precise noticer (he is trained to notice), with an apparently stable, calm, pedantic, and "relentless" (his wife's word) temperament, given only to outbursts against, as he sees it, female instability and hysteria.

Remarkably, Rush manages to make us believe that he is indeed a Milton scholar, that he loves language, and especially seventeenth-century language. During the course of the book, Ray uses words such as "hellmouth," "pismire," and "slumgullion," all in entirely natural ways. When he complains to himself about his wife, he uses a formulation that has Rush's verbal quirkiness, and yet remains true to Ray's calling as a teacher of literature: "It looked like the universal conspiracy of women, stanza nine billion, on the face of it." That word "stanza" is perfect for the kind of man wielding it; and again one notices Rush's staggering of the sentence, the jumpy rhythm of thought. Later, when Ray again returns to the question of women, and to the idea that women never forget anything, he thinks to himself: "But here it was again, the past that lives forever, in detail, with women, like the women in Joyce, The Dead, ruining everything." The jerky rhythm is there again, with that repetition of "women," but there is also something delicate about the way Rush has Ray think not "in Joyce's 'The Dead'" or "in Joyce's story," but "in Joyce, The Dead," which reproduces the crawling movement of identification by which thought moves.

Ray's way of thinking to himself, or speaking to himself, combines the precision of a spy, the language of a scholar, and the officialese of a bureaucrat. Rush has fun inventing Ray's patois, and the pleasure is contagious. Talking to Boyle, who is a standard-issue CIA type, full of agency folklore, Ray realizes that he "was going on too long and he knew it, but he couldn't make himself stop . . . He hated the slings and arrows of staircase wisdom." A little later, he thinks: "Boyle was normally laconic, and laconic at a completely standard middle-class level of word choice." When Ray notices a sheathed *TLS*, Rush puts it with apt pedantry: "He had two *Times Literary Supplements* still in their glassine sleeves." Ray's wife, Iris, is clever like Ray, but unlike him she is witty (she refers to Kleenexes by a bogus Latin plural, "Kleenices"). She, too, speaks an utterly contemporary American discourse, a mixture of the slangy and the overeducated or theoretical: "He can't get rid of the furniture without it being a critique of his own project." Or: "He's a very good writer, but he has an imprimatur problem" (meaning: he's unpublished).

This marriage is at the core of the novel, which is, despite its many interests, a traditional novel of adultery. In a sense, the book inverts *Othello*. Ray, a white man, suffers excruciating sexual jealousy as he imagines his white wife involved in an affair with the black American Davis Morel. For a good part of the novel, Ray's sexual jealousy, like Othello's, seems unjustified, and it is only when Ray meets Morel in the Kalahari Desert that his fears are finally confirmed. Ray is concerned with the perfection of his marriage, to an obsessive degree. At times Rush seems to overdo the vitality of Ray and Iris's marriage, as if to convince us of the horror of Iris's eventual adultery. There is a little too much about how Iris has "perfect parts" and perfect breasts, how fabulous they are in bed, how she would regularly cut Ray's toenails "out of love," and how "Iris could look at him and tell if he was hungry whether he said anything or not." When Rush tells us that Ray had never been able to finish *Madame Bovary* "because the idea of a wife committing adultery was upsetting to him," one feels that he is throwing too many eggs into his pudding.

After all, Rush has already suggested, much more subtly, that Ray is unstable on the question of his wife, and that his idea of the marriage may be rather different from hers. Ray's reading of "The Dead," for instance, was slightly self-aggrandizing. The idea that female memory, which never forgets, "ruins everything," especially for men, is exactly what the protagonist of "The Dead," Gabriel Conroy, thinks. But Joyce's point is that the overfastidious Gabriel Conroy is himself a hysteric, and Ray's identification with Gabriel suggests that Ray is also something of a hysteric. He is consumed by visions of female conspiracy, but he of course belongs to that great male club of conspiracy, the CIA. (His work for the agency has come between him and his wife; she is more liberal than he is and longs for him to disengage.) One realizes that in a novel dominated by a single consciousness there is very little of anything resembling objectivity.

Rush's characterization of Ray's marriage is really Ray's characterization of it, and Ray cannot be wholly believed: Iris's eventual un-
happiness and infidelity cast doubt on Ray's credibility. He is a
first-class noticer, but not, perhaps, of his own wife.

The novel's machinery is properly started when Iris reveals to
Ray that she has been depressed and that she has started having
therapy with Davis Morel. Ray knows about Morel, because he has
tried to argue to Boyle that the CIA should be interested in this
seductive African-American rabble-rouser, who has recently quit
Cambridge for Gaborone. But Boyle has ignored Ray's entreaty and
has instead asked him to keep tabs on Samuel Kerekang, the leader
of a grassroots movement that mixes Ruskinian socialism with African nativism. When Ray learns about Iris's sessions with Morel, he
is immediately suspicious. His wife has been acting secretively; an
affair would explain much. He broods on this question, and the
great accomplishment of the novel lies in the way in which we are
made to inhabit Ray's brooding.

Rush achieves this with a superb combination of free indirect
style—the technical term for third-person narration that is so close
to a character's thought that it resembles first-person monologue—
and stream-of-consciousness. In order to demonstrate Rush's skill,
one has to quote at length. Here, Ray is sitting opposite his loathed
CIA chief, Boyle, and beginning to drift away. He thinks of how
much he loves his wife:

> It came to him then that probably one of the best things, or
> at least one of the simplest good things, you could do with
> your mortal life would be to pick out one absolutely first-
> rate deserving person and do everything you could conceive
> of in the world to make her happy, as best you might, and
> never be an adversary on small things . . .
>
> And the idea was to let this single flower bloom with-
> out notifying her of what was going on. Because it would be
> on the order of a present because it was only fair reciproca-
> tion for someone who enthralled you and who had inciden-

tally saved you from your demons. Or the idea was to so charge her life with his appreciation that some morning she would sit up and say What the fuck is going on with us, I am so happy. The idea was to let this single flower bloom until it was something monstrous, like an item in a Max Ernst collage, something that fills the room and the occupant says *Oh, this is you, this is you, my beloved friend, my love, now I see*, something along those lines. He was going to float her in love and she would be like those paper flowers that open up. Water rising around her. She didn't know about him that he could get an erection just thinking in passing about her and that on one occasion he had to claim that he was having a hamstring problem, sitting facing Boyle was when it had happened, sitting facing Boyle and saying Ow and massaging his Achilles tendon so he could sit there until it was decent to get up. Boyle was divorced, or rather separated, since he was a Roman Catholic. He was in some null state with his wife, was the story. A lot of regular officers in the agency were divorced. A divorce would kill Ray. Maybe the evaporation of Russia would make this easier. He wasn't sure what he meant, unless it was that a certain pressure had gone out of that sector of his work. He couldn't believe it was over with the Russians, leaving only bullshit antagonists on the horizon, it looked like now. Maybe they could all relax some. And the joke of it was that Russia had gone up in mist not because of anything the agency had done, really. The agency had been amazed, startled. All this would probably never lead to a verbal event, where she says Good God, I seem to be floating in love. It would be enough if she just thought it, or something like it. No, he had been too average in his attitude and all that toward her in the past, and now he knew it and so would she, soon enough, although she would feel it before she truly knew it, but he was repeating himself. So this would be his new secret work. It would be like adding,

say, potted blue hyacinths, one pot at a time, to a shelf or a
ledge in the living room, one at a time, until the atmosphere
was paradisiacal.

Reading this fantastical passage—there are many like it in the
book; indeed, it is the book's very mode of narration—one recalls
what fiction can supremely do with the mind, and how very rare is
this kind of mastery, let alone this preoccupation, in current American writing. Look again at the passage: it is both lyrical (ending
with the image of the hyacinths) and awkward (that repeated "because"); one sees how easily Ray passes from thinking about his
wife to Boyle (who is sitting opposite him), to Boyle's marriage, to
the geopolitical status of the world, and then, in what seems like
a non sequitur, back to his wife: "All this would probably never lead
to a verbal event, where she says Good God, I seem to be floating
in love." Notice also how Rush moves Ray's thought from third person to first person and back again: "And the joke of it was that Russia
had gone up in mist not because of anything the agency had done,
really. The agency had been amazed, startled." (There is also the
oddity of the phrase "gone up in mist," rather than the more usual
"gone up in smoke"—the curious way we customize clichés when
we pass them through our minds.) And how much, too, this single
page of the novel tells us about Ray: not only about his anxious devotion, but also about his secret agent's tendency to control. It is characteristic, after all, that Ray would think of letting the single flower
of his wife bloom, "without notifying her of what was going on." Ray
may love his wife to death, but we understand, thanks to passages
like this, why she might want to escape this mixture of control and
withholding.

   Rush is a fine manipulator of what Conrad knew as *progession
d'effet*—the steady intensification of plot and meaning as the novel
builds toward its climaxes. As Ray becomes more certain that Iris
is being unfaithful, his mental thought becomes less a drift than a
tattoo, drumming again and again on the unblemished skin of his

"perfect" marriage. The passage in which Ray comes up with the vaguely Miltonic word "hellmouth" is a fine example. He begins by reflecting on the childlessness of his marriage:

> He had never been captivated by the idea of reproducing himself. But he had wanted it very much, for Iris. He had, despite the fact that children exposed you to hellmouth, which was the opening up of the mouth of hell right in front of you, without warning, through no fault of your own. It was the mad gunman shooting you at lunch and it was the cab jumping the curb and crushing you. It was AIDS and it was the grandmother, the daughter, the granddaughter tumbling through the air, blown out of the airplane by a bomb, the three generations falling and seeing one another fall, down, down, onto the Argolid mountains. With children you created more thin places in the world for hellmouth to break through. Morel was hellmouth for him. Hellmouth was having the bad luck to be born in Angola anytime after 1960. And hellmouth was Bertrand Russell coming home from a bicycle ride and announcing to his wife that he had decided he didn't really love her, like that. That was hellmouth, too.

About halfway through the book, the story shifts gear. Ray is sent north, to the Kalahari Desert, to report on the activities of Samuel Kerekang's men, who have been burning villages and killing livestock. What might be, in another kind of novel, an obvious attempt to splash some action into a rather floating psychological narrative, seems anything but expedient here. The novel's bulk has already so properly ballasted Ray, has made his mind so present to us, and has filled in so many elements of his life, that we travel with Ray rather than travel merely with Rush to the Kalahari. Ray has a job of surveillance to do, but his mind is consumed by his suspicions of his wife. In addition, he has been sent to spy on Kerekang, but unlike his station chief, Ray likes Kerekang, rather approves of him, and enjoys his old-fashioned socialist's devotion to rousing nineteenth-century poetry. He is much more interested in doing surveillance on the suspected adulterer Davis Morel. Moreover, he is thinking remorsefully of his gay brother, Rex, whom he suspects is dying of AIDS in California. He has a manuscript of his brother's, a kind of novel, a vast modernist assemblage with the title *Strange News*. (Rush, who has a gift for pastiche and parody, reproduces pages of this book in all its vivid, ambitious awfulness. It has sections with titles like "All Power to the Country Clubs!" and "Titles," a chapter devoted to possible titles of unwritten books. One of the titles is *Out to Luncheon: Notes Toward a More Elegant Mode of Disparagement*.) Ray has always loathed and feared his clever, bitchy, somewhat feckless younger brother. At first, he feels the same way about *Strange News*. But his terrible experiences in the Kalahari change him, and by the end of the novel he is carrying the manuscript around with him, strapped to his chest, as a kind of penance.

The two hundred or so pages in which Rush describes what is in effect a small African civil war seem to me some of the most extraordinary pages written by a contemporary American novelist. Again, one admires the precision of Rush's effects, which keeps his lyricism on a tight budget. For example: "The horizon seemed to be writhing"—a marvelous description of the hazy, sun-battered rims of a very hot country. Or: "Cooking fires wagged in some of the lolwapas" (a lolwapa is a traditional courtyard; Rush's verbs are often potent like this). Or: "The blackness around them felt irregular, like a fabric being shaken. It was bats at work, swerving and fluttering their ugly wings."

Ray is captured by soldiers organized and funded by the South Africans and interrogated by a Boer named Quartus. He is thrown into a makeshift prison and joined a day later by Davis Morel, who has come north, at Iris's insistence, to find out what has happened to Ray. It is in their hutlike prison that the two men confront each other. Morel confirms that he and Iris are lovers, and that Iris wants to leave her husband and live with Morel. Ray must absorb this devastating news while trying to save Morel and himself from death. The two escape, are snatched up with Kerekang's forces, and fight a fierce battle against Quartus and his irregulars. Rush's writing is tautly exciting; there are tremendous swirls and billows of prose. The Conradian alienation principle is brilliantly employed: when Ray finds himself back in the interrogation room—the compound has now been abandoned by Quartus and company—he notices that the floor is full of "cigarette butts and empty soda cans and, here and there, roses. He was amazed, but only until he realized that the roses were wads of bloodstained tissue." Eventually, Ray comes face-to-face with his former interrogator, struggles with him, and finally shoots him clumsily, in the hip: "Quartus screamed and let go. His jodhpurs were filling with blood, one leg of them was." Might there have been, in the back of Rush's mind, the famous image in *Heart of Darkness*, when the helmsman is killed by a spear and falls at the feet of Marlow, who notices that "my feet felt so very warm and wet that I had to look down . . . my shoes were full; a pool of blood lay very still"?

In this gripping second section of the book, Rush blends Conradian action—the warfare is as involving and convincingly haphazard as that at the end of *Lord Jim*—with his sustained interest in the contents of Ray's mind. His ability to sketch the different political allegiances of Kerekang, of his young supporters—teenagers with Kalashnikovs—of the American quack Morel, of the received wisdom of the CIA chief, and of many others is impressive, since a high level of analysis never insults the hospitality of storytelling. *Mortals* is above all a novel, not an essay or an ideological thriller (as, say, Didion's political novels are). The book becomes a study of a man finally subjecting himself to examination, and not enjoying what he finds.

It is really the story of a man disengaging himself from conspiracies. By the end of the tale, Ray has decided to leave the CIA. His experiences in the north, his proximity to death, his anger at the way the CIA has bungled what ought to have been an easy task in largely peaceful Botswana, and his wife's terrible decision that

she can apparently live without him—all these experiences con-
spire against him, reduce him, humble him. At last he is on his own,
and wants to remove himself from the two institutions that have
sustained him, his marriage and the agency: "Ray thought that he
would be willing to die if it was going to be pitch black, hell zero,
diving through the zero like a clown through a burning hoop and
then nothing. He hoped to God the atheists were right. Because if
there was an afterlife it would be institutional because somebody
would have to run it and he couldn't go through that again. And the
only worse thing would be reincarnation and back to the ocean of
human institutions again."

Ray returns several times to a glorious line of John Webster's:
"like diamonds we are cut with our own dust." "Dust," in Webster's
diction, has the sense of death, the dust of death, and Rush clearly
wants the line to make resonant the book's title. In the Kalahari,
Ray does begin to think of himself as a "dying animal." But Webster's line has a simpler application, too: If we are truly cut with
our own dust, then perhaps this means that Ray is really the reason for the breakup of his marriage? And does it not suggest likewise that the CIA tends to create the problems that it wants to
solve?

Mortals is a deeply serious, ambitious book. Like all such books,
it is not without faults. Ideologically speaking, Ray, the liberal who
eventually leaves the agency, is perhaps too good to be true, so that
one wonders about the likelihood of such a right-thinking (or,
rather, left-thinking) fellow ever joining the CIA in the first place.
And the novel has the air at times of a once fatter man whose thinner
frame is now making his skin sag a bit: there are abrupt transitions
and sudden deposits of information. But big books flick away their
own failings and weaknesses, make insects of them. And how much
is accomplished here! For once, knowledge in an American novel
has not come free and flameless from Google, but has come out of a
writer's own burning; for once, knowledge is not simply exotic and
informational, but something amassed as life is amassed, as a pile
of experiences rather than a wad of facts. (Botswana is never a back-

drop but always the fabric of Rush's fictions, and he clearly knows and loves the country.) And for once intelligence is not mere "smartness," but an element inseparable from the texture and the movement of the novel itself. For once it is novelistic intelligence, for which we should give thanks.

CORMAC McCARTHY'S
THE ROAD

I.

In addition to the 9/11 novel, and the 9/11 novel that is pretending not to be a 9/11 novel, an old genre has been reawakened by new fears: the post-apocalyptic novel (which may well be, in fact, the 9/11 novel pretending not to be one). The possibility that familiar, habitual existence might be so disrupted within the next hundred years that crops will fail, warm places will turn into deserts, and species will become extinct—that areas of the earth may become uninhabitable—holds and horrifies the contemporary imagination. This fear may not be as present, acute, or knife-edged as the fear of nuclear annihilation that produced novels such as *A Canticle for Leibowitz* and *On the Beach* and movies such as *Fail-Safe* and *The Day After*, but it is more fatalistic and in its way more horrible, precisely because the catastrophe that climate fear imagines may be inevitable and incorrigible. And the temporal reprieve, the deferral of the worst to later generations, may not be any consolation at all. It may, strangely enough, increase the fear: are you more agonizingly afraid of something that will happen to yourself or of something that will happen to your children?

This—the increasingly well-documented horror that precedes all the "greening" that is around us—may in part explain the recent cluster of new movies and novels that are set in a future world catastrophically changed or almost posthuman: *The Children of Men*; the

global warming horror movie *The Day After Tomorrow*; Kazuo
Ishiguro's novel about cloning, *Never Let Me Go*, Jim Crace's novel
The Pesthouse, and Cormac McCarthy's *The Road*. In his book *The
Revenge of Gaia*, the scientist James Lovelock presents this hideous
picture of the warmed world, sometime in the middle of this century:

> Meanwhile in the hot arid world survivors gather for the
> journey to the new Arctic centres of civilization; I see them
> in the desert as the dawn breaks and the sun throws its
> piercing gaze across the horizon at the camp. The cool fresh
> night air lingers for a while and then, like smoke, dissipates
> as the heat takes charge. Their camel wakes, blinks and
> slowly rises on her haunches. The few remaining members
> of the tribe mount. She belches, and sets off on the long un-
> bearably hot journey to the next oasis.

Note the word "survivors": post-apocalyptic minimalism is assumed.
    Minimalism can be very good for the life of fiction: description,
thrown back onto its essentials, flourishes as it justifies its own existence. Words are returned to their original function as names. The
J. M. Coetzee who admires the way that Daniel Defoe has the ship-
wrecked Robinson Crusoe notice "two shoes, not fellows" on the
island shore, as proofs of other deaths, is the novelist who, in *Life &
Times of Michael K*, thrillingly described, from the ground up as it
were, Michael K's desperate, starving, solitary roaming through the
dry wastes of rural South Africa. How will Michael K find his next
meal? Where will he sleep? Prison fiction works in the same way.
One day of Ivan Denisovich's will suffice for the telling, not just because Ivan's every day is the same, but because the fiction has slowed
down to notice the smallest details, just as time has slowed down for
Ivan. Inside prison, the scale of everything has changed: a decent
piece of bread would be an unimaginable luxury for Ivan, and worth
the lengthiest savoring.
    In some ways, and despite Cormac McCarthy's reputation as an
ornate stylist, *The Road* represents both the logical terminus and a

kind of ultimate triumph of an American minimalism that became
well known in the 1980s under the banner of "dirty realism." This
was a prose of short declarative sentences, in which verbs docked
quickly at their objects, adjectives and adverbs were turned away,
parentheses and subclauses were shunned. An antisentimentality,
learned mainly from Hemingway, was so pronounced as to constitute
a kind of male sentimentality of reticence. Basic, often domestic
activities were honored in sentences of almost painfully repetitive
simplicity. A generic parody might sound like this:

> He took the glass from the cupboard and set it on the table.
> He poured the bourbon into it, but did not drink it. In-
> stead, he went to the door and listened. Nothing except far
> away a squeal of tires, over on Route 9 probably. He walked
> back heavily to the table. Through the wall he could hear
> them arguing again.

This style, which quickly reaches the limits of its expressivity, produced one indisputably significant writer, Raymond Carver, and a
thousand thin cousins. In 2005, it was born again in Cormac Mc-
Carthy's cynical, very bloody, very stripped-down thriller, *No Country for Old Men*, which abounded in lucid, hard little paragraphs
devoted to male activity—say, a man painstakingly dressing a wound
or slowly cleaning his gun or chasing another man down a street.
That book was slick and merely cinematic, but in *The Road* the same
kind of minimalism comes alive. Dirty realism was sometimes
unwittingly excruciating because one felt that the chosen fictional
worlds—even impoverished ones, all those motels and trailers—
deserved richer prose. But in *The Road* something strange happens
to this ordinary descriptive language—the book describes a world
without reference, without things, but does so in a language we associate with reference and domestic normality: the father pitches a
tent, makes a home, the boy eats some beans, or washes himself, in
a descriptive language little different from Hemingway's in the Nick
Adams stories: "He fixed dinner while the boy played in the sand"

(a sentence not from Hemingway but from this novel). There is a powerful tension between reference (things, context) and its absence. McCarthy writes at one point that the father could not tell the son about life before the apocalypse: "He could not construct for the child's pleasure the world he'd lost without constructing the loss as well and he thought perhaps the child had known this better than he." It is the same for the book's prose style: just as the father cannot construct a story for the boy without also constructing the loss, so the novelist cannot construct the loss without the ghost of the departed fullness, the world as it once was.

Roughly ten years before the opening of the action of the novel, some kind of climacteric occurred: "The clocks stopped at 1:17. A long shear of light and then a series of low concussions." A kind of nuclear winter now grips an America—and presumably a world—that is largely unpeopled. Animals have disappeared, there are no birds, no cities—just burned-out buildings—no cars, no power, nothing. Corpses are everywhere. Black ash covers everything, and the weather is always gray: "By day the banished sun circles the earth like a grieving mother with a lamp." A father and a son, who remain unnamed, are making their way southward, in America, toward the sea, in the hope that they might find human community or just some activity on the coast. We learn that the son was born ten years ago, and that the boy's mother committed suicide rather than wander the world as a survivor. So the boy has never known anything else. The father has his memories of ordinary life before the catastrophe, but these are horridly incommunicable, and McCarthy beautifully catches the alienation between the two generations.

Short phrasal sentences, often just fragments, savagely paint the elements of this voided world. Food and survival are the only concerns. With no animals alive, the best chance is to come upon some old cache of tinned food in an abandoned house or farm: "Mostly he worried about their shoes. That and food. Always food. In an old batboard smokehouse they found a ham gambreled up in a high corner. It looked like something fetched from a tomb, so dried and drawn. He cut into it with his knife." McCarthy is not without a sense of the comic, and he knows how to keep his punch lines dry until the last moment. The couple rake through an old supermarket, for instance, and eventually come upon an unopened can of Coke. The boy does not know what this is; his father promises him it will be a treat:

> On the outskirts of the city they came to a supermarket. A few old cars in the trashstrewn parking lot. They left the cart in the lot and walked the littered aisles. In the produce section in the bottom of the bins they found a few ancient runner beans and what looked to have once been apricots, long dried to wrinkled effigies of themselves. The boy followed behind. They pushed out through the rear door. In the alleyway behind the store a few shopping carts, all badly rusted. They went back through the store again looking for another cart but there were none. By the door were two soft-drink machines that had been tilted over into the floor and opened with a prybar. Coins everywhere in the ash. He sat and ran his hand around in the works of the gutted machines and in the second one it closed over a cold metal cylinder. He withdrew his hand slowly and sat looking at a Coca Cola.
>
> What is it, Papa?
> It's a treat. For you.
> What is it?

Surely McCarthy is knowingly playing here—not only with the American iconicity of the Coke can, but with iconic artworks about American icons, like Edward Hopper's *Gas* (his painting, from 1940, of the archetypal American gas station), and Andy Warhol's Campbell's soup tins.

The Road will not let the reader go, and will horribly invade his dreams, too. The apocalyptic fiction genre is not a very distinguished one. It relies on formulaic scenery (those piles of burning tires always seen in films, those gangs of feral children), and generally rather lazy or incoherent political futurism: for instance, if Britain, in *The Children of Men*, twenty years hence, is ruled by a totalitarian dictator who can round up immigrants and put them in cages, why can't this same all-powerful ruler clean up the garbage? It is an interesting question as to why McCarthy succeeds so well. The secret, I think, is that McCarthy takes nothing for granted.

It is the common weakness of novels such as Walter Miller's *A Canticle for Leibowitz*, Doris Lessing's *The Memoirs of a Survivor*, P. D. James's *The Children of Men*, or even *A Clockwork Orange* and *1984*, that they are all to some extent science fiction allegories in which the author extrapolates from the present, using hypothetical developments in the future to comment on crises that he or she sees as already imminent in contemporary society. Thus, in the postnuclear age of *A Canticle for Leibowitz*, secularism will triumph and religions die; in Burgess's and Lessing's worlds, juvenile violence and waywardness have spun out of control (these two novels were written in 1962 and 1974, early in the two decades of "the Sixties"); in James's Britain of twenty years hence, males have become infertile and immigrants are rounded up by a totalitarian government and put in cages. There is nothing wrong with any of this, except that some essential illusionistic pressure is taken off the novelist, who can then merely describe the life that we know but with a twist, the old world that most of us recognize but that is suddenly more horrid to live in.

McCarthy's vision is not much like this. *The Road* is not a science fiction, not an allegory, and not a critique of the way we live now, or of the-way-we-might-live-if-we-keep-on-living-the-way-we-do. It poses a simpler question, more taxing for the imagination and far closer to the primary business of fiction making: what would this world without people look like, feel like? From this, everything else flows. What would be the depth of one's loneliness? What kind of tattered theology would remain? What would hour-to-hour, day-to-day experience be like? How would one eat, or find shoes? These questions McCarthy answers magnificently, with the exception of the theological issue (about which more in a moment).

McCarthy's devotion to detail, his Conradian fondness for calmly described horrors, his tolling, fatal sentences, make the reader shiver with fear and recognition. The Coke can is a good example: McCarthy is not afraid to stint the banal, and we are always aware of the contemporary American civilization that has been overthrown by events; it pokes up out of the landscape like fingerposts. There is a barn in a field "with an advertisement in faded ten-foot letters across the roofslope. See Rock City." (So we are in Tennessee, the scene of many of McCarthy's novels.) There are old supermarkets, and abandoned cars, and guns, and a truck the father and son sleep a night in, and even a dead locomotive in a forest. The narrative is about last-ditch practicality, and is itself intensely practical. In one of the houses they enter, the father goes upstairs, looking for anything useful. A mummified corpse is lying in a bed, a blanket pulled up to its chin. Without sensitivity, the man rips the blanket from the bed and thieves it. Blankets matter. There is even a light meter, and the way McCarthy deals with this gives an idea of his patience with things. The man is reflecting on how monotonous the diurnal thin gray light has become:

> He'd once found a lightmeter in a camera store that he thought he might use to average out readings for a few months and he carried it around with him for a long time thinking he might find some batteries for it but he never did.

Again there is the slightly droll humor—the nonexistent batteries kept for the punch line. This sort of ordinariness anchors the book. Jim Crace's *The Pesthouse*, by contrast, is finely written but afraid of banality. Mysteriously, in Crace's vision of life after catastrophe— his book is also set in America and also involves a couple trying to get to the coast—we have returned to the Middle Ages, as if all plastic and technological proof of our former existence had been utterly extinguished. McCarthy's single can of Coke, hallowed like a fossil, seems of course much more plausible than Crace's "biblical" voiding of memory and evidence. Reviewers endlessly speak of McCarthy's biblical style, but in fact this novel is sagely humdrum.

McCarthy's prose combines three registers, two of which are powerful enough to carry his horrors. He has his painstaking minimalism, which works well here. Again and again, he alerts us, in this simpler mode, to elements of hypothetical existence we had not thought about: how angry we might be, for instance, at the world before our catastrophe. The man comes across some old newspapers and reads them: "The curious news. The quaint concerns." He remembers standing in the charred ruins of a library, where books lay in pools of water: "Some rage at the lies arranged in their thousands row on row." In this mode the novel succeeds very well at conjuring into life the essential paradox of post-apocalyptic struggle, which is that survival is the only thing that matters, but why bother surviving?

The second register is the one familiar to readers of *Blood Meridian* or *Suttree*, and again seems somewhat Conradian. Hard detail and a fine eye is combined with exquisite, gnarled, slightly antique (and even slightly clumsy or heavy) lyricism. It ought not to work, and sometimes it does not. But many of its effects are beautiful—and not only beautiful, but powerfully efficient as poetry. The shape of a city seen from far away, standing "in the grayness like a charcoal drawing sketched across the waste." The father and son stand inside a once grand house, "the peeling paint hanging in long dry sleavings down the columns and from the bucked soffits." The little boy has "candlecolored skin," which perfectly evokes his gray, undernourished whiteness, in a gray light that is itself undernourished and entirely reliant on candlepower. The black ash that blows everywhere is seen as resembling a "soft black talc," which "blew through the streets like squid ink uncoiling along a sea floor."

When McCarthy is writing at his best, he does indeed belong in the company of the American masters. In his best pages one can hear Melville and Lawrence, Conrad and Hardy. His novels are full

of marvelous depictions of birds in flight, and *The Road* has a gorgeous paragraph, like something out of Hopkins:

> In that long ago somewhere very near this place he'd
> watched a falcon fall down the long blue wall of the moun-
> tain and break with the keel of its breastbone the midmost
> from a flight of cranes and take it to the river below all
> gangly and wrecked and trailing its loose and blowsy plum-
> age in the still autumn air.

One of the most moving passages in the book concerns the eventual
arrival of father and son at the sea. It is a great disappointment:
their discovery reverses the ancient classical cry, in Xenophon, of
"Thalassa! Thalassa!" There is no one and nothing there, except a
huge gray watery waste, and of course the loneliness of the couple is
vilely exaggerated by the endless gray water—what McCarthy calls
"the endless seacrawl." The sea is covered in ash.

> Beyond that the ocean vast and cold and shifting heavily like
> a slowly heaving vat of slag and then the grey squall line of
> ash. He looked at the boy. He could see the disappointment
> in his face. I'm sorry it's not blue, he said. That's okay, said
> the boy.

Yet McCarthy's third register is more problematic. He is an American ham. When critics laud him for being biblical, they are hearing sounds that are more often than not merely antiquarian, a kind
of vatic histrionic groping, in which the prose plumes itself up and
flourishes an ostentatiously obsolete lexicon. Blood Fustian, this style
might be called. The father and son are here described as "slumped
and cowled and shivering in their rags like mendicant friars," that
word "mendicant" being one of McCarthy's regular favorites. He is
almost always prompted to write like this by metaphor or simile,
which he often renders as hypothesis or analogy, using the formulation "like some": so the man, his face streaked with black from the

rain, looks "like some old world thespian" (an especially flagrant example here, since the son is looking at his father at this moment, and the fancy language stubbornly violates a child's point of view). In the following sentence, the word "autistic," while comprehensible, seems simply incorrect, and somehow a little adolescent, and shakes one's confidence in the writer: "He rose and stood tottering in that cold autistic dark with his arms outheld for balance while the vestibular calculations in his skull cranked out their reckonings." It begins to snow at one point, and "he caught it in his hand and watched it expire there like the last host of christendom."

Still, as in Hardy and Conrad, who were both at times terrible writers, there is a sincerity, an earnestness, in McCarthy's vaudevillian mode that softens the clumsiness, and turns the prose into a kind of awkward secret message from the writer. Conrad, after all, was capable of this description of money, in *The Secret Agent*: it "symbolized the insignificant results which reward the ambitious courage and toil of a mankind whose day is short on this earth of evil." In the same novel, a cheap Italian restaurant in London is said to have "the atmosphere of fraudulent cookery mocking an abject mankind in the most pressing of its miserable necessities." Moreover, McCarthy's writing tightens up as the novel progresses; it is notable that the theatrical antiquarianism belongs largely to the first fifty or so pages, as the writer pushes his barque out into new waters.

II.

All of McCarthy's remarkable effects notwithstanding, there remains the matter of his meanings. There is another vaudevillian strain in *The Road*, a troubling one, in the way the novelist manipulates his theological material. McCarthy's work has always been interested in theodicy, and somewhat shallowly. Here the comparisons to Melville and Hardy are rather embarrassing. He likes to stage bloody fights between good and evil, and his commentary tends toward the easily fatalistic. There is nothing easy about the machinery of this book—the mise-en-scène, the often breathtaking writing, the terrifying concentration of the evocation—but there is something perhaps a little showy about the way that questions of belief are raised and dropped.

The questions could not have been avoided. A post-apocalyptic vision cannot but provoke dilemmas of theodicy, of the justice of fate; and a lament for the *Deus absconditus* is both implicit in McCarthy's imagery—the fine simile of the sun that circles the earth "like a grieving mother with a lamp"—and explicit in his dialogue. Early in the book, the father looks at his son and thinks: "If he is not the word of God God never spoke." There are thieves and murderers and even cannibals on the loose, and the father and son encounter these fearsome envoys of evil every so often. The son needs to think of himself as "one of the good guys," and his father assures him that this is the side they are indeed on.

About halfway through *The Road*, the couple run into a pitiful old man in rags named Ely. The father asks Ely, in another of McCarthy's examples of drollery, how one would know if one were the last man on earth. "I don't guess you would know it. You'd just be it," replies Ely. "I guess God would know it," says the father, which suggests that some measure of faith has survived the end. Ely flatly asserts, "There is no God," and continues: "There is no God and we are his prophets." A little later in the conversation, the father again suggests that he sees his son as divine: "What if I said that he's a god?" Ely replies: "I hope that's not true what you said because to be on the road with the last god would be a terrible thing so I hope it's not true." Ely suggests that it will be better when everybody has died. "Better for who?" asks the father. For everybody, says Ely, closing the scene with a rather lovely peroration, of the kind that gives this book its clear, deep sound: "When we're all gone at last then there'll be nobody here but death and his days will be numbered too. He'll be out in the road there with nothing to do and nobody to do it to. He'll say: Where did everybody go? And that's how it will be. What's wrong with that?"

But the idea that the boy may be the last god—an eschatological plot that is a kind of more philosophical version of *The*

Terminator—lingers in the book, and is caught up again at the end of the book. It is this ending that has surely prompted *USA Today* to draw attention to "something vital and enduring about the boy's spirit," and the *San Francisco Chronicle* to talk of McCarthy's "tale of survival and the miracle of goodness." I wonder what "redemptive" gloss, what little uplifting lesson, Oprah Winfrey, who selected the novel for her remorselessly edifying book club, read into the novel's final pages? The father, who has been ailing, dies, and the son realizes this in the morning. McCarthy's prose is movingly chaste; the reticent power of his minimalism is exactly what is needed:

> He slept close to his father that night and held him but when he woke in the morning his father was cold and stiff. He sat there a long time weeping and then he got up and walked out through the woods to the road. When he came back he knelt beside his father and held his cold hand and said his name over and over again.

Especially fine is the withheld passion of "held his cold hand and said his name over and over again," because, in the rest of the novel, we rarely, if ever, witness the son calling his father "Father" (or any intimate equivalent); those words of tenderness burst through only now, at the end of the novel, and only in reported description.

So the boy is alone, but not for long. He meets a man on the road. "Are you one of the good guys?" he warily asks him. Yes, says the man. "You dont eat people," says the boy. "No. We dont eat people." So he joins the man's group, and in the novel's penultimate paragraph, a woman is seen embracing the boy, and saying, "Oh . . . I am so glad to see you." It is the only moment in the book in which anyone other than the boy's father has embraced him.

> She would talk to him sometimes about God. He tried to talk to God but the best thing was to talk to his father and he did talk to him and he didnt forget. The woman said that was all right. She said that the breath of God was

his breath yet though it pass from man to man through all
of time.

The woman seems to affirm that God, or some kind of God, still
exists, and is not annihilated by the end of his creation. The boy is
indeed a kind of last God, who is "carrying the fire" of belief (the
father and son used to speak of themselves, in a kind of familial
shorthand, as people who were carrying the fire: it seems to be a
version of being "the good guys"). Since the breath of God passes
from man to man, and God cannot die, this boy represents what
will survive of humanity, and also points to how life will be rebuilt.

There is no obligation for *The Road* to answer an unanswerable
dilemma like theodicy. But the placement of what looks like a paragraph of religious consolation at the end of such a novel is striking,
and it throws the book off balance a little, precisely because theology has not seemed exactly central to the book's inquiry. One has a
persistent, uneasy sense that theodicy and the absent God have
been merely exploited by the book, engaged with only lightly, without much pressure of interrogation. When Ely says "There is no
God and we are his prophets," the phrase seems a little trite in its
neat paradox of negation; when exactly the same phrase was used
by the nineteenth-century Danish novelist Jens Peter Jacobsen, in
his novel *Niels Lyhne*, it vibrated powerfully, because it arose out of
an extended, vehement, and utterly engaged treatment, crucial to
nineteenth-century life, of the question of God's existence.

In this respect, to compare McCarthy to Beckett, as some reviewers have done, is to flatter McCarthy. His reticence and his
minimalism work superbly at evocation, but they exhaust themselves when philosophy presses down. The style that is so good at
the glancing, the lyrical, the half-expressed, struggles to deal ade-
quately with the very metaphysical questions that apocalypse raises.
Beyond tiny hints, we have no idea what the father and son believe
about God's survival, so there is no dramatized rendition, no aesthetically responsible account, of such a question.

The theological question stirred by apocalypse is, How will all this end? What will result? "Please don't tell me how the story ends," the father silently implores, early in the book. It is not the truth about the end of the world that he refers to, but the knowledge that it may end with him killing his son. He is haunted by this apprehension, and he cannot do it: that is why he dies and tells his son to go on without him. That the question of endings is transferred onto this personal dilemma is precisely what makes the novel, and especially its conclusion, so painfully affecting. But the end of the world is more than a personal matter; and what *The Road* gains in human interest it loses by being personal at the moment when it should be theological. The question of endings in apocalypse must be philosophical as well as merely personal, even in a novel. Will it be heaven or hell? Will it last forever, or be over in flash?

Apocalyptic narrative is necessarily paradoxical. The end threatens, but in order for narrative to exist, in order for narrative to continue narrating, apocalypse must always be postponed. Behind much of *The Road* one can feel the pressure of Edgar's lines from *King Lear*: "the worst is not / So long as we can say 'This is the worst'"; as long as language can be used to recount the worst, then the worst has not arrived. Has "the worst" already occurred (the destruction of *almost* everything we recognize as human), or is worse still ahead? And would *that* then be "the worst"? When does narrative, language end? *The Road*'s solacing theological optimism blurs and finally evades these deepest of questions.

EDMUND WILSON

I.

In the photograph by Irving Penn, he stares remorselessly at his fashionable torturer. He is sixty-five, and looks every day of it. Two sparse claws of sandy hair lie on the back of his head, leaving a large, dense, unencumbered brow. His small eyes, alive with irritable clarity, look sore and weary: they are multiply rimmed. The heavy jowls are at once mannish and babyish, like his downturned mouth, a fallen crescent. The strong, broad chin, exactly his mother's, pushes forward to confront the weaker world. He looks confident, uncomfortable, impatient, and sourly lucid.

When Edmund Wilson sat for Penn in 1960, most of his great work was behind him: *Axel's Castle* (1931), that still superbly clear-eyed introduction to symbolism and the modernism that was its child; the long, pioneering essays on Pushkin, Dickens, Kipling, Wharton, and Hemingway, collected in *The Triple Thinkers* (1938) and *The Wound and the Bow* (1941); and *To the Finland Station* (1940), a massive and spacious account of radical thought from Vico and Michelet to Marx and Lenin. The three years between 1938 and 1941, in which Wilson published those last three books, must constitute the greatest period of critical productivity in American letters, and one of the greatest periods of creative productivity, too.

In these early books, Wilson had established his characteristic personality and intellectual temperament. Isaiah Berlin, one of

Wilson's friends, once remarked that other critics writing at this time wrote "just intelligent sentences," while Wilson's, which came out of his discomfort with himself, were always "filled with some kind of personal content." Wilson's criticism is marked by its eighteenth-century robustness, by its glinting, pugnacious clarity, by its need to turn analysis into narrative, by its exhaustive and sometimes exhausting scholarship, and by the tense, prosaic music of its sentences. It can, at first, seem like a flat style, one unfit for permanent criticism—which lasts, after all, only if it, too, becomes literature. The abundant literary journalism, often written weekly for *The New Republic* magazine and *The New Yorker*, has at times a hasty lusterlessness, but Wilson polished and revised the literary portraits that filled his books, and often we find a beautifully restrained and classically elegant expository prose. The chapter on Proust, from *Axel's Castle*, is an astonishing thirty-page summary of *À la recherche du temps perdu*, and ends with a paragraph that used to be famous:

> Proust is perhaps the last great historian of the loves, the society, the intelligence, the diplomacy, the literature and the art of the Heartbreak House of capitalist culture; and the little man with the sad appealing voice, the metaphysician's mind, the Saracen's beak, the ill-fitting dress-shirt and the great eyes that seem to see all about him like the many-faceted eyes of a fly, dominates the scene and plays host in the mansion where he is not long to be master.

Finer still, perhaps, are the closing words of Wilson's portrait of Oliver Wendell Holmes, from *Patriotic Gore* in 1962, his last great book, in which he discusses Justice Holmes's bequest of his entire fortune to the government of the United States:

> He had fought for the Union; he had mastered its laws; he had served in its highest court through a period of three decades. The American Constitution was, as he came to declare, an "experiment"—what was to come of our democratic

society it was impossible for a philosopher to tell—but he had taken responsibility for its working, he had subsisted and achieved his fame through his tenure of the place it had given him; and he returned to the treasury of the Union the little that he had to leave.

Wilson several times called himself a man of the eighteenth century, and one can hear in the balanced periods, the long semicolons, and the finely paradoxical compression—"plays host in the mansion where he is not long to be master"; "returned to the treasury of the Union the little that he had to leave"—both Gibbon and Johnson. And behind them is the Latin of Tacitus and Cicero: this is how, until quite recently, if not with such eloquence, English classics teachers of the old school used to write their term reports, and Wilson, almost uniquely among American literary journalists, had a solid training in Greek and Latin, languages that he maintained throughout his life. The tendency to defer the verb and object, to wave them on to the middle or end of the line, to interrupt the shapely sentence with subordinate and prepositional clauses, is clearly Latinate: "The abstractions of German philosophy, which may seem to us unmeaning or clumsy if we encounter them in English or French, convey in German, through their capitalized solidity, almost the impression of primitive gods. They are substantial, and yet they are a kind of pure beings; they are abstract, and yet they nourish." Gibbon, with a greater, more silvery exhibitionism, does the same thing:

> While Petrarch indulged these prophetic visions, the Roman hero was fast declining from the meridian of fame and power; and the people, who had gazed with astonishment on the ascending meteor, began to mark the irregularity of its course, and the vicissitudes of light and obscurity. More eloquent than judicious, more enterprising than resolute, the faculties of Rienzi were not balanced by cool and commanding reason; he magnified in a tenfold proportion the

objects of hope and fear; and prudence, which could not
have erected, did not presume to fortify, his throne.

Wilson disliked the kind of piecemeal quoting I am doing. He
called it "anthologizing," and his own prose, built of solid blocks of
exegesis and description, is correspondingly difficult to parcel up.
Unlike, say, Randall Jarrell—or Hazlitt, or Woolf—he had almost
no interest in witty or metaphorical one-liners. In his essay "Is Verse
a Dying Technique?" he rebukes Matthew Arnold and T. S. Eliot
for their habit of selecting a line or two of a poet's work, so making
fetishistic touchstones of these now "anthologized" poets: "The old
critic, when he reads the classic, epic, eclogue, tale, or play, may
have grasped it and enjoyed it as a whole; yet when the reader reads
the comment of the critic, he gets the impression . . . that the *Divine Comedy*, say, so extraordinarily sustained and so beautifully
integrated, is remarkable mainly for Eliot-like fragments."

Wilson's method was likewise to eschew the fragmentary, to
strive for integration, and it is both a strength and a weakness in
his work. He wrote a huge essay, such as the one on Dickens, which
is almost twenty-five thousand words long, by reading everything,
and then by clearing an exegetical path through the many large
novels in order to turn Dickens's career into a story, consisting of
biography and description. For the kind of summarizing and con-
clusive portraits Wilson did, this method is majestically good, and
truly makes him an heir to Johnson and Macaulay. He seems to rear
panoptically above his subjects, like a statue overseeing a city square,
sternly, anciently surveying the busy activity, compressing and elu-
cidating vast amounts of mobile information. His letters become
rather wearisome to read because of his need to whale his corre-
spondents with his learning; as someone in the Goncourt journals
remarks about a minor French writer, "Yes, yes, he has talent, but
he doesn't know how to make people forgive him for having it."
A letter to Gilbert Highet, after the publication of the latter's
The Classical Tradition in 1949, runs to many pages, and sixteen

numbered points: "2. I think that there is something more to the influence of Virgil on Dante than your account of it indicates . . . 3. You say, on page 79, that Dante makes Statius a Christian 'doubtless because of the medieval tradition of his conversion' . . . But apparently no such tradition is known." And this was an admiring letter. A typical missive to Lionel Trilling, written in 1953, proceeds thus: "Not only George Orwell but Eliot has been under the delusion that runcible is not a real word. I suppose you know that a runcible spoon was a three-tined spoon (I think, three) for extracting pickles from jars . . . Have you ever gone into [Edward] Lear aside from his nonsense rhymes? I think he is very attractive, and I do hope some day to write about him." As late as 1971 (he died a year later), he was writing to Erich Segal: "Thank you very much for the Plautus . . . You have been extremely successful in catching the sense and following the meter . . . I don't quite like 'Greeking it up,' 'Boozing it up,' etc. (Wouldn't 'going Greek' be better?)" And to Angus Wilson in the same year: "I enjoyed your book on Dickens. I suppose that you have discovered that an illustration by Catermole is attributed to Cruickshank." And to Vladimir Nabokov, with whom he had quarreled over Pushkin, Wilson wrote, also in 1971: "I am just now getting together a volume of my Russian articles. I am correcting my errors in Russian in my piece on Nabokov-Pushkin; but citing a few more of your ineptitudes."

He admired the independence of a historian such as Michelet, or the much more scattered learning of an American oddity such as John Jay Chapman. Though he taught occasionally—a course on Dickens at Chicago, a term at Princeton, and some lectures at Harvard—he disliked lecturing, and was not very good at it, and his career was conducted, during the great era of the encroaching university, in prickly independence from academia. What he wrote about Michelet, in *To the Finland Station*, can also be applied to himself: "The impression he makes on us is quite different from that of the ordinary modern scholar who has specialized in some narrowly delimited subject and gotten it up in a graduate school: we

feel that Michelet has read all the books, been to look at all the
monuments and pictures, interviewed personally all the authorities,
and explored all the libraries and archives of Europe; and that he
has it all under his hat."

Wilson's grand, all-seeing approach, while ideal for narrative, is
something of a weakness in literary criticism. He was never drawn
to the kind of close textual reading that was going on around him in
and out of the universities, and his unwillingness to quote from the
texts that he is discussing gives his criticism, at times, a rather syn-
optic voraciousness, as if texts exist to be paraphrased and sum-
marized, to be crushed into clarifying prose. In his essay "Seeing
Chekhov Plain," one of his weakest, he argues, without much evidence, that Chekhov's late stories were attempting to cover the
whole of Russian society, like Balzac's novels did France. He briskly
marches through several of Chekhov's most exquisite tales:

> "Peasants" is a study of the peasant world, which Chekhov
> is far from idealizing . . . A peasant from the *izba*, who has
> bettered himself to the extent of becoming a waiter in
> Moscow, falls ill and returns with a wife and child to his
> family in the village . . . In a companion piece, "In the Ra-
> vine," Chekhov deals with the brutalizing influence of the
> kulak, prosperous peasant, class. In this somewhat better-
> off family, the shopkeeper father sells bad meat, one of his
> sons passes bad money, and an enterprising daughter-in-
> law, who is building a brickyard on her father-in-law's land
> and who fears that she may be deprived of it, eliminates the
> infant grandson to whom he proposes to leave it by scald-
> ing him to death with boiling water . . . In "The Bishop,"
> the next-to-last story that Chekhov lived to complete, he
> fixes on his slide a specimen of the not quite diseased yet
> not very vigorous tissue of the Greek Orthodox Church: a
> dying peasant priest, who has risen above the level of his
> parents but now finds he has nobody close to him . . . In

these, and in the stories that immediately precede them, are presented a variety of other types of peasants, ex-peasants, and the lower middle class that were called in Russia *meshchane*, together with doctors, professors, petty provincial officials, and—given the full-scale treatment in "The Duel" of 1891—the pretentious and inept intelli-gentsia.

It is true that Wilson was trying, in such hard descriptions, to coun-ter the Anglo-American idea of Chekhov, then prevalent, as a misty poet of dreamy despair. Yet the lack of attention to detail, in a writer whose greatness rests supremely on his use of detail, the un-willingness to talk of fiction as if narrative were a special kind of aesthetic experience and not a reducible proposition, the conver-sion of the complicated long story "The Duel" into what sounds like a mere exposé of intellectuals, is rather scandalous. One reads Wil-son on Chekhov without any sense that beauty is involved, or that the critic wants to account for it. One feels only that yet another writer has been mastered. The "specimen" Wilson refers to—an unfortu-nate metaphor to use in connection with "The Bishop," which is so full of Chekhovian tenderness and sympathy—is not Chekhov's bishop but Chekhov himself, who is here being used to fulfill an ideological requirement of comprehensiveness.

Three men influenced Edmund Wilson's youth and constructed his sensibility: his father; the nineteenth-century French historian Hippolyte Taine, whom Wilson read as a teenager, and whose *His-tory of English Literature* was the first criticism he ever read; and Christian Gauss, the teacher of Dante and Flaubert whom he en-countered as a student at Princeton, and with whom he corresponded until Gauss's death. It might be said that, among many things, Wil-son received, respectively, from these three: an abiding interest in, and personal involvement with, neurotic collapse; a sense that literature should above all be accounted for historically; and a deep, neoclassical suspicion, amounting to an incomprehension, of ro-manticism.

One of Wilson's finest essays is "The Author at Sixty," a portrait not really of the writer but of his father. It is written with Wilson's lovely stern objectivity; the impulse is not to bathe in memory, but to see his father whole, to comprehend him as Pushkin or Marx or John Jay Chapman are also comprehended. Edmund Wilson Sr. was a successful trial lawyer who became attorney general of New Jersey, and who was once sounded out for a Supreme Court position by President Wilson. But like Virginia Woolf's father, though much more drastically, he was a neurotic who had a breakdown in midlife and never quite functioned properly again. He was learned, severe, hypochondriacal, and inaccessible. "He was undoubtedly a very self-centered man, and, when sunk in his neurotic periods, would be shut in some inner prison where he was quite beyond communication," wrote his son. These periods of withdrawal could last as long as a year, broken only by his wife's insistence that he take on another case, to fill the family coffers. As a lawyer, the elder Wilson was formidable, and his son reckoned that the success had partly to do with rhetorical power and with imperturbable confidence, traits that he himself would inherit: "The reason for his success was undoubtedly that he never undertook a case which he did not think he could win, and that his judgment about this was infallible. He would cause [the jury] to live through the events of the crime or supposed crime, he would take them through the steps of the transaction, whatever that was, and he would lodge in their heads a picture that it was difficult for his opponent to expel."

His son, who had a breakdown at the same age his father was first afflicted, would develop what amounts to a theory about the connection between artistic production and personal suffering—"the wound and the bow"—and would become expert at brilliantly lodging in the minds of his readers "a picture" of his subjects. It was a talent that both Taine and Gauss possessed, too. Wilson discovered Taine's book, in translation, on his father's shelves. From the first, he was enthralled by his mixture of belletristic criticism and biographical verve—the way, for instance, Taine began his chapter on Swift (in Van Laun's translation):

In 1685, in the great hall of Dublin University, the professors engaged in examining for the bachelor's degree enjoyed
a singular spectacle: a poor scholar, odd, awkward, with
hard blue eyes, an orphan, friendless, poorly supported by
the charity of an uncle, having failed once before to take
his degree on account of his ignorance of logic, had come
up again without having condescended to read logic . . .
and the professors went away, doubtless with pitying smiles,
lamenting the feeble brain of Jonathan Swift.

Taine's French positivism involved studying works of literature
"scientifically," by setting them in their historical and biological
context—in what he called "*la race, le milieu et le moment.*" Though
Wilson did not subscribe as faithfully as Taine to a belief in the
causative powers of history and race, he employed such categories
when it suited him (particularly when writing about Russians). Like
Taine, he believed that literature could be studied as a "specimen"—
that word used by Wilson to describe Chekhov's dying bishop—and
he learned from the French tradition the importance of clear, objective scrutiny.

Born just inside the nineteenth century, in 1895, Wilson was a
man both of that epoch and of the eighteenth century, and in some
ways he remained fiercely loyal to his background. Just as his father,
in later years, had taken to spending time alone in the old family
house, in Talcottville, New York, so his son, in his later years, would
spend bookish weeks alone in Talcottville, despite the hostility and
the absence of his wife. He loved Swift, as Taine did, and like Taine
he had a tendency, reinforced by his education at Princeton, to con-
descend to Wordsworth and Shelley, using the more classical Goethe
and Dante as sticks with which to chastise the romantics' spilt religion. Just as George Saintsbury, the breezy Victorian scholar of English literature whom Wilson read as a young man, disdained George
Eliot, so Wilson would confess to never having read *Middlemarch*.

He encountered Christian Gauss in his final year at Princeton
and wrote a fine memoir of him after his death. Gauss was a greatly

learned professor of French and Italian, born in Michigan to German parents. "He seemed to be able to summon almost anything he wanted in prose or verse, as if he were taking down the book from the shelf," wrote his distinguished pupil. He transmitted to Wilson a lifelong love of Dante, and a neoclassical aesthetic. "Shakespeare was not one of the authors whom Christian had lived in or on; and he always made us feel that that sort of thing [Shakespeare's messiness] would never come up to literature that was polished and carefully planned and that knew how to make its points and the meaning of the points it was making." Likewise, Wilson never gives the impression of one who lives in, or on, Shakespeare. Virgil, Dante, and Flaubert were his great navigators. "This non-English, this classical and Latin ideal, became indissolubly associated in our minds with the summits of literature," he writes in his memoir.

Faithfully, Wilson would use this "non-English, this classical and Latin ideal" as a standard by which to judge much literature. It is how he thought Flaubert should be read, thus squeezing the romanticism out of that writer, and he rather strangely praised Henry James for "his classical equanimity in dealing with diverse forces . . . his combination, equally classical, of hard realism with formal harmony." He disliked the romantic aestheticism in Arnold's and Eliot's criticism, and he liked in Michelet that "he gave the world, not as his romantic contemporaries did, personal exaltations and despairs swollen to heroic volume, but the agonizing drama of the emergence of the modern world out of feudalism." He would read Marx as perhaps the ideal nineteenth-century romantic, a child of the Enlightenment who united rationalism and a properly submerged personal struggle. Most happily, Wilson would rightly find in Pushkin, whose greatness he pressed on a largely ignorant Anglo-Saxon world, a Mozartean blend of the classical and romantic.

If we were to use Taine's categories of milieu and moment, we would have to admit that when Wilson left Princeton in 1916, European and American modernism had found its ideal critic. As modernist writing would draw some of its chastened lyricism from the trauma of the Great War, so Wilson, who served in the hospitals in

France, dressing the wounds of men whose genitals had been burned by mustard gas, would be deeply affected by his wartime experience. At Princeton, the young man had added French to his Greek and Latin, and this would enable him to trace a line from the aestheticism of Mallarmé and Villiers de l'Isle-Adam to Proust, Eliot, and Joyce. Above all, modernism's own classicism, its formal rigor and allusive snobberies, its Homeric and Virgilian aspirations, would fall right into the lap of a young critic with deep historical eyesight and his own distrust of "personality."

So began the two great decades of Wilson's career, first at *Vanity Fair*, and then, from 1925 and through the 1930s, at *The New Republic*. He moved between relentless amounts of work and equally relentless eroticism. (He did not lose his virginity until he was twenty-five, to Edna St. Vincent Millay, but he made up for lost time in the next decade.) Nowadays, as people run around town yelling about reviewers' "snark," it is invigorating to be reminded of how steely and objective Wilson was as a critic, and how the writers he pressed to give the best of themselves came to rely on the critic's clear-running judgment. F. Scott Fitzgerald, a Princeton classmate, received harsh criticism for *This Side of Paradise*, but wrote to Wilson that "I am guilty of its every stricture and I take an extraordinary delight in its considered approbation." Wilson wrote the first review in America of Hemingway's work, in 1924, and would write with great insight over the next twenty years about this novelist. The two became friendly, but this would not stop Wilson from severely criticizing Hemingway's masculinist fantasies. Yet Hemingway, like Faulkner after a similar bruising, eventually wrote to Wilson in a spirit of solidarity. None of them went to quite the lengths of Anaïs Nin, who slept with Wilson in order to win his critical approval of her work. Fitzgerald probably spoke for many when he called Wilson the literary conscience of the age.

Most impressive, perhaps, were Wilson's early reviews of *The Waste Land* and *Ulysses*. He would go on to defend Joyce in particular (Eliot's conservative politics irritated him), and to write wonderfully and acutely about *Finnegans Wake*, seeing in that book

a new Joycean lyricism. Wilson was always independent, but in
modernism he had found his creed, or it had found him. He was
blindfolded, like Justice herself, so that he could see beyond the
Manhattan horizon. His criticism, at once partisan and Olympian,
manages the extraordinary feat of being disinterestedly interested.

II.

The other creed that found Wilson was Marxism, which permeated
his literary judgments. Wilson's radical politics had a long literary
afterlife, too. Many years after he had drifted away from any belief
in Marxism's survival in Soviet Russia, his notion of literature was
apt to be skewed by old loyalties. His long essay on Chekhov, written in 1952, is an example, in which Chekhov is turned out as a
writer who usefully shows us scenes of peasant life and the idiocies
of the prerevolutionary intelligentsia. His essay on Flaubert, published in 1938, is bizarrely determined to see the novelist as a kind
of unconscious Marxist: "In his novels, it is never the nobility—
indistinguishable for mediocrity from the bourgeois—but the peasants and working people whom he habitually uses as touchstones to
show up the pretensions of the bourgeois." He can at times sound
like the much more orthodox Marxist Georg Lukács, who was writing at the same time about the bourgeois novel. In Wilson's forced
reading, *Madame Bovary* becomes an attack on capitalist nostalgia:
"What cuts Flaubert off from the other romantics and makes him
primarily a social critic is his grim realization of the futility of
[Emma's] dreaming about the splendors of the Orient and the brave
old days of the past as an antidote to bourgeois society . . . She will
not face her situation as it is, and the result is that she is eventually
undone by the realities she has been trying to ignore." That last
rather moralistic sentence reminds us of the brutally summarizing
Wilson, the Wilson who will happily gut a living novelistic organism
with the blunt blade of précis. In this case, his classical resistance to
Flaubert's romanticism combines with his worthy political belief
that Flaubert ought to be on the side of the good, to blind him to

the quality of ironic nullification, the conservative misanthropy that is so disturbing in Flaubert.

Wilson is determined to see something "positive" and "objective" in Flaubert, as he rightly found many positive elements in Dickens. These socialist loyalties would obstruct, at times, his friendship with Nabokov. When the Russian complained, in 1946, that André Malraux, Wilson's newest literary "find," was not a great novelist, Wilson confidently replied that "Silone and Malraux now emerge, I think, as the masters of the political-social-moral semi-Marxist school of fiction that is the great development in its field since the analytical psychological novel." Wilson was bringing the cultural news; but one can only imagine what Nabokov thought of the headlines: "the political-social-moral semi-Marxist school of fiction," indeed.

The fruit of his interest in communism was his astonishing history of radical thought, *To the Finland Station*, which he began in 1934 and finished in 1940. It began life as a series of articles for *The New Republic* on Vico, Michelet, Taine, Fourier, Marx, Engels, and Trotsky. The labor involved was prodigious; Louise Bogan wrote to a friend about counting eighty-six volumes of Michelet's writings lined up on a shelf in Wilson's study. He visited Russia in 1935, and in the next two years taught himself both Russian and German. There is something very moving about Wilson's independence, his erotic curiosity for knowledge—though the conquistador of knowledge, bedding one fact after another, can become tiresome to the reader after a while. Wilson moved out of New York, to Stamford, Connecticut, where most of the book was written, and as late as 1939 he was writing to Trilling to ask him to find, in a New York library, Marx's pamphlet on Palmerston.

To the Finland Station is still an enthralling book. Wilson conveys, with something approaching joy, the experience of reading Michelet, or *Das Kapital*, or Trotsky's history of the revolution. The book is full of vivid portraits, which are etched like woodcuts: Marx and his family, evicted from their Soho lodgings; Engels, and his almost French liveliness and buoyant rationalism; Trotsky, with his amazing confidence, sitting in prison and posing for a photograph, "not abashed, not indignant, hardly even defiant, but like the head of a great state who has still at a time of crisis to give the photographer a moment." Wilson is convinced that Marxism is the great second flowering of the Enlightenment, and that Marxism-Leninism still holds the possibility of founding, in Russia, the first "truly human" society.

Of course, the book is also spiked with premonition, for he could now see, despite his own golden reports during his visit, that Stalin's Russia was far from being a truly human society. Little jabs of warning protrude like fingerposts every so often: "There are many respects in which Marx and Engels may be contrasted with the crude pedants and fanatics who have pretended to speak for the movement which Marx and Engels started."

But he believed that it was not Marxism so much as something rotten in the Russian system, even the Russian psyche, that was to blame. "The problem is not Marxism but the incompatibility of certain national psychologies to Marxism," he wrote to John Dos Passos. As Paul Berman has shown, Wilson had come under the tutelage of the historian Max Eastman, for whom the culprit was Marx's mysticism, and for whom Lenin was a hero. This explains the romanticizing, at the end of Wilson's book, of Lenin, who is seen as the gentlest and most selfless of men, a lover of Beethoven and *War and Peace* who once, Wilson moistly reports, refused to shoot a fox because he thought it "beautiful." A pity then, wrote Nabokov tartly, that Russia was homely.

Wilson could see that it was psychologically credulous of Marx to believe that when the proletariat took over it would simply be on its best behavior. What was the evidence for this? Why would the worker not want what the capitalist plutocrat had had? Marx, he reflects, "did not know the United States," and thus begins four glorious pages in which Wilson's difficult, crooked, ornery love of America, which would become more and more of a passion in his later years, is flowingly confessed:

What Karl Marx had no clue for understanding was that the absence in the United States of the feudal class background of Europe would have the effect not only of facilitating the expansion of capitalism but also of making possible a genuine social democratization; that a community would grow up and endure in which the people engaged in different occupations would probably come nearer to speaking the same language and even to sharing the same criteria than anywhere else in the industrialized world. Here in the United States, our social groupings are mainly based on money, and the money is always changing hands so rapidly that the class lines cannot get cut very deep . . . we have the class quarrel out as we go along . . . We are more lawless [than Europe], but we are more homogenous; and our homogeneity consists of common tendencies which Marx would have regarded as bourgeois, but which are actually only partly explicable as the results of capitalist competition. The common man, set free from feudal society, seems to do everywhere much the same sort of thing—which is not what Marx had expected him to do because it was not what Marx liked to do himself.

Wilson continues in this powerful vein, finally landing on a devastating sentence: "In other words, Marx was incapable of imagining democracy at all."

Yet he cannot get around the problem that Marxism seems to have failed in Russia, and he seems unsure where to place the blame—sometimes at Marx's door, more often at the feet of those "pedants and fanatics" who have distorted Marx's humanism. In this regard there are two telling omissions in *To the Finland Station*: Rousseau and Dostoevsky. It is strange to write a history of radical political thought that only briefly mentions the thinker most influential on the prime movers of the French Revolution, whose own work alleges that society began to go downhill when a single man first declared that his patch of land was private property, whose notion of the "general will" could be described by a later historian as "totalitarian democracy."

But Rousseau's speculative theology of the fall of man only forces the very question that Wilson cannot face in Marx. If man was once good, in his state of nature, and is now bad, in his state of society, how exactly did he begin to corrupt? Did he become bad because human nature is corrupt, or because society corrupted his goodness? If the latter, what is the hope for a utopian restoration of man? How do we get back—or back and forward at once—to the ideal state of man? Likewise, did the revolution of 1917 go bad because corrupt human nature cannot be trusted with revolutionary despotism, or because violent revolution is at its heart a corrupt idea? And if the answer to either question is yes, the question fudged by Rousseau returns: how do we reach utopia; how do we—in Rousseau's terms—restore what has been lost?

Dostoevsky, only once, and briefly, mentioned in Wilson's book, is in some ways the more flagrant omission, for in *The Possessed*, fictionalizing the rabid cruelty of the revolutionaries Nechaev and Bakunin, he produced a prophetic, highly conservative account of what Leninism would become. It is hard to read the novel without feeling that, in Peter Verkhovensky, arrogant, contemptuous, bullying, murderous, one has really met Lenin. Wilson was not given to theoretical questioning like this, and had very little time for the kind of theological answers that such questions tend to prompt. So Rousseau and Dostoevsky, in their different ways religious, hem Wilson from two sides, both of them finally pessimistic about worldly utopia (though Rousseau did not think he was), and both waving before his eyes the tattered flags of radical defeat.

III.

Rereading Edmund Wilson, one's admiration for him both expands and contracts. His literary portraiture is remarkable, and lastingly fine. Meyer Schapiro once remarked that Wilson's subjects are rendered like "the great fictional characters of literature," and it is true that Wilson extends to Marx, to Chapman, to Dickens, to Holmes, to Ulysses Grant, to his father, a kind of negative capability that he never truly summoned in his own fiction: he is willing to give these men the benefit of the doubt, to leave them in a dapple of ambiguity rather than drag them out into any prematurely decisive light of judgment.

He follows the eccentricities and brilliances of a man such as John Jay Chapman with fascinated tact. Chapman, like Wilson's father, had roared out of his upper-class confinement into the political and legal world, only to withdraw into inexplicable obscurity. As a young man, he lost his arm by thrusting it into a fire—he was morbidly in love—and then entered New York politics. Highly literate and refined, he wrote a biographical study of Emerson, and many brilliant essays on literature and philosophy. Wilson does not really know why Chapman withdrew from political and social life. He simply describes it:

> Given the fineness of Chapman's equipment, the overpowering nature of his emotions, and the relentless clarity of his insight—and given the inescapable conviction of his superiority . . . there was nothing for him to do but break. And the permanent psychological damage which he had inflicted upon himself by beating his head against the gilt of the Gilded Age was as much one of the scars of the heroism of his passionate and expiatory nature as the hand he had burnt off in his youth.

This is very good; it does what Wilson's father achieved as a lawyer—it fixes in our mind a picture, as in the close of the essay, in which Wilson remembers seeing Chapman, now a middle-aged man, in New York in the 1920s:

> One used to see him, during those years, in New York, in company a figure of a distinction almost exotic for the

United States, with his fine manners, his sensitive intelligence, his clothes with their attractive suggestion of the
elegance of another era, his almost Jove-like beard and
brow, his deep and genial laugh; or for a moment under a
quite different aspect, when one had happened to meet
him in the street: walking alone, head drooping and brooding, with his muffler around his neck, in his face dreadful
darkness and sadness and fear, as if he were staring into
some lidless abyss.

What is most surprising, perhaps, in light of Wilson's reputation, is
that he is sometimes, in the major essays, a disappointing literary
critic. The negative capability that he extends to his people—to
their ambiguities, their abysses, their neurotic hollows—he often
refuses to extend to texts themselves. Indulgent toward biographical ambiguity, he is actually hostile to it when it emerges in literature. To my knowledge, his only published words on William
Empson are found in a letter to Louise Bogan, in 1938: "He has one
of those untrustworthy minds which in their more uncontrollable
forms prove that Bacon wrote Shakespeare." It is telling that Wilson had no time for the great theorist of ambiguity and contradiction, whose "seventh category" of ambiguity in *Seven Types of
Ambiguity* occurs when the two meanings of a word "are the two
opposite meanings defined by the context, so that the total effect is
to show a fundamental division in the writer's mind." Empson con-
cedes that many will presume that contradiction always forms "a
larger unity if the final effect is to be satisfying. But the onus of
reconciliation can be laid very highly on the receiving end"—that
is, readers may want to push reconciliation onto a text, but this may
be just our fantasy of wholeness, not the text's, which may want to
persist in being contradictory.

It was just this "onus of reconciliation," this need to tidy up
ambiguities, that seemed to make Wilson so restless as a critic,
and to push him out of the twentieth century and back into the

nineteenth or eighteenth. Recall the words with which Wilson me-
morialized his mentor at Princeton. Christian Gauss, he wrote, always made them feel that Shakespeare would never quite equal a
classical literature "that was polished and carefully planned and
that knew how to make its points and the meaning of the points it
was making." This sounds very much like Wilson's own criticism;
but it is a weak foundation on which to judge modern literature,
with its ironies and its veils. It is the desire to force literature to
"make its points and the meaning of the points it is making" that
leads Wilson into the coercions of paraphrase again and again.

That coercion is there in the Chekhov essay, and also in his essay on Gogol. It makes the essay on Flaubert dogmatic. It makes a
scandal of his essay "The Ambiguity of Henry James." Wilson peculiarly uses *The Turn of the Screw* as the key to unlock what clearly
irritates him in James—which is James's apparent refusal to decisively judge his characters, to come down on one side or another.
The Aspern Papers is praised because "there is no uncertainty
whatever as to what we are to think of the narrator"; but in *The Sa-
cred Fount*, as in *The Turn of the Screw*, "the fundamental question
presents itself and never seems to get properly answered: What is
the reader to think of the protagonist?" James, Wilson decides, was
not "clear" in his own mind.

Flaubert is favorably contrasted with James. In *Sentimental
Education*, for instance, "Flaubert is quite emphatic in his final
judgment of Frédéric. He considers Frédéric a worm." But this
pugilistic confidence is surely misplaced. It is by no means certain
what Flaubert thinks of his lax hero, precisely because of the ironic
ambiguity of Flaubert's writing, and indeed Henry James himself
worried that Flaubert was not entirely in control of these ambiguities. But Wilson tends to revert to biography, and to reductive biography, when he gets into such critical abysses, and sure enough he
decides that James's ambiguities really flow from his repressed
homosexuality. In a barbarous postscript for a second edition, dated
1948, Wilson digs himself further in by bizarrely accusing James of

being fond of describing the sexual violation of children. He reports
that he has shown *The Turn of the Screw* to an Austrian novelist
who remarked: "The man who wrote that was a *Kinderschander*
[child molester]." Wilson seems to concur: "There was always in
Henry James an innocent little girl whom he cherished and loved
and protected and yet whom he later tried to violate, whom he even
tried to kill . . . In his impatience with himself, he would like to destroy or rape her."

His much-praised essay on Kipling seems to me similarly reductive, tracing weaknesses in the work to Kipling's childhood trauma
of being sent away at the age of six to stay with cruel relatives in
England. Wilson's political hostility to Kipling's work is far more
virulent than Orwell's; unlike Orwell, who in his sensible essay on
Kipling eschews this kind of biography mongering, he decides that
Kipling's politics can best be explained with reference to an originating wound. (The essay appeared in *The Wound and the Bow*.)
Kipling, it seems, learned at an early age to cower before authority
and to bully the weak; there was something wrong with "the basic
courage and humanity of his character." He was even, so Wilson reports, bossed around by his wife. Here, as in the James essay, Wilson
sounds much more Victorian, much more moralistic, than he probably wished to sound. He attacks the weakest stories, and then, too
late, praises the great late tales, such as "Mary Postgate" and "The
Gardener." But these are briskly celebrated, unlike the poorer stories, which are lovingly excoriated, and there is no really discrimi-
nating account of what makes Kipling so exciting to read. The reader
has to go to Jarrell's and Trilling's brilliant essays on Kipling for any
sense of aesthetic pleasure.

So Wilson's three great childhood inheritances—his interest in
neurotic collapse, his neoclassical aesthetic, and his belief in a posi-
tivist historicizing of literature—frequently lead him away from an
aesthetic account of a work toward biographical speculation and
cultural instruction. Wilson is a superb elucidator of the pleasures
to be had on first looking into Proust or *Das Kapital*, but it is hard

to find any sustained analysis of deep literary beauty in his work. What was ideal "equipment," to use his word from the Chapman essay, for writing about modernism, about the shock of recognition indeed, was comparatively blunt on other surfaces, and it is perhaps no surprise that he began to decline as a critic after World War II. The essays in *A Window on Russia* (1972), mostly written in the 1950s and 1960s, are a great disappointment. Not for the first time, reading about Tolstoy, Chekhov, and Gogol, one has the uneasy sensation that the more one knows about the subject, the less helpful Wilson becomes. Often, it is a matter of tone as much as of comprehension. "In all Tolstoy's talk about love and God," Wilson writes in "Notes on Tolstoy," "it is a little hard to know what he means by either. He does not seem very much to love others; and what is his communion with God?" This is right, as far as it goes, but phrasing it like this, as if merely asking the irritable question is to have irritably answered it, is not to go very far.

At other moments, the most basic comprehension seems to desert him. In the same book he attacks Nabokov's fiction for its addiction to schadenfreude: "Everybody is always humiliated." In *Pnin*, writes Wilson, "he goes so far as to bring in himself to humiliate in prospect in his own person his humble little Russian professor, who dreads Nabokov's brilliance and insolence." Moving at too rapid a speed, Wilson misses the great comic sympathy extended to Pnin by Nabokov, and fails to see that Nabokov beautifully engineers the novel so that Pnin finally escapes the clutches of the Nabokovian narrator, a narrator who is deliberately made to seem untrustworthy, snobbish, cruel, and not as dear a friend of Professor Pnin as he tiresomely claims to be. The Wilson who could do this to *Pnin* is the same Wilson who found the narrative strategies of late James and Conrad frustrating and needlessly obscure: "the unnecessary circumlocutions and the gratuitous meaningless verbiage."

By this time, of course, the struggle with Nabokov had become personal. In the 1940s and 1950s, Wilson had shown great generosity to the Russian émigré, newly arrived in America. He introduced his new friend to other writers and editors, and properly chivvied him when Nabokov was about to dismiss—out of almost perfect ignorance, it should be said—Jane Austen or Henry James. It is thanks to Wilson that Nabokov chose to teach *Mansfield Park* and *Bleak House* to his students at Wellesley and Cornell.

What now seems a frail bridge joined the two men until Wilson, in 1954, told Nabokov that he did not think much of *Lolita*; it crumbled slowly for almost a decade, and then spectacularly collapsed when Wilson, with his usual confidence, reviewed Nabokov's translation of *Eugene Onegin* in *The New York Review of Books* in 1963. Wilson was right about the awkwardness of Nabokov's literal English version—though it has many superb and canny triumphs—but he unwisely presumed to set Nabokov straight about his "ineptitudes" in Russian. Nabokov replied by pointing out that Wilson's own piece made several errors in Russian. It was a fight that apparently only Wilson, who read Russian fluently but could barely speak it, thought he could win.

The episode, a sad one for those who, like Mary McCarthy, had witnessed the "joy" that Wilson radiated in "Volodya's" company, is usually read in a spirit of tart Shakespearean symmetry: the two palatial egos deserved this plague on both their houses. But the conflict was deeper rooted than mere ego. Wilson and Nabokov had never agreed about Russia, about socialism, and had never agreed on how to read fiction. From the very beginning, Wilson had felt that Nabokov's book on Gogol was too aestheticizing, too decadent. They would disagree vehemently about the quality of *Dr. Zhivago*, which Wilson championed and Nabokov thought second-rate. Isaiah Berlin thought that the clue was that Wilson "was a moral being," while Nabokov "was purely aesthetic," as if this were the last word. But to throw away a friendship for the sake of a few thousand bullyingly corrective words in *The New York Review* was not a very moral act, and Nabokov was by no means purely aesthetic, as his fiction, which so often reflects morally on the dangers of freewheeling aestheticism, beautifully demonstrates.

Curiously, though, if Wilson became a poorer critic as he aged, bullishly brushing aside complexities and ambiguities, restlessly exploring one promising cultural site after another—Israel, Canada, Haiti, the Iroquois reservations—he became, if anything, a better writer. As he swerved away from journalism, from the weekly or monthly treadle of reviewing, and into memoir and the writing of his journals, so his prose took on a new lyricism. It was in the 1950s that he wrote the lovely memoirs of his father, and of D. S. Mirsky, the Russian critic and aristocrat whom Wilson had visited in Moscow, and who was arrested in the purges of 1937, dying sometime after that in northeast Siberia. The old stone family house in Talcottville, so full of sublime childhood memories, and where the now aged critic spent more and more of his waning years, always stimulated him. There is a passage in his journal, *The Sixties*, in which Wilson describes a watery hollow just off Route 12, near the Talcottville house. It was June 1970, exactly two years before his death. The portly and wheezing man of letters, always on the qui vive for erotic adventure, was newly infatuated with a young female neighbor and had gone with her to the hollow. But he is content to watch. He sees her take off her dress—"I saw her slim brownish figure from behind, and she looked very pretty." Then he paints, in words, as his admired Turgenev so often did, the landscape. The graceful, lucid, lyrical writing has all the virtues of Wilson's determination to see and to describe, his fortifying curiosity and his sure sense that language can objectively capture galaxies of disparate data—natural, literary, political, even sexual:

> You find yourself in a high-walled chasm of stratified limestone rock, which is feathered with green fern and lined in the cracks with green moss. Birds flit back and forth between the rapids. The cliffs where they overhang are dripping with springs, and across the river, the farther one goes, the more densely they are plumed, grown with trees: ash, feathery hemlock, elm—bushes of sumac. A dead tree droops down over the stream. The cascade is white, rather

> crooked and dragged . . . A stretch of primitive landscape in-
> visible and little frequented just off the traffic of Route 12.
> Above the chasm, against the blue, the coverlet of small dap-
> pling clouds crawls slowly below the sky.

Wilson preferred to be called a journalist rather than a critic, and there is an attractive wholesomeness to this preference. In the end, his name will last because of everything he wrote—the paradox being, then, that his reputation will persist because of many pieces of work that have not lasted. Already out of print and likely to remain so are much of the travel writings, the hundreds of book reviews, the political journalism, the books on Canadian literature, on the Iroquois, on Haiti, on the Dead Sea Scrolls, and so on. The journal-chronicles of the decades, especially *The Sixties*, deserve to live. But a literary world that does not keep the great nineteenth-century diarist H. F. Amiel in print is unlikely to feel much compassion about the much looser, much scrappier chronicler of Talcottville.

Wilson's desire to be called a journalist, which would have been redundant before the twentieth century, becomes more problematic in an era marked by the rise of academic criticism. For Wilson's literary criticism, with its introductory relish, its recourse to biographical speculation, and its swerve away from aesthetic questions, now looks more journalistic than it once did. V. S. Pritchett seems to me to have had a more literary sensibility, and a more natural understanding of how fiction works its effects; William Empson explains poetry with a far richer respect for ambiguity; Lionel Trilling imbricates ideas and aesthetics with greater skill; and Randall Jarrell accounts for beauty with more devoted vivacity. Wilson's criticism, by contrast, exposes the limits of literary journalism in an age when journalism was no longer the only way of attending to literature. Wilson's robust will to mastery, his comprehensive and solitary scholarship, sometimes seem to substitute for an equivalent critical rigor in matters of aesthetics, philosophy, and religion. There was a short revolution that almost exactly coincided with Wilson's life, in

which literary criticism briefly became both an art and a philosophical discipline—that moment between, say, Eliot's essays of the
1920s and the decline of the New Criticism in the 1950s. Wilson's
work stands somewhat to the side of that efflorescence, proudly independent as he always wished it to be, but now a little more isolated than he ever thought it would become.

ALEKSANDAR HEMON

In Joseph Roth's novel of the Austro-Hungarian empire, *The Radetzky March*, there is an extraordinary scene when the varied soldiers of that vast, improbable portmanteau parade in Vienna before the Hapsburg emperor, Franz Joseph. Uniformed men stream by, Austrians, Italians, Hungarians, Slovenians—and most remarkably and most exotically, Bosnians, vivid in their "blood-red fezzes," which seemed to glow, writes Roth, like bonfires lit by Islam in tribute to the emperor himself. Those blood-red fezzes are all Roth needs to conjure the distant romance of the Bosnian subjects, who, of course, disappear from the novelistic pageant as quickly as they flashed by.

Nearly eighty years after *The Radetzky March* was published, the writer Aleksandar Hemon, who was born in Sarajevo and now lives in Chicago, seems to return Roth's compliment in his story "The Accordion," when he uses the same phrase: the Archduke Franz Ferdinand is riding in a carriage through Sarajevo, and he sees "the blood-red fezzes—much like topsy-turvy flower pots with short tassels—and women with little curtains over their faces." The archduke has an appointment with history: at any moment, a man will emerge from the crowd and shoot him, and the long fuse that exploded in the First World War will be lit. But before that encounter, the archduke's attention is caught—in Hemon's spirited telling—by a man with an accordion. The instrument is missing a key, and the archduke idly wonders if one could play a tune without it. The narrator remarks triumphantly that the man with the accordion "was none other than my great-grandfather, freshly arrived in Bosnia from Ukraine." He goes on to tell us that the accordion lived another fifty years, expiring when "my blind uncle Teodor" threw himself onto a bed where it lay. The story ends with stark abandon: "Uncle Teodor is now stuck in the Serb part of Bosnia. Most of my family is scattered across Canada. This story was written in Chicago (where I live) on the subway, after a long day of arduous work as a parking assistant, A.D. 1996."

Hemon's writing shares with Joseph Roth's an interest in the extremities and borderlands of the Hapsburg Empire, and both writers delight in rich, fantastical metaphor (the fezzes like bonfires and flower pots). Whether Hemon had Roth in mind or not, his piece of family lore, grandly fanciful yet fiercely grounded in political actualities and personal hardship, seems to thumb its Bosnian nose at Roth's romantic Orientalism. Where Roth sees in the Bosnians only color and loyalty, Hemon sees the comfortable disdain of the archduke for his outlandish subjects. Roth, who was born in Ukraine and worked in Vienna, was sentimentally nostalgic for an unreal empire, for the livery and insignia of Viennese pomp. Hemon, whose paternal ancestors moved from Ukraine to Sarajevo, and who came to America in 1992 for a short visit only to find that the siege of Sarajevo prohibited his return, is complicatedly nostalgic for a real city he grew up in and left—or that left him, once the war began.

As Roth's work is shadowed by the pivot of 1914, that moment at which the empire began to unravel, 1992 comes down again and again like a scimitar of fable in Hemon's work: it was the year that he realized he could not go home. Serbian snipers had taken their positions in the gods, above the city, and Sarajevo was their toy theater. Hemon is both a relentless demystifier and a playful mythologist, so he is probably amused by the way that the story of his enforced American exile (which no one disputes) has become its own irresistible shilling life: the young Bosnian writer, merely visiting Chicago, unable to return to his native city, and forced to watch, along with the more-or-less titillated West, the images on CNN of bloody sneakers and exploded marketplaces. Hemon's fictional creation and almost alter ego Jozef Pronek, who appears in his first book of stories, *The Question of Bruno*, and is the protagonist of his first novel, *Nowhere Man*, arrives in the States from Sarajevo in January 1992. The customs officer at JFK flips through his Yugoslav passport "as if it were a gooey smut magazine." No one in America has the slightest conception of where he comes from: the least idiotic hazard a reference to Kundera and Czechoslovakia; others tell him what a great country America is and suggest that maybe General Schwarzkopf can sort it all out. Young Pronek gets a succession of dismal jobs in Chicago, while squatting in seedy digs with a girl named Andrea and her hideous boyfriend, Carwin:

> Jozef Pronek decided to stay in the United States, possibly for the rest of his life, in the middle of a snowy night, as snowflakes were pressing their crystal faces against the window pane, after Carwin dropped a pot of rotting spaghetti on the floor and said: "Fuck!"

That is characteristically Hemon-like comic deflation, but the verb "decided" may ascribe too much agency. A more piercing sentence later in the same story ("Blind Jozef Pronek & Dead Souls") suggests less volition, and the portable provincialism of exile: Jozef watches the CNN pictures of his besieged city, but, writes Hemon, "he only watched the images to recognize the people in them."

> Once he thought he saw his father, running down Sniper's Alley, but he couldn't be sure, because the man hid his head behind a folded-up newspaper.

When he arrived in the States, Hemon had what his publisher calls only a "basic command" of English. Eight years later, *The Question of Bruno* appeared, stories written in an English remarkable for its

polish, luster, and sardonic control of register. In the Hemon my-
thology, this conversion is "Nabokovian," and indeed Hemon's writing sometimes reminds one of Nabokov's. (Hemon has said that he
learned English by reading Nabokov and underlining the words he
didn't recognize.) Yet the feat of his reinvention exceeds the Russian's. For Nabokov grew up reading English and had been educated at Cambridge. When his American career began in 1940, he
was almost middle-aged and had long experience in at least three
languages. Hemon, by contrast, tore through his development in
the new language with hyperthyroidal speed.

And it needs to be stressed that Hemon did not become, in
those eight years, merely a proficient but a superb stylist. Sometimes,
his English has the regenerative eccentricity of the immigrant's,
restoring buried meanings to words like "vacuous" and "petrified."
A sentence like this one stands at a slight angle to customary English
usage: "I piled different sorts of blebby pierogi and a cup of limpid
tea on my tray." "Blebby" is wonderful, but perhaps more wonderfully, how many native English speakers would ever describe tea as
limpid? Occasionally, he flourishes a lyrically pedantic Nabokovian
bloom, as in "she has fenestral glasses."

But more often he uses his astonishing talent to notice the
world with sarcastic precision, a precision and worldliness that is
then put in tension with his love of surreal metaphor. Thus the
horse that is pulling the archduke drops turds that are "like dark,
deflated tennis balls." A shower head looms over a bathtub "like a
buzzard head," and pubic hairs are stuck to the side of a toilet bowl
"as if climbing up." Jozef Pronek, newly arrived in America, is amazed
at how smoothly toilets work, and watches, in his Quality Inn, "how
the water at the bottom was enthusiastically slurped in, only to rise,
with liquid cocksureness, back to the original level." When he and
Andrea have sex, the language registers, with impeccable sureness,
the erotic ordinariness of the event: "They breathed into each other's
faces and let their abdomens adhere. Then their little sex unit fis-
sioned, and she went to the bathroom." And there is much beauty
on every page—the "sooty tapestry" of Pronek's hairy torso, or his

skin first thing in the morning, "soft, with crease imprints, the fossils of slumber."

Often, Hemon's narratives stall, and then stutter into magnificent lists of noticed or remembered details, loosely joined by semicolons. (He likes tall tales, but has a refreshing lack of interest in conventional novelistic plot.) One has the sense, as one does in Nabokov's case, of the stylist urgently preserving in exile details that might disappear if unnoticed. In his story "Exchange of Pleasant Words," for instance, he writes fondly about a Hemon family reunion in 1991—what they call "the Hemoniad"—when two sides, the Hemons and the Hemuns (a branch of the writer's grandfather's brother) are reunited. It is a warm summer day, filled with rustic drinking and eating, and much outrageous storytelling. Uncle Teodor, the unofficial family historian, addresses the conclave, mentioning Hemons who, according to him, appear in *The Iliad*; and a Breton soldier named Alexandre Hemon, who fought with Napoleon; and a Hemon who went to America and got rich. The young Aleksandar Hemon is charged with recording this mythical party on a video camera, has "one drink too many," and eventually collapses. But not before he manages to notice the following list of "discontinuous memories":

> the noxious, sour manure stench coming from the pigsty; the howling of the only piglet left alive; the fluttering of fleeting chickens; pungent smoke, coming from moribund pig-roast fires; relentless shuffling and rustle of the gravel on which many feet danced; my aunts and other auntly women trodding the *kolomiyka* on the gravel; their ankles universally swollen, and their skin-hued stockings descending slowly down their varicose calves; the scent of a pine plank and the prickly coarseness of its surface, as I laid my cheek on it and everything spun, as if I were in a washing machine; my cousin Ivan's sandaled left foot tap-tap-tapping on the stage, headed by its rotund big toe; the vast fields of cakes and pastries arrayed on the bed (on which my grandmother had

expired), meticulously sorted in chocolate and non-chocolate phalanxes.

One of the most appealing and intriguing aspects of Hemon's fiction is the paradoxical way in which he is grounded in pungent realities and simultaneously drawn toward the most playful fiction-alizing. On the one hand, he finishes "The Accordion" with infor-mation about his family's diaspora and the news that he wrote it on the subway after a hard day's lowly work, and on the other, he offers an anecdote about an accordion-playing ancestor that might be en-tirely fictitious, and is grandly unverifiable. He likes to use his fam-ily name in his fiction, and to refer recurrently to certain relatives and family histories, but the autobiographical veracity of that fiction seems architectural rather than foundational. Yet more than any other American novelist I can think of, he has made a kind of run-ning autobiographical fiction of his actual circumstances—the child-hood in Sarajevo, the exile in America, the early hardships in Chicago. He is a fabulist but not really a postmodernist; or rather, he is a postmodernist who has been mugged by history. When he lays bare the device (an old Russian formalist phrase for the technique of playful fictive self-consciousness), he opens a wound. During "the Hemoniad," his mother remarks: "The trouble with the Hemons . . . is that they always get much too excited about things they imagine to be real." The formulation is canny: a good proportion of reality consists of what we freely imagine; and then, less happily perhaps, we discover that that reality has imagined us—that we are the vas-sals of our imaginings, not their emperors or archdukes.

Hemon's cunningly ambitious novel *The Lazarus Project* is a further installment in his autobiographical fictionalizing. Its narra-tor, Vladimir Brik, came from Sarajevo to the States in 1992, and describes himself as "a reasonably loyal citizen of a couple of coun-tries." Like one of the narrators of *Nowhere Man*, he has taught English as a second language. His grandfather came to Bosnia from Ukraine. He writes a column about his immigrant experiences, which people like partly because they find "the quirky immigrant language endearing." At a dinner to celebrate Bosnian Independence Day, Brik meets Susie Schuettler, a board member of Glory Foundation, which agrees to fund Brik's research. Hereafter, he refers to the largesse of "the Susie grant" (a jokey reference, in part, to Hemon's MacArthur Fellowship of 2004).

Brik wants to research an actual event that took place on March 2, 1908, in Chicago, when a Jewish immigrant, Lazarus Averbuch, paid a visit to George Shippy, the chief of Chicago police, and was shot dead. No one knew why Averbuch visited Shippy, nor exactly why or how he died, but his involvement with anarchist circles solved, for many Chicagoans, the mystery: he had obviously intended to assassinate the prime representative of law and order. There was a hysterical fear of anarchism at this time, frothed up by the newspapers—"the war against anarchism was much like the current war on terror," Brik tells us. The Chicago Historical Society has a number of photographs of Averbuch, and Hemon reproduces them and other photos throughout his novel, including a shocking one, in which Chief Shippy stands behind the recently deceased Averbuch, who appears to be sitting in a chair, his head kept from lolling by Shippy's hands, which are placed on the top of his victim's head and underneath the chin, as if exhibiting a rare archaeological find. Averbuch's eyes are not quite closed, his lips are pursed in vague puzzlement, and, rather than dead, he looks slightly disgruntled at the prospect of being woken.

Hemon is clearly fascinated by the story of this man with the biblically suggestive name who survived the Kishinev pogrom of 1903, in what is now Moldova, and who came with his sister to Chicago, only to be killed by an American policeman. The fragility of the immigrant's status, the mere sand of his grounding, has been one of Hemon's great themes; it has a metaphysical cast in his work. One of the narrators of *Nowhere Man* has the feeling that "things will go on existing whether I lived or died. There was a hole in the world, and I fit right into it; if I perished, the hole would just close, like a scar healing." Vladimir Brik is afraid when his American wife leaves the house, "for somehow her absence opened up the possibility that my life and all of its traces had vanished." Lazarus Averbuch belonged nowhere, and though Brik describes himself as a reasonably loyal citizen of two countries, he is better described as an angry citizen of neither. With an old childhood friend from Sarajevo, Brik uses the Susie money to go on a research trip—first to Ukraine, where his grandparents lived, then to Czernowitz, present-day Chernivtsí, where Averbuch was briefly in a refugee camp, and then to Kishinev, present-day Chişinău. In Chernivtsí, Brik reflects cynically on identity, and its center:

> Everybody imagines that they have a center, the seat of their soul, if you believe in that kind of thing. I've asked around, and most of the people told me that the soul is somewhere in the abdominal area—a foot or so above the asshole. But even if the center is elsewhere in the body— the head, the throat, the heart—it is fixed there, it does not move around. When you move, the center moves with you, following your trajectory. You protect that center, your body is a sheath; and if your body is damaged, the center is exposed and weak. Moving through the crowd at the bus station in Chernivtsi, I realized that my center had shifted—it used to be in my stomach, but now it was in my breast pocket, where I kept my American passport and a wad of cash. I pushed this bounty of American life through space; I was presently assembled around it and needed to protect it from the people around me.

Hemon's fiction has always been daring: *Nowhere Man* uses three or maybe four different narrators to rub in the silhouette of Jozef Pronek's complicated life. *The Lazarus Project* is in some ways bolder still. It alternates chapters describing Brik's travels with chapters imagining Lazarus Averbuch's existence in the early twentieth century. It is both a historical fiction and an inquiry into the limits of historical fictionalizing: whereas, say, Susan Sontag, in her novel of Polish immigrants, *In America*, apologized for the brazenness of historical fiction and then just brazenly forgot about her own reservations, the better to produce a skein of intellectual costume drama, Hemon is more systematically skeptical, more philosophical, alternating one kind of experimental fiction (essentially a travelogue) with another (essentially an archival fantasy). Perhaps, though, he remembers his reservations too much, and the narrative moves a bit too essayistically, from argument to counterargument. Brik is pursuing his "Lazarus Project," whereby Hemon can pursue *his* "Lazarus Project," and the book's photographs represent another kind of mimetic project, which is a few projects too many.

One of the reasons the novel feels argumentative is that Brik is so angry—chiefly at America and at his wife, Mary, a neurosurgeon at Northwestern Memorial Hospital. Mary, a hardworking Catholic from a standardly provincial American family, is made to represent much of what Brik dislikes about this country since the events of 9/11—a culpable innocence, a benign complacency about intentions and consequences. "She had the bright, open face that always reminded me of the vast midwestern welkin." Anger blackens these pages, and political anger at that: Hemon wants us to see the connection between the treatment of anarchists and immigrants in 1908 and the treatment of vulnerable groups now, even at the cost of making this parallel very . . . parallel. For Mary, evil is barely comprehensible, and good intentions matter. Brik tells us that he and his wife argued over the Abu Ghraib pictures. For her, the American prison guards were decent, corrupted kids "acting upon a misguided belief they were protecting freedom, their good intentions going astray." For her Bosnian-American husband, at home in neither place, the good intentions were precisely the problem: "What I saw was young Americans expressing their unlimited joy of the unlimited power over someone else's life and death. They loved being alive and righteous by virtue of having good American intentions." The fictional argument, lightly fictionalized as it is, has the feel of a real, remembered one, outside the book.

Angry, Vladimir Brik is relatively unappealing; he could borrow some of Jozef Pronek's bumbling, Pnin-like charm. (In a Ukrainian cemetery, Brik finds the stone of one Oleksandr Pronek, 1967–2002, the latter date being the year of the publication of *Nowhere Man*.) Angry and lost, homeless in two continents, Brik is poignant, and the novel is never more moving than when its narrator seems a little unhinged because a little unhoused. In his earlier work, Hemon circled around *King Lear*, and Shakespeare's great phrase "unaccommodated man," the naked human animal Lear finds on the heath. Physically and metaphysically unaccommodated, Brik even imagines the biblical Lazarus as a kind of unaccommodated man— the emblem of all immigrants. When he was raised by Jesus from the dead, he muses, did Lazarus remember being dead? Or did he just begin again? "Did he have to disremember his previous life and start from scratch, like an immigrant?" That beginning all over again would be the true "Lazarus project."

One of the fascinations of Hemon's work is that he makes a new and strange kind of postcolonial literature out of the long, occupied history of Bosnia-Herzegovina. The Eastern European itinerary of Brik and his friend—Ukraine, Moldova, Bukovina—is not just a tour of devastated, post-Holocaust Jewry, but a kind of sly homage to Joseph Roth, who was born in what is now Ukraine, on the eastern edges of the Austro-Hungarian Empire, and who became that empire's greatest celebrant. Again and again, Hemon reaches back into Sarajevo's curious imperial past, back into the Hapsburg nineteenth century, back into Russian imperial history, so that his modern Bosnian characters are not just immigrants to America—prickly with estrangement and alienation—but also appear, slightly magically, as deracinated escapees from an ancient European empire. This double aspect—characters at once immigrant and emigrant, the tortured relation of the colonist and the colonized—is familiar enough in African, Indian, Pakistani, and West Indian writing in English, but it is bewildering to encounter some of the same motifs in a writer for whom the reality of empire is not even a distant memory, and in a context in which race (the burning issue of most postcolonial literatures) is not really an issue. But then, consider again the context of Hemon's removal to America in 1992—a nationalistic oppressor, keen to assert the rights of an ancient empire, a war premised on racial and religious sectarianism, and tiny multiethnic Sarajevo besieged and menaced. Suddenly, the witty and oblique sense of imperial history in Hemon's work seems to take on a different, and more urgent, coloration.

BEYOND A BOUNDARY: *NETHERLAND* AS POSTCOLONIAL NOVEL

Fiction has an entrepreneurial element, akin to the inventor's secret machine, elixir, or formula. Many novelists have experienced that moment when they fall upon the perfect controlling image or scene or character, the one that will breed meaning and metaphor parthenogenetically throughout the book or story. Gogol surely knew that he had invented a devastating symbolic structure when he came up with the story of a devil figure who travels around Russia buying up the names of dead serfs; he carefully garaged his secret—in a letter, he refuses to name the title of his imminent novel, apparently aware that *Dead Souls* might give the game away. When we read *Herzog*, we think: how brilliant and simple, like the best of inventions, to have turned something we all do (writing letters in our heads to other people) into a new way of representing consciousness. And when we read *Midnight's Children*, we feel that Salman Rushdie has found a powerful controlling image in the impending midnight of Indian partition, the clock's hands meeting in prayer.

I don't know whether Joseph O'Neill jumped out of his bath in Manhattan shrieking "Eureka!" when he suddenly realized that, of all the possible stories in the world, he *had* to write a novel about playing cricket in New York City, but he should have. For, paradoxically, despite the seeming parochialism or irrelevance to America of cricket, the game makes *Netherland* a large fictional achievement, and one of the most remarkable postcolonial books I have read. Cricket, like every sport, is an activity and the dream of an activity, thus a fact and an ideology, badged with random ideals, aspirations, and memories. It popularly evokes long English summers, newly mown grass, the causeless boredom of childhood. Its combat is so temperate that, more explicitly than other sports, it also encodes an ethics: in Britain, the phrase "it's not cricket" means something like "it's not kosher." But cricket in this novel is much more than these associations: it is an immigrant's imagined community, a game that unites, in a Brooklyn park, Pakistanis, Sri Lankans, Indians, West Indians, Australians, and so on; it is an émigré's community, since these immigrants are playing a sport whose radical un-Americanness accentuates their singularity; and, most poignantly, for one of the characters in the novel, cricket is an American dream, or perhaps a dream of America, for this man is convinced that, as he puts it, cricket is not an immigrant sport but "the first modern team sport in America . . . a bona fide American pastime," played in New York since the 1770s.

That man's name is Chuck Ramkissoon, and we first hear of him as a corpse. It is 2006, and the novel's narrator, a Dutch banker named Hans van den Broek, receives a call in London from a *New York Times* reporter. The remains of Khamraj Ramkissoon—"It's Chuck Ramkissoon," corrects Hans, on the phone—have been found in the Gowanus Canal, and wasn't Hans a business partner of the victim? No, just a friend, says Hans. Later, to his wife, Rachel, Hans describes Chuck as "a cricket guy I used to know. A guy from Brooklyn." We don't know it yet, but the novel has just unfurled its great theme: this "cricket guy," an Indian from Trinidad, is a large American visionary—Chuck, not Khamraj—and cricket is the macula of that mad vision, and *Netherland* has opened by starting where *The Great Gatsby* ends, with its forlorn dreamer facedown in the water.

The unhappy news prompts Hans to recall his years in New York, and the moment he first met Chuck, on a cricket field in

Walker Park, Staten Island, in the summer of 2002. Hans and his wife and son had been living in the Chelsea Hotel, their domicile after the September 11 attacks, "staying on in a kind of paralysis even after we'd received permission from the authorities to return to our loft in Tribeca." Hans has his own kind of paralysis: large and fair, he is apparently one of nature's flâneurs, willing to be swept along by powerful events and people, fastidiously curious about the world and yet also a bit complacent, and this reflective sluggishness maddens Rachel, who, already on edge after September 11, announces that she is leaving him and America. Hans drifts, visiting his wife and son in London twice a month, amiably acquainting himself with some of the eccentrics at the Chelsea Hotel, and eventually taking up cricket, the game of his Dutch childhood.

There are moments when Rachel's hostility seems a little undeveloped, and one suspects her absence from New York as merely the necessary fictional trigger for Hans's hospitable sloth. But as in *Sentimental Education*, one will forgive in this novel a lot of stasis when the verbal rewards are so very high. As Hans takes the measure of his newfound city, so O'Neill's prose finds its own calibrations. O'Neill writes elegant, long sentences, formal but not fussy, punctually pricked with lyrically exact metaphor. Here Hans recalls the days not long after September 11, when the city was an acoustic sensorium:

> Around the clock, ambulances sped eastward on West Twenty-third Street with a sobbing escort of police motorcycles. Sometimes I confused the cries of the sirens with my son's nighttime cries. I would leap out of bed and go to his bedroom and helplessly kiss him . . . Afterward I slipped out onto the balcony and stood there like a sentry. The pallor of the so-called hours of darkness was remarkable. Directly to the north of the hotel, a succession of cross streets glowed as if each held a dawn. The taillights, the coarse blaze of deserted office buildings, the lit storefronts, the orange fuzz of the street lanterns: all this garbage of light had been

refined into a radiant atmosphere that rested in a low silver heap over Midtown and introduced to my mind the mad thought that the final twilight was upon New York.

It is a pleasure to be reading an attentive prose about New York in crisis that is not also a prose in crisis—in other words, that is not exaggerated or solipsistic or puerile or sentimental or solecistic, or in some way straining to be noticed. It takes a steady hand and a good ear to dare the paradox of "all this garbage of light," in which the noticer is both enraptured and faintly alienated, and which accurately tracks the forked European perspective of the novel's narrator. The eye that sees the "orange fuzz" of the streetlights is the eye that, elsewhere in the novel, alights on the "molten progress of the news tickers" in Times Square, the "train-infested underpants" of Hans's little boy, "a necklace's gold drool," the "roving black blooms of four-dollar umbrellas," and that sees, in one lovely swipe of a sentence, a sunset like this: "The day, a pink smear above America, had all but disappeared."

Perhaps Joseph O'Neill is the writer this city has been awaiting: an émigré-immigrant born in Ireland, raised in Holland, educated in England, and resident in Manhattan. If his writing has an English ease and classicism, it also has a world-directed curiosity, an interest in marginal lives that might owe something to O'Neill's Turkish origins. (His mother is Turkish. His Irish and Turkish grandfathers were separately arrested by the British, one in Ireland and one in British Palestine, a history he related in his spacious memoir *Blood-Dark Track*.) As Hans moves around the city, he sees, with O'Neill's loaned lenses, both natural and human wonders. There is the Hudson, covered in ice:

Ice was spread out over the breadth of the Hudson like a plot of cloud. The whitest and largest fragments were flat polygons, and surrounding these was a mass of slushy, messy ice, as if the remains of a zillion cocktails had been dumped there. By the bank, where the rotting stumps of an old pier projected like a species of mangrove, the ice was shoddy, papery rubble, and immobile; farther out, floes moved quickly towards the bay.

But there is also Coney Island Avenue:

> that low-slung, scruffily commercial thoroughfare that stands in almost surreal contrast to the tranquil residential blocks it traverses, a shoddily bustling strip of vehicles double-parked in front of gas stations, synagogues, mosques, beauty salons, bank branches, restaurants, funeral homes, auto body shops, supermarkets, assorted small businesses proclaiming provenances from Pakistan, Tajikistan, Ethiopia, Turkey, Saudi Arabia, Russia, Armenia, Ghana, the Jewry, Christendom, Islam: it was on Coney Island Avenue, on a subsequent occasion, that Chuck and I came upon a bunch of South African Jews, in full sectarian regalia, watching televised cricket with a couple of Rastafarians in the front office of a Pakistani-run lumberyard.

It is Chuck Ramkissoon who tutors the narrator in the wonders of this ethnic "miscellany" when he decides to help Hans pass his driving test by appointing the Dutchman his unofficial chauffeur, responsible for ensuring that Chuck gets to his various appointments in his 1996 Cadillac, "a patriotic automobile aflutter and aglitter with banners and stickers of the Stars and Stripes and yellow ribbons in support of the troops." Chuck is reminiscent of Dr. Tamkin in Bellow's *Seize the Day*, one of the noisy urban braggers, probably a charlatan, but mysteriously seductive. Unlike Tamkin, Chuck has charm, and it was this that Hans fell for in the summer of 2002, when he first met him on Staten Island and heard him talk about how cricket is "a lesson in civility," and how "Benjamin Franklin himself was a cricket man." Like the reader, Hans wants to know more about this dark-skinned Trinidadian, whose family came originally from Madras and who wants so deeply to make himself an American.

Chuck bristles with enterprises. He has a kosher sushi restaurant, runs a private lottery (it is probably this activity that gets him killed and thrown in the canal), and has designated himself president of what he grandly calls the New York Cricket Club. O'Neill parentally rations our exposure to Chuck, using the length of his novel, and its apparent formlessness—it moves back and forth between 2001, 2002, 2003, when Hans returns to London, and 2006, when Hans hears of Chuck's death—to give us suggestive pictures of the man's flamboyance and anxious yearning. The danger with self-exaggerating characters is exaggerated writing, but O'Neill knows how to sign rather than autograph. When Chuck says, at one moment, with his usual confidence, "Just ask Mike Bloomberg," that brash "Mike" does exactly what needs to be done. Similarly, we get a quick sense of the man—both of his appeal and of his type— when he tells Hans that he needs a permanent wife and a permanent mistress: "Anne and me . . . we've known each other since we were babies. She's been with me through thick and thin . . . So we're together for life. But my theory is, I need two women . . . One to take care of family and home, one to make me feel alive. It's too much to ask one woman to do both."

One day in January 2003, Chuck takes Hans to the field he has leased in Brooklyn. This is where his New York Cricket Club will be—at what Chuck names Bald Eagle Field ("It's got scale. It makes it American.") Hans looks at the frozen, snowy space and is silently skeptical. It is an "immense white emptiness." I have little interest in cricket, but I can't help being drawn into the complex way that cricket generates meaning in the novel. For O'Neill is alive, as Hans perhaps is not yet, to the larger implications of Chuck's desire. The immigrant is trying to choose his plot of ground, and calling it his, as the original colonists did with their America. (Like the first European colonists, Chuck also needed to exterminate: "The first thing we did, in the summer, was kill everything with Roundup," he tells Hans, referring to his taming of Bald Eagle Field with weed-killer; one of the fields, where Pakistanis play cricket, is called Dutch Kills.) This is where *Netherland* becomes subtle. Hans tells us that when he plays cricket in New York, he is "the only white man I saw." He plays with people from Trinidad, Guyana, Jamaica, India, Pakistan, and Sri Lanka, and becomes an honorary brown man. But as a white Dutchman, educated in classics at Leiden and raised in a conservative family in The Hague, Hans is not a "colonial" like his fellow cricketers, but inescapably a *colonist*, part of the history of Dutch imperialism that has marked places as different as Java and America. Chuck talks about how cricket "civilizes," because he needs to believe in this colonial ideology, as his (overeager) way of belonging; but Hans can talk unselfconsciously about how one of the players is a specialist in "fizzing Chinamen" (a "Chinaman" is an unorthodox left-arm bowl) without registering the political awkwardness of the locution. Enormous gulfs—the gulfs of privilege, race, class; of geographical accident and geopolitical event—separate these two men.

Cricket in America puts all of this, quite literally, in play. Hans, the white banker, can only be an honorary immigrant, something O'Neill cleverly acknowledges by teasing out the question of Hans's American driving test. It takes him the entirety of the novel to pass it, and he finally succeeds only at the moment when he no longer needs a license—weeks before his departure. A document that would be utterly crucial to a Chuck Ramkissoon is a bit of a joke to a Hans van den Broek. O'Neill beautifully counterposes the different origins and expectations of these two men, united by cricket: the upper-class Hans, who can come and go in America on a banker's whim and is paralyzed by the expensive torpor of his marital woes, and the modest Trinidadian, dynamic with designs, ever eager to be grounded in America. Chuck is excited by Hans's Dutchness, and compliments him, in his usual showy way, on being, after the Native Americans, a member of New York's "first tribe." This ideological affection arises partly from Chuck's determination to argue for cricket's aboriginal status as the first American sport. The immigrants playing cricket on Bald Eagle Field are the real Americans, Chuck thinks; the true natives, at once colonials and the first colonists. The colonial wants to become a colonist, killing everything with Roundup; Hans, the ancestral colonist, wants only to be a colonial: in the summer of 2003, he is gripped by "real cricket madness." In the end, both men fail at their projects: Chuck cannot become a colonist, cannot become what he is not; and Hans cannot become a colonial, cannot become what he is not. But only for one of the pair will this failure to belong, this fatal homelessness, matter. Privileged Hans can go anywhere he wants in the world, equally at home and equally homeless; immigrant Chuck cannot go anywhere he wants in the world, and wants only to be at home in America. Yet despite the eager patriotic rhetoric, Chuck is not a very successful American. He can't rid himself of his Trinidadian-Indian background (which is also an English colonial background); it is Chuck who snobbishly tells Hans that the escort agency he uses employs "girls with refinement, from the islands. College graduates, nurses. Not your American rubbish."

It is this postcolonial dimension that was missed or slighted by the novel's first eager critics, and was missed by Zadie Smith in her widely read essay "Two Paths for the Novel," about *Netherland* and Tom McCarthy's *Remainder*. The early reviewers liked *Netherland* and Zadie Smith didn't, really; but both insisted on seeing it as a post-9/11 novel. Smith writes sardonically that "it's the post–September 11 novel we have hoped for." Smith's essay is a suggestive critique, and she is not wrong about the novel's willingness to reach for bursts of epiphany and fine writing as ways for the flâneur-like narrator to authenticate and anchor himself (or at least to *try* to authenticate himself, a distinction that matters when an unreliable narrator is narrating a novel). Her argument, in part, is that though *Netherland* is properly intelligent and self-questioning and ironic (one should imagine an implied "blah-blah-blah" here), in the end it "wants to offer the authentic story of a self." That self can't be Hans, who is too uncomfortable as a white, well-off, liberal stand-in for the author to announce the authenticity he obviously feels is his birthright; the real authenticity belongs to Chuck, who "has no such anxieties. He is unselfconscious. He moves through the novel *simply being*." Chuck is used by O'Neill to say those things that the novel daren't say, for fear of seeming naive. For instance, it is Chuck who openly states the central metaphor of the novel, that cricket is "a lesson in civility."

Smith implies that O'Neill uses Ramkissoon's unselfconscious authenticity to authenticate Hans's wealthy, self-conscious inauthenticity; in other words, O'Neill believes that Hans's self is authentic but can't quite say so: Chuck must be used to enable the white man's lovely epiphanies. Smith credits *Netherland* for being alive to a certain anxiety about its fundamentally old-fashioned, liberal humanist project; but in the end, it's one of those clever liberal attempts at recuperation: it announces anxieties only to annul them. There may be a lot of stuff about colonial politics and immigration and the color of one's skin, but that is really just a feint, because the real goal of *Netherland* is to affirm the bottomless authenticity of the liberal self: "In *Netherland*, only one's own subjectivity is really authentic, and only the personal offers this possibility of transcendence." And this metaphysical conservatism, Smith continues, is premised on the book's antique narrative realism, a mode of writing that believes in and depends upon "the transcendent importance of form, the incantatory power of language to reveal the truth, the essential fullness and continuity of the self."

There is plenty that is intelligent and probing about Smith's essay, not least the fact that it is always good to put proper pressure on realism's unquestioned conventions. And she is right that, as so often in first-person novels of a flâneur-ish nature, there is an awkward contradiction between the likely voice of the narrator (in this case a well-educated but not obviously literary banker), and the hyperliterary writer who has hijacked his narrator's voice and fills the book with "fine writing." But by ignoring or occluding the fraught politics of the novel, she reads it almost back to front. Indeed, her essay makes *Remainder* sound far more radical than it actually is, and *Netherland* far more conservative than it actually is. For obviously enough, Chuck may be unselfconscious, but he is not authentic. How can one say that he moves through this novel *simply being*? As Mr. Biswas moves through Naipaul's novel *simply being*? As Gatsby moves through Fitzgerald's novel *simply being*? Chuck craves a political authenticity, a groundedness, a sense of belonging; but the very exaggeration of his identifications bespeaks an intense insecurity. It is not simply that he is a blusterer and blowhard. It is that he is an Indian Trinidadian who has attached himself to the colonist's game (English cricket), while simultaneously attaching himself to the absurd notion that the colonist's game is really the great American (and thus democratic) game. Awkwardly, he belongs not in Trinidad nor in England nor in America (recall the telling detail of his patriotically emblazoned Cadillac). He longs to be buried in a Brooklyn cemetery, but we know that will never happen.

Smith thinks that O'Neill uses Chuck as "an authenticity fetish," as a way to smuggle into the novel those metaphysical and political affirmations that it would be too embarrassing to admit, but that a brown-skinned immigrant can be allowed to confess. "Through Chuck, idealisms and enthusiasms can be expressed without anxiety." One of her examples is a moment when Chuck announces that he loves the eagle: "I love the national bird . . . The noble bald eagle represents the spirit of freedom, living as it does in the boundless void of the sky." So absurd and outlandish is this statement that Hans comments: "I turned to see whether he was joking. He wasn't." And this is one of the "enthusiasms" that Smith thinks is being confessed without anxiety? Surely the whole point about Chuck's inflated rhetoric at this moment is not just that it draws attention to the rampant fakery of this "enthusiasm," but also to the anxiety of Chuck's exaggerations, the awkward obedience, the overdone conformism of his identifications. Chuck's "idealism" is closer to brainwashed propaganda than to authentic enthusiasm. (*Are you a good American? Well, then, you must admire the noble bald eagle!*) V. S. Naipaul has written often about such characters, usually within the Trinidadian colonial context: the young Indian who goes off to Oxford, and who returns to the island wearing Oxford "bags" and saying

things like "I loathe T. S. Eliot's verse." Naipaul and O'Neill understand the anxious, inauthentic semiotics of this kind of too-good-to-
be-true citizenship, understand the shame and cravenness of the
obedient gesture. Chuck, of course, is not in any way an authenticity
fetish: he is an inauthenticity fetish.

And I also doubt that Hans is just an easy alter ego of the authorial flâneur. Hans's narration is self-serving, politically complacent, solipsistic, privileged, and unreliable—and is supposed to be.
His nickname, after all, is "Double Dutch," a term, he tells us, that
has entered banking parlance to describe some financial sleight of
hand. He may describe the frozen Hudson River very beautifully,
but when he does so he compares the filthy ice unfavorably to the
"pure canal ice of The Hague," an image he says comes partly from
"paintings of Dutch life through the centuries." He may describe
the Manhattan skyline very well, but he likens the skyscrapers to his
precious (and tellingly European) childhood box of Caran d'Ache
crayons. He sees well, but not well enough: at the very end of the
novel, his son tells him to look at something, and says, "See, Daddy?"
And Hans comments (it is the book's last line): "Then I turn to look
for what it is I'm supposed to be seeing."

What, indeed? Actually, O'Neill goes out of his way (almost too
didactically, I would complain) to push the novel's actual politics
of immigration and homelessness up against Hans's unquestioned
banker's right to come and go as he pleases. The little story of what
that American driving license might mean to these two very different
men—a story easily missed—is such an example. Another is offered,
unwittingly, by Smith. Hans is sitting in a train that has left New York
City for Toronto, and is traveling through the Hudson Valley. Looking out the window, Hans notices, in the enormous forests that
border that sealike river, a "near-naked white man. He was on his
own. He was shuffling through the trees wearing only underpants.
But why? What was he doing? Why was he not wearing clothes?"

Hans thinks he might be hallucinating. The train speeds on,
and he never sees the man again. Smith uses this moment as an

example of what is detestable about the realist novel. It is a "rule of lyrical Realism: that the random detail confers the authenticity of the Real." But first of all, is this a random detail, or does it not remind us that realism always has a tendency to slide into the allegorical and symbolic? Consider the context: Hans, a rich, entitled Dutch part-time colonist in America, is traveling through one of those areas of natural America that reminds one, inescapably, of the America that existed before the arrival of Dutch and European colonists. He is reading a packet that Chuck has given him, about the Dutch colonial presence in early America. He reads a Dutch-American poem that Chuck has included, titled "The Christmas Race, a True Incident of Rensselaerwyck," and realizes with a start that this is precisely the area—with its colonial Dutch names—that he is traveling through. And of course Chuck's packet of papers is part of his larger propaganda effort, which is to convince Hans that cricket is not so much a British colonial game as an American one. And in this context, Hans looks up and sees . . . a white savage, a blanched Native American, a half-naked aboriginal! This is not a random detail but a rather overdetermined one, if anything. And just as it is not a random detail, it does not confer the authenticity of the real. It is another of the many reminders in this book of the inauthenticity, the instability, the illegibility of the "real."

In a strange, inverted way, Smith is exactly right: Hans does indeed use Chuck to affirm his own mysterious authenticity. And this is what is unpleasant about Hans: she is absolutely right to be suspicious of him, even to find him a bit repellent. She just refuses to see the novel as engaged in any kind of similar critique of its narrator. Yet far from affirming the bottomless (but safely conservative) depths of the liberal humanist soul, *Netherland* pursues an almost obsessively deconstructive argument about the groundlessness of our existence. Again and again, the novel presses the idea that Netherland (Bottom-land) has no real bottom, no stable foundation. Beneath the concrete of Manhattan and the "nether regions" of Brooklyn are the murky depths of the Hudson and the filth of the

Gowanus Canal; and beneath these is the old landscape of the Native Americans; and beneath this are the old "trout rivers" of human prehistory. (Hans enjoys the sight of a man who works for a fish-and-tackle store on West Twenty-third Street, and who wanders out every so often from his shop to practice his fly-fishing technique with a rod, so that "it became possible to envision West Twenty-third Street as a trout river.")

Cricket is bound up with an ideology both of nature (this is how things *just are*—lovely green fields and ideal blue skies and cricket as the very emblem of this natural order) and of cultivation (the "marvelously shorn Surrey village greens" that Hans characteristically thinks of when he imagines cricket). But the two ideologies work against each other: if you have to cultivate nature, you have to change it, and then nature isn't quite a natural order anymore. The black Trinidadian critic and writer C.L.R. James, obsessed with cricket all his life, once wrote a wonderful essay about the West Indian cricketer Garry Sobers, and about how Sobers was important because he was the "first genuine native son" to be made captain of the West Indian team, "without benefit of secondary school, or British university." James continues: "The roots and ground he now covers (and can still explore further) go far down into our origins, the origins of all who constitute the British version of Western civilization." James, alert to the overlapping (and sometimes diverging) ideologies of cricket and colonialism, chooses his words with care when he counterposes Sobers's West Indian "roots" and "ground" with the roots and ground that might be "cultivated" at a British university, and by "the British version of Western civilization." (The doubleness of the pun on "ground" is unavoidable because in British usage large cricket fields are known not as fields but as "cricket grounds.") James knows that Garry Sobers's West Indian roots and ground are very different from an Englishman's, and yet ineradicably similar, too—linked and affected by the impress of British colonialism. Chuck does not know this, or has chosen to repress these historical affinities in his headlong rush toward forgetful American belonging; and it is the acute intelligence of this novel—both a political intelligence and a *human* intelligence—that it understands the hidden personal wound of this unknowing. That wound is successfully hidden from Hans (who complacently talks about how cricket makes him feel "naturalized" in America), and successfully hidden, it would seem, from Zadie Smith. But it is not hidden from Joseph O'Neill. It is why he wrote his book, which is not importantly a novel about Hans, but about Khamraj "Chuck" Ramkissoon. *What is the ground of Chuck's being?* That is the question that *Netherland* asks. Surely that question is not apolitically "humanist" or "metaphysical" in the way that Zadie Smith fears, but inescapably both human and political.

Nature is always being modified, fields cropped and mowed. That is why *Netherland* mentions the word "aftermath" on its second page, and provides the slightly pedantic definition "a second mowing of grass in the same season." The entire novel exists in the shadow and knowledge of aftermath—superficially, the "aftermath" of 9/11; more deeply, the "aftermath" of constant change and modification. This is the significance of the three visits to Chuck's playing field: visits to a changing piece of ground. Three times O'Neill takes us to Bald Eagle Field. The first time, it is Chuck's snowy dream ("an immense white emptiness"—note again the loaded political charge of that adjective "white"). The second time, sixty pages later, it is the summer of 2003, and Hans is astounded: the field is green and tended. "Jesus," he says to Chuck, "you did it." The colonial has successfully colonized his green breast of America. A hundred pages later, in 2006, Hans has left the States, is reunited with his wife in London, and has heard the news about Chuck's demise. He sits at his computer and uses Google Earth to zoom over the old cricket field, and finds that it has browned:

There's Chuck's field. It is brown—the grass has burned—but it is still there. There's no trace of a batting square. The equipment shed is gone. I'm just seeing a field. I stare at it for a while. I am contending with a variety of reactions, and consequently with a single brush on the touch pad I flee upward into the atmosphere and at once have in my sights the physical planet, submarine wrinkles and all—have the option, if so moved, to go anywhere. From up here, though, a human's movement is a barely intelligible thing. Where would he move to, and for what? There is no sign of nations, no sense of the so-called work of man. The USA as such is nowhere to be seen.

The field is still there, but the ground has disappeared.

WOUNDER AND WOUNDED

The public snob, the grand bastard, was much in evidence when I interviewed V. S. Naipaul in 1994, and this was exactly as expected. A pale woman, his secretary, showed me in to the sitting room of his London flat. Naipaul looked warily at me, offered a hand, and began an hour of scornful correction. I knew nothing, he said, about his birthplace, Trinidad; I possessed the usual liberal sentimentality. It was a slave society, a plantation. Did I know anything about his writing? He doubted it. The writing life had been desperately hard. But hadn't his great novel, *A House for Mr. Biswas*, been acclaimed on its publication, in 1961? "Look at the lists they made at the end of the 1960s of the best books of the decade. *Biswas* is not there. Not there." His secretary brought coffee and retired. Naipaul claimed that he had not even been published in America until the 1970s, "and then the reviews were awful—unlettered, illiterate, ignorant." The phone rang, and kept ringing. "I am sorry," Naipaul said in exasperation, "one is not well served here." Only as the pale secretary showed me out, and novelist and servant briefly spoke to each other in the hall, did I realize that she was Naipaul's wife.

A few days later, the phone rang. "It's Vidia Naipaul. I have just read your . . . careful piece in *The Guardian*. Perhaps we can have lunch. Do you know the Bombay Brasserie? What about one o'clock tomorrow?" The Naipaul who took me to lunch that day was different from the horrid interviewee. Stern father had become milder uncle. "It's a buffet system here. Don't pile everything onto one plate. That is vulgar. Put one small thing onto a plate, and when you have finished it they will come and take it away." I didn't think that he was making amends for his earlier behavior, nor that he had so admired my piece that he was compelled to meet me off duty. I thought he was merely curious to talk to someone in his late twenties about writing, and that the habits of a lifetime—the brilliant noticer, the committed world-gatherer—were asserting themselves almost automatically: he was working. He was also lecturing, and enjoying it. "If you want to write serious books," he said to me, "you must be ready to break the forms, break the forms. Is it true that Anita Brookner writes exactly the same novel every year?" It is true, I said. "How awful, how awful."

The Indian social theorist Ashis Nandy writes of the two voices in Kipling, the saxophone and the oboe. The first is the hard, militaristic, imperialist writer, and the second is Kipling's "Indianness, and his awe for the culture and the mind of India." Naipaul has a saxophone and an oboe, too, a hard sound and a softer one. These two sides could be called the Wounder and the Wounded. The Wounder is by now well known—the source of fascinated hatred in the literary world and postcolonial academic studies. He disdains the country he came from—"I was born there, yes. I thought it was a mistake." When he won the Nobel Prize in 2001, he said it was "a great tribute to both England, my home, and India, the home of my ancestors." Asked why he had omitted Trinidad, he said that he feared it would "encumber the tribute." He has written of the "barbarism" and "primitivism" of African societies, and has fixated, when writing about India, on public defecation ("they defecate on the hills; they defecate on the riverbanks; they defecate on the streets"). When asked for his favorite writers, he replies, "My father." He is socially successful but deliberately friendless, an empire of one: "At school I had only admirers; I had no friends."

The Wounder, we learn from Patrick French's superb biography of Naipaul, used and used up his first wife, Patricia Hale, sometimes depending on her, at other times ignoring her, often berating and humiliating her. In 1972, Naipaul began a long, tortured, sado-masochistic affair with an Anglo-Argentinian woman, Margaret Gooding. It was an intensely sexual relationship, which enacted, on Naipaul's side, fantasies of cruelty and domination. On one occasion, jealous because Margaret was with another man, he was "very violent with her for two days with my hand . . . Her face was bad. She couldn't really appear in public."

The Wounded Naipaul is the writer who returns obsessively to the struggle, shame, and impoverished fragility of his early life in Trinidad; to the unlikely journey he made from the colonial rim of the British Empire to its metropolitan center; and to the precariousness, as he sees it, of his long life in England—"a stranger here, with the nerves of a stranger," as he puts it in *The Enigma of Arrival* (1987). This wound is the death that makes possible the great life of the books. Again and again, Naipaul extends a sympathy seemingly reserved only for himself to others, and manages, without condescension or vanity, to blend his woundedness with theirs: the empire of one is colonized by his characters. They range from the major to the minor, from the educated to the almost illiterate, but they are united by their homelessness. They are the men in *Miguel Street* (1959), a book of linked stories rich in comedy and dialect, based on the street in Port of Spain, the capital of Trinidad, where Naipaul spent his formative years. Elias, for instance, dreams of being a doctor. "And Elias waved his small hands, and we thought we could see the Cadillac and the black bag and the tube-thing that Elias was going to have." To become a doctor, Elias must escape the island, and to do that he must sit a British scholarship exam. A friend comments excitedly: "Everything Elias write not remaining here, you know. Every word that boy write going to England." Elias fails the exam, and sits it again. "Is the English and litricher that does beat me," he confesses. He fails it again. He decides to become a sanitary inspector. He fails that exam. He ends up as a cart driver, "one of the street aristocrats." And there is Santosh, who narrates one of the stories in *In a Free State* (1971), a servant from Bombay

who accompanies his master to Washington, D.C., and is quite lost
away from his old home. He wanders the American streets, sees
some Hare Krishna singers, and for a moment thinks that they are
Indians. And his mind yearns for his old life:

> How nice it would be if the people in Hindu costumes in
> the circle were real. Then I might have joined them. We
> would have taken to the road; at midday we would have
> halted in the shade of big trees; in the late afternoon the
> sinking sun would have turned the dust clouds to gold; and
> every evening at some village there would have been wel-
> come, water, food, a fire in the night. But that was the dream
> of another life.

Instead, as an Indian restaurant owner tells Santosh: "This isn't
Bombay. Nobody looks at you when you walk down the street. Nobody cares what you do." He means it consolingly—that Santosh is
free to do whatever he likes. But Naipaul is alert to Santosh's negative
freedom, in which nobody in America cares what he does because
nobody cares who he is. Santosh leaves his master, marries an American, becomes a citizen. He is now "in a free state," but ends his tale
like this: "All that my freedom has brought me is the knowledge
that I have a face and have a body, that I must feed this body and
clothe this body for a certain number of years. Then it will be over."

   And above all there is Mohun Biswas, the protagonist of Naipaul's greatest novel, *A House for Mr. Biswas*, who is born into
poverty in Trinidad, begins his professional life as a signwriter
("IDLERS KEEP OUT BY ORDER" is his first commission), miraculously becomes a journalist in Port of Spain, and ends his life at the
age of forty-six, lolling on his Slumberking bed and reading Marcus
Aurelius—a homeowner but barely housed: "He had no money . . .
On the house in Sikkim Street Mr. Biswas owed, and had been ow-
ing for four years, three thousand dollars . . . Two children were at
school. The two older children, on whom Mr. Biswas might have
depended, were both abroad on scholarships." Naipaul ends the

short prologue to that novel with a deep autobiographical shudder: Imagine if Mr. Biswas had not owned this poor house, he suggests to his comfortable readers. "How terrible it would have been, at this time, to be without it . . . to have lived without even attempting to lay claim to one's portion of the earth; to have lived and died as one had been born, unnecessary and unaccommodated." How much land does a man need? asks Tolstoy in a fierce late tale. Six feet, just enough to be buried in, is that story's reply. Mr. Biswas had a little more than that; but he had so narrowly avoided being the "unaccommodated man," the naked savage found on the heath in *King Lear*.

Unnecessary, unaccommodated—and unnoticed, until Naipaul made him the hero of his book. The shudder is autobiographical, because Mr. Biswas is essentially Vidia Naipaul's father, Seepersad Naipaul, and the fictional house on Sikkim Street is the real house on Nepaul Street from which Vidia was launched, at nearly eighteen, on his enormous journey to England—"a box," writes Patrick French, "a hot, rickety, partitioned building near the end of the street, around 7 square metres on two floors with an external wooden staircase and a corrugated iron roof." Seepersad's father was an indentured laborer, shipped from India to Trinidad in order to fill out the workforce on the sugarcane plantations. Indentured servitude differed from slavery in that it was theoretically voluntary, and families were allowed to stay together. After five or ten years, the laborer could return to India or stay and take a small plot of land. At the time of Vidia Naipaul's birth, in 1932, the literacy rate among Trinidadian Indians (then about a third of the island's 400,000) was 23 percent. For the entire island, there were four British government scholarships, which paid for study at a British university, and Vidia felt that this was his only chance to escape. He had won his first scholarship at the age of ten; he won his last in 1949, and left for Oxford the next year.

From this world, Naipaul's father, Seepersad, made a career as a reporter and columnist for *The Trinidad Guardian*, and published a book of fictional stories about his community, written with a simplicity and comedy and attention to detail that his son would admire and emulate. It was an extraordinary achievement, but judged by wider standards it was also a relative failure, because Seepersad never left the island, and had to live vicariously through his clever children, who did. (He died in 1953, aged forty-seven, while Vidia was still at Oxford.) That double assessment—pride and shame, compassion and alienation—is the stereoscopic vision of *A House for Mr. Biswas* and, in a sense, of all Naipaul's fiction, and it is why he is a writer who has a conservative vision but radical eyesight. The Wounded, radical Naipaul burns with rage at the cramped colonial horizon of his father's life, and seeks to defend his accomplishments against the colonist's metropolitan sneers; but the conservative Wounder has got beyond the little prison of Trinidad, and now sees, with the colonist's eye and no longer the colonial's, the littleness of that imprisonment. Naipaul is enraging and puzzling, especially to those who themselves come from postcolonial societies, because his radicalism and conservatism are so close to each other—each response is descended from the same productive shame. Naipaul plays the oboe and the saxophone with the same reed.

In his writing, Naipaul is simultaneously the colonized and the colonist, in part because he never seriously imagines that the former would ever want to be anything but the latter, even as he uses each category to judge the other. Thus a pompous English Oxford student of the early 1950s might have seen Seepersad's achievement as absurdly minor, and Vidia Naipaul would certainly have agreed with him; but the bitterness of Seepersad's struggle would also have qualified that Oxonian complacency. How could Vidia not have wanted to defend his father as soon as the Oxonian looked down his nose at him? This dialectic seems familiar because it may have less to do with race and empire than with class; it is the classic movement from province to metropolis, whereby the provincial, who has never wanted to be anywhere but the metropolis, nevertheless judges it with a provincial skepticism, while judging the provinces with a metropolitan superiority. In *A House for Mr. Biswas*, the Wounded and the Wounder are hard to disentangle, and Naipaul often adopts a kind of cool summary omniscience that he uses to provoke our rebellious compassion. There is an extraordinary moment early in the book when he offers a flash-forward, and tells us that Mr. Biswas's fate would probably be that of a laborer, working on the estates like his brother, Pratap, "illiterate all his days." Pratap, he writes, would become "richer than Mr. Biswas; he was to have a house of his own, a large, strong, well-built house, years before Mr. Biswas." And then he changes course:

> But Mr. Biswas never went to work on the estates. Events which were to occur presently led him away from that. They did not lead him to riches, but made it possible for him to console himself in later life with the *Meditations* of Marcus Aurelius, while he rested on the Slumberking bed in the one room which contained most of his possessions.

Naipaul is here communicating, almost esoterically, with his presumed non-Trinidadian audience: You are the sort of people, he seems to say, who might disdain Mr. Biswas, but you are also the kind of people who know that Pratap's "riches" are not as important as Biswas's "riches"; that Marcus Aurelius on a Slumberking bed, small as it is, is better than a Slumberking bed without Marcus Aurelius.

Nowadays, V. S. Naipaul spends so much time being disagreeable and superior, is so masked and armored, that it can be hard to remember the young writer's woundedness. The letters he sent from Oxford to Trinidad, preternaturally confident, occasionally show a chink, as when he writes: "I want to come top of my group. I have got to show these people that I can beat them at their own language." Patrick French shrewdly dips into the Oxford student magazine *Isis* to give us an idea of "these people," and thus of the world Naipaul had to join and beat. For instance, the magazine offered a portrait in its "Americans-and-Colonials" series, of an Indian undergraduate, Ramesh Divecha: "This fine specimen of Hindu manhood is equally at home theorising on the secrets of his success in Vincent's or fingering his native chapattis in the Taj . . . He returns to the jungle in August to study for his Bar Finals."

To the jungle. Thus joked Pox Britannica.

Naipaul had a breakdown at Oxford, and the years immediately after his graduation as he looked for work in London were intensely difficult. The hardship was softened by his relationship with Patricia Hale, whom he had met at Oxford in 1952. They were in some ways well matched. Like him, she was from modest circumstances—her father was a clerk in a lawyer's office, and the family lived in a small two-bedroom flat in a suburb of Birmingham. She was the only girl at her school to win a state scholarship to Oxford. They were both twenty-two when they married, and neither family was notified. But whereas Naipaul careened from confidence to anxiety (a year after meeting Pat, he told her that "from a purely selfish point of view you are the ideal wife for a future G.O.M."—Grand Old Man—"of letters"), Pat was stable, supportive, a willing helpmeet. Years later, Naipaul reread his early correspondence with Pat, and made notes. Characteristically, he did not spare himself. He had got too quickly involved with Pat, he wrote; he had been in too deep and could not get out. It would have been better if he had married someone else. Pat "did not attract me sexually at all." He decided that the relationship, on his side, "was more than half a lie. Based really on need. The letters are shallow & disingenuous."

Pat sometimes seems to have aspired to the condition of the Athenian women adjured by Pericles, in his funeral oration, to "think it your greatest commendation not to be talked of one way or other." Her presence in this biography is a hush around Vidia's noise; her job is merely to hold the big drum of his ego in the right position, the better for him to strike the vital life-rhythm. "I am not much good to anyone and Vidia is probably, almost certainly right when he says I have nothing to offer him," she would write in her diary, many years on in their marriage. Unassertive, Englishly reticent, a little milky and bland, she became steadily obsessed with his writing—even as she would half mockingly call him "The Genius" in private—and enjoyed being his spur and amanuensis. There are six thrilling pages, in a biography full of intimate and moving revelations, in which Patrick French, with the help of Pat's diaries, shows us the genesis and progress of Naipaul's novel A *Bend in the River* (1979), probably the only rival to *Biswas*. One evening, in the fall of 1977, after watching television, he informed his wife that he wanted "to be alone with my thoughts." Half an hour later she entered his room, and he told her that the novel would begin with these lines: "My family came from the east coast. Africa was at our backs. We are Indian ocean people." Then he outlined for her the story and the main characters. Over the next months, he said pleadingly that he could not write the book without her presence, and her diary documents its swift, difficult passage. Sometimes he read to her and sometimes he dictated to her, calling her into his bedroom, like Churchill with his secretaries, at one o'clock in the morning. The novel moved fast, and in May 1978 he asked her to come into his room at twelve thirty at night and "spoke the end of the book. It took an hour to an hour and a half."

A *Bend in the River* is narrated by Salim, a Muslim Indian merchant who has moved to a trading town on the bend of a great river in a newly independent African country. In 1966, Naipaul had spent time in Uganda, Kenya, and Tanzania, and in 1975 he traveled to Mobutu's Zaire. In Kisangani, Tanzania, he happened to meet a young Indian businessman whose deracination was striking. The essence of his novel, he said, is: "What is this man doing here?" Like so many of Naipaul's characters, Salim feels his status to be precarious. "I was worried for us. Because, so far as power went, there was no difference between the Arabs and ourselves. We were both small groups living under a European flag at the end of the world." An old friend of Salim's named Indar, who has been educated at a British university, arrives to do research at the town's polytechnic. Indar tells Salim about his journey to England, and once again Naipaul returns to the two beguilingly traumatic stories he has never escaped—the abbreviated short story of his father's journey, and the arpeggiated long story of his own journey. (Indar "will be me," he told Pat.)

Indar tells Salim that "when we land at a place like London Airport we are concerned only not to appear foolish." After university, he tries to get a job with the Indian diplomatic service, but is humiliated at the Indian High Commission in London. The officials there seem to him cringing minor pomposities, yet one of them is bold enough to ask Indar how he can possibly represent India when he comes from Africa: "How can we have a man of divided loyalties?" Indar tells Salim that "for the first time in my life in London I was filled with a colonial rage. And this wasn't only a rage with London or England; it was also a rage with the people who had allowed themselves to be corralled into a foreign fantasy." He decides, in London, that he will be a Naipauline empire of one. He realizes that he is homeless, that he cannot go home, that he must stay in a place like London, that "I belonged to myself alone." He consoles himself, however:

> "I'm a lucky man. I carry the world within me. You see, Salim, in this world beggars are the only people who can be choosers. Everyone else has his side chosen for him. I can choose . . . But now I want to win and win and win."

Yet near the end of the book, Salim hears that Indar has not exactly won and won and won. His academic gig has folded because the Americans pulled the funding. Now "he does the lowest kind of job. He knows he is equipped for better things, but he doesn't want to do them . . . He doesn't want to risk anything again."

The Naipaul who wrote Indar's incandescent monologue is the Naipaul who, many years earlier, had written this fierce letter to Pat:

> I want you to put yourself in my place for a minute . . . If my father had 1/20 of the opportunity laid before the good people of British stock, he would not have died a broken, frustrated man without any achievement. But, like me, he had the opportunity—to starve. He was ghettoed—in a sense more cruel than that in which Hitler ghettoed the Jews. But there was an element of rude honesty in the Nazi approach; and they at any rate killed swiftly. The approach

of the Free World is infinitely subtler and more refined.
You cannot say to a foreign country: I suffer from political
persecution. That wouldn't be true . . . But I suffer from
something worse, an insidious spiritual persecution. These
people want to break my spirit. They want me to forget my
dignity as human being. They want me to know my place.

Naipaul in this letter resembles no writer so much as Frantz
Fanon, the radical analyst of the "insidious spiritual persecution"
wrought by colonialism on the colonized. "The colonized subject,"
writes Fanon in *The Wretched of The Earth* (1961),

is constantly on his guard: Confused by the myriad signs of
the colonial world he never knows whether he is out of line.
Confronted with a word configured by the colonizer, the
colonized subject is always presumed guilty. The colonized
does not accept his guilt, but rather considers it a kind of
curse, a sword of Damocles.

Fanon is a very different political animal from the conservative
Naipaul. Fanon believed in violent revolution, but Naipaul's radical
pessimism meets Fanon's radical optimism at that point where the
cut of colonial guilt, angrily resisted by both men, is converted into
the wound of colonial shame—"a kind of curse." And Naipaul's long
novella *In a Free State* is practically a working demonstration of
Fanon's argument that "the colonist is an exhibitionist. His safety
concerns lead him to remind the colonized out loud: 'Here I am
master.' The colonist keeps the colonized in a state of rage, which
he prevents from boiling over." In that spare, bleak, burning novella, a white Englishman and Englishwoman drive through an African country resembling Uganda. The man is an administrative
officer in a government department. In the course of their journey
they perpetrate, and also witness, flamboyant acts of colonial rage
on black Africans, acts whose raison d'être seems to be white self-
reassurance. Impotent exhibitionists in Fanon's sense, these white

intruders are at once predatory and fearful, constantly supplicating an assumed black "rage" that they themselves actually feel, and constantly provoke. At a decrepit hotel, an old English colonel humiliates Peter, a black assistant, while his white visitors look on. One day, he warns Peter, you will come to my room to kill me, but you won't get past my door, because I'll be waiting for you: "I'll kill you, I'll shoot you dead."

Naipaul's sympathy for the political and emotional fragility of his characters did not extend, alas, to his wife. His brutally fulfilling affair with Margaret Gooding—"I wished to possess her as soon as I saw her," he tells his biographer—gradually voided a marriage that had never been sexually fulfilling. In the mid-1970s, husband and wife began to spend more and more time apart as Naipaul traveled on ceaseless journalistic assignments. Naipaul's sister, Savi, suggests that once Pat realized she would not have children and that her husband was committedly unfaithful, she lost her confidence as a woman. Patrick French had access both to Pat's diaries and to searching interviews with V. S. Naipaul, whose candor is formidable: as always, one feels that while Naipaul may often be wrong, he is rarely untruthful, and indeed that he is likely to uncover twenty truths on the path to error. Pat's diaries make for painful reading: "I felt assaulted but I could not defend myself." "He has been increasingly frenzied and sadly, from my point of view, hating and abusing me." Pat died of breast cancer in 1996. "It could be said that I had killed her," Naipaul tells French. "It could be said. I feel a little bit that way."

The day after Pat's cremation, Nadira Alvi, the well-heeled daughter of a Pakistani banker, soon to be the novelist's second wife, arrived in Wiltshire, at the house so recently vacated by her predecessor; and Naipaul wrote to his literary agent: "She is part of my luck, and I would like you to meet her." This is where French's masterly, mournful book ends, and it seems hideously just, in a life story so consumed by social and racial anxieties and so transcendent of them, too, that we should see V. S. Naipaul ending his life with a haughty woman who tells Patrick French that she thinks her husband's relatives are "jumped-up peasantry" and that her father "would be shocked that I found happiness with an indentured labourer's grandson."

In *The Enigma of Arrival*, the long book that Naipaul wrote about the Wiltshire countryside in which he has lived, intermittently, since 1971, there is a searing parenthesis in which he tells us about two derelict cottages he has been converting into a new home. One day, a very old lady is brought by her grandson to look at the cottage where she once spent a summer. Confused by Naipaul's renovations, she thinks she has come to the wrong place. Naipaul is "ashamed," and so "I pretended I didn't live there." But what is the real source of the shame? Is it his building project or his very presence in the English countryside? He lives there but is ashamed to live there; the house for Mr. Naipaul in England, as for Mr. Biswas in Trinidad, is a homeless house. The man is still unaccommodated.

ROBERT ALTER AND
THE KING JAMES BIBLE

In the beginning was not the word, or the deed, but the face. "Darkness was upon the face of the deep," runs the King James Version in the second verse of the opening of Genesis. "And the Spirit of God moved upon the face of the waters. And God said, Let there be light: and there was light." Two uses of "face" in one verse, and a third implied face, surely: God's own, hovering over the face of his still uncreated world. The Almighty, looking into the face of his waters, might well be expected to see his face reflected: it is profoundly his world, still uncontaminated by rebellious man.

The committees of translators appointed by James I knew what they were doing. The face of God and the face of the world (or of mankind) will become a running entanglement throughout the five Books of Moses (Genesis, Exodus, Leviticus, Numbers, and Deuteronomy). Man will fear to look upon God's face, and God will frequently abhor the deeds of the people who live on the face of his world. Once Cain has killed Abel, and has been banished by God, he cries out: "Behold thou hast driven me out this day from the face of the earth; and from thy face shall I be hid." When the Almighty decides to flood his world, he pledges to destroy every living thing "from off the face of the earth." After wrestling with a divine stranger all night, Jacob "called the name of the place Peniel: For I have seen God face to face, and my life is preserved." Jacob dies happy that he has seen his son Joseph's face, and Moses, of course, spoke to God "face to face, as a man speaketh unto his friend." The Book of Numbers contains the little prayer so beloved of the Christian liturgy: "The Lord bless thee, and keep thee: The Lord make his face shine upon thee: The Lord lift up his countenance upon thee, and give thee peace." He casts his now kindly face upon ours. The Hebrew word for "face" is the same in all these verses, so the seventeenth-century translators were being exact; but they were also perhaps telling us something about God's circular ownership of his creation, his face above and his face below. Perhaps when they chose "the face of the waters" they had in their ears John's description of the Lord in Revelation: "and his voice as the sound of many waters."

In his translation of the Pentateuch, Robert Alter eschews "face" to describe the surface of the world at the start of Genesis, and I miss the cosmic implications, but his first two verses compensate with their own originality: "When God began to create heaven and earth, and the earth then was welter and waste and darkness over the deep and God's breath hovering over the waters, God said: 'Let there be light.' And there was light." The King James Version has "without form and void" for Alter's Anglo-Saxonish "welter and waste," but Alter, characteristically, provides a diligent and alert footnote:

> The Hebrew *tohu wabohu* occurs only here and in two later biblical texts that are clearly alluding to this one. The second word of the pair looks like a nonce term coined to rhyme with the first and to reinforce it, an effect I have tried to approximate in English by alliteration. *Tohu* by itself means "emptiness" or "futility," and in some contexts is associated with the trackless vacancy of the desert.

Alter brings this kind of sensitivity to bear on moment after moment of his translation, and the result greatly refreshes, sometimes productively estranges, words that may now be too familiar to those who grew up with the King James Bible.

The Pentateuch, or Torah, contains the great narratives of our monotheistic infancy. It tells the stories of the creation; of Adam and Eve and their children, Cain and Abel; of the Flood and Noah's escape and God's promise never to destroy the earth again; of Abraham and God's covenant with him and his people; of Isaac and his sons Esau and Jacob; of Jacob's wrestle with God and God's anointing of Jacob as Israel; the story of Joseph and his brothers; the sojourn of the Israelites in Egypt and their exodus, led by Moses; the handing down of the law from the mountain at Sinai; the elaboration of the law or teaching (*torah* means "teaching"); and finally the death of Moses as his people are on the verge of the promised land.

Biblical style is famous for its stony reticence, for a mimesis that Erich Auerbach called "fraught with background." This reticence is surely not as unique as Auerbach claimed—Herodotus is a great rationer of explanation, for example—but it achieves its best-known form in the family stories of Genesis. The paratactic verses with their repeated "and" move like the hands of those large old railway-station clocks that jolted visibly from minute to minute: time is beaten forward, not continuously pursued. Yet it is often the gaps between these verses, or sometimes between the clauses of a single verse, that constitute the text's "realism," a realism created as much by the needy reader as by the withholding writing itself. For example, after the Flood, Noah starts a new occupation: "And Noah began to be an husbandman, and he planted a vineyard. And he drank of the wine, and was drunken; and he was uncovered within his tent." Noah is a lush. This is not without crooked humor of a kind, and the gap-filled rapidity of the narration is the reason for the smile it raises.

Likewise, though generating pathos rather than comedy, the laconic report of Joseph's response to his brothers works by starving us of information. Joseph, installed by Pharaoh as his right-hand man in Egypt, receives in an official capacity his brothers, who have traveled from Canaan in search of food. He recognizes them but disguises himself. Three times he weeps, twice turning away from them and a third time openly. The first time, "he turned himself about from them, and wept." The second time is more agitated:

"And Joseph made haste; for his bowels did yearn upon his brother: and he sought where to weep; and he entered into his chamber, and wept there." Finally, after various ruses, he can stand it no longer and asks his servants to leave him alone while he "made himself known unto his brethren. And he wept aloud: and the Egyptians and the house of Pharaoh heard." The beauty is that the final episode, the apparent climax, is as terse as the first: secret weeping is no different in this account from public weeping, and revelation is as hidden as disguise. Joseph is no longer hidden from his brothers, but he is still hidden from the reader: that surely is the thrust of the narration. And note, too, how our desire to witness this open crying, to bathe in authorial emotion, is reticently, and very movingly, transferred to another, less involved audience: "and the Egyptians and the house of Pharaoh heard."

I quoted from the King James Version here, but Alter's translation honors both the text's grave simplicity and its almost novelistic attention to different literary registers. Abraham's wife, Sarah, is for a long time barren, so she proposes that her maid Hagar sleep with Abraham to provide him with an heir. Hagar conceives, and when she sees that she is pregnant, "her mistress was despised in her eyes." It is one of those intensely human biblical moments: the servant, proud of her plump fertility, cannot but help look down on her withered mistress. But Alter improves on the King James Version's "despised": "And she saw that she had conceived and her mistress seemed slight in her eyes." That "slight," for obvious reasons, is very subtle.

Or take the little adjustment Alter makes to the Jacob and Esau tale. Esau is so hungry for the lentils that his brother has that he sells his birthright for a mess of pottage: "And Esau said to Jacob, Feed me, I pray thee, with that same red pottage: for I am faint." Alter's version is more literal, and more natural: "And Esau said to Jacob, 'Let me gulp down some of this red red stuff, for I am famished.'" In a footnote, he explains his choice:

Although the Hebrew of the dialogues in the Bible reflects the same level of normative literary language as the surrounding narration, here the writer comes close to assigning substandard Hebrew to the rude Esau. The famished brother cannot even come up with the ordinary Hebrew word for "stew" (*nazid*) and instead points to the bubbling pot impatiently as (literally) "this red red." The verb he uses for gulping down occurs nowhere else in the Bible, but in rabbinic Hebrew it is reserved for the feeding of animals.

There are many examples like this of choices deeply pondered and painstakingly explained; reading Alter's scripture is a slow business only because one stops so often to put down into the well of one of his life-giving footnotes.

Though the King James Version is sometimes inaccurate, it is generally thought to be, of all English translations, the one that best captures the quiddity of the Hebrew. Early seventeenth-century English—and mid-sixteenth-century English, since the KJV stands on the shoulders of Tyndale, Coverdale, and Cranmer—was not afraid of antisentimental reticence (my favorite is perhaps Exodus 13:17, "And Joshua discomfited Amalek and his people with the edge of the sword"); it followed the parataxis of the Hebrew narration (the "and" that so often begins a new verse or clause); it understood, as a literary principle, that to repeat a word can be enrichment, not exhaustion, and that repetition subtly changes the sense of the repeated word if not its sound (modern versions, like the flat Revised Standard Version, invariably flee from repetition); and it relished the pungent physicality of Hebrew, which often inheres in the verbs.

Alter's translation brings delight because it follows the precepts of the committees of King James, but is founded on a greatly deeper conversance with Hebrew than the great seventeenth-century scholars could summon. (Of course, no Jew was involved in the King James committees.) And Alter, who has been at the forefront of the rise of what might be called literary biblical studies, and who has educated two or three generations of students and readers in the art of biblical appreciation, brings to his own English a scholarly comprehension of the capacities of literary usage.

In his introduction he says that among the great twentieth-century English stylists such as Joyce, Woolf, Nabokov, Faulkner—he might have added Lawrence, by far the most biblical writer of twentieth-century English—"there is not one among them whose use of language, including the deployment of syntax, even vaguely resembles the workaday simplicity and patly consistent orderliness that recent translators of the Bible have posited as the norm of modern English." Thus Alter is happy to follow the precedent of the KJV when he feels that it cannot be bettered: his Adam also "knew" Eve, and his Israelites also "murmured against" Moses in the wilderness and lament that they have left behind "the fleshpots" of Egypt. As ever, he usefully defends his reasons. About the "fleshpots," he writes: "The Hebrew indicates something like a cauldron in which meat is cooked, but the King James Version's rendering of 'fleshpots' ('flesh,' of course, meaning 'meat' in seventeenth-century English) has become proverbial in the language and deserves to be retained." Well, it became proverbial, but is it still? The word always makes me smile because when I was growing up, albeit in a highly scriptural household, my family used to talk of my grandparents' house—where I was allowed unlimited sweets—as the "fleshpots of Egypt."

Especially fine is the way Alter seems to dig into the earth of the Hebrew to recover, in English, its fearless tactility. When Pharaoh has his first dream, of seven good ears of corn and seven bad, "his heart pounded," which, Alter informs us in a footnote, follows the Hebrew, whose literal meaning is "his spirit pounded." (The usually concrete KJV has the softer "his spirit was troubled.") The dream comes to pass, and there are seven fat years and seven lean years. "During the seven plenteous years the earth brought forth abundantly," runs the Revised Standard Version, itself a wan starveling of the more robust and accurate KJV: "And in the seven plenteous years the earth brought forth by handfuls." But Alter is more

literal: "And the land in the seven years of plenty made gatherings."
A footnote girds the apparent oddity of "gatherings":

> The Hebrew *qematsim* elsewhere means "handfuls," and
> there is scant evidence that it means "abundance," as sev-
> eral modern versions have it. But *qomets* is a "handful"
> because it is what the hand gathers in as it closes, and it is
> phonetically and semantically cognate with *wayiqbots*, "he
> collected," the very next word in the Hebrew text. The
> likely reference here, then, is not to small quantities (hand-
> fuls) but to the process of systematically gathering in the
> grain, as the next sentence spells out.

Or take the moment at the end of chapter 2 of Exodus where the
Bible writer tells us that God began to hear the groaning of the Israelites in their Egyptian bondage: "So God looked on the Israelites
and was concerned about them," says the New International Version.
The King James has: "And God looked upon the children of Israel,
and God had respect unto them." Alter has: "And God saw the Israelites, and God knew." Notice that the New International Version
shies away from repeating the word "God," something that fazes
neither the KJV nor Alter. But Alter's reading is at once elegantly
emphatic—"and God knew"—and accurate. He informs us that the
Hebrew verb has no object, and that Greek translators mistakenly
tried to "correct" it. How majestic and indeed divine that objectless
"knew" is. And Alter's version allows one to make new connections
with biblical-sounding texts. Saul Bellow, who grew up reading the
Hebrew Bible, and whose English was profoundly influenced by
both the Tanakh and the King James Version, was very fond of that
objectless verb "knew." Tommy Wilhelm, the hero of *Seize the Day*,
is haplessly surrounded by people he fears are the kinds of people
who "know" (as opposed to the confused hero): "Rubin was the kind
of man who knew, and knew and knew," Tommy thinks to himself.
Mr. Sammler's Planet ends with the eponymous hero reflecting that

he has met the terms of his life contract, those terms "that we all know, God, that we know, that we know, we know, we know." This always *sounded* biblical to me, but Alter's translation of the line in Exodus has given me chapter and verse.

To read the Pentateuch right through is an extraordinary education in early theology. These five books revert obsessively to questions of fertility, rebellion, and polytheism, and the three concerns are tightly linked. Again and again, Yahweh tells his people that they must worship no other gods but him, and that the consequences for failing this charge will be death and destruction. God's chosen people repeatedly failed to keep this law, most famously at Sinai, when Aaron persuaded them to worship the golden calf, saying: "These are your gods, O Israel, who brought you up from Egypt." The five books are anxiously shadowed by the threat of polytheism, which surrounded the Israelites in Egypt and Mesopotamia, and which provided some of the mythic texts that Genesis and Exodus seem to remember. God goes by several names in the Torah, some of the differences having to do with different Bible writers working in different centuries. He first appears in Genesis as Elohim, but is switched to Yahweh Elohim (usually translated as "the Lord God"). When he appears in chapter 17 of Genesis to tell Abraham that he will be "a father to a multitude of nations," he announces himself as "El Shaddai," an archaic name used five times in the Pentateuch that may have associations with fertility or mountains. In Numbers, the word "El" seems to be used as a synonym for Yahweh: El is a Hebrew word meaning God, but it is also the name of the chief of the Canaanite gods. And after the parting of the Red Sea, when the Israelites give thanks in their Song of the Sea, the following verses occur (in Alter's translation):

> You blew with Your breath—the sea covered them over.
>   They sank like lead in the mighty waters:
> Who is like You among the gods, O Lord,
>   who is like You, mighty in holiness?

At times like these, and in its insistent warnings against worshiping other gods, the Pentateuch reflects the effort of wrenching monotheism out of the polytheistic context: monotheism is known nowhere else in antiquity and is, on the face of it, a peculiar notion (so peculiar, perhaps, that one chosen god must be matched by one chosen people). It cannot have been easy to have renounced—if indeed such a renunciation took place—the comforting cosmogony wherein various parts of the natural world were represented by different all-powerful gods, and junior "personal" deities looked after one's daily interests. Frank Moore Cross and Jean Bottéro, among many others, have shown the Pentateuch's indebtedness to Egyptian and Babylonian mythic narratives. In *Religion in Ancient Mesopotamia*, Bottéro gives an account of the *Atrahasis*, a Mesopotamian poem written, most likely, before 1700 B.C. In it, the gods meet in council and agree to follow the god Enki's plan to create human beings out of clay. In these early years, as in the days of Noah, people live for hundreds and even thousands of years. But mankind multiplies so effectively that its noise disturbs the sleep of the irascible king of the gods, Enlil, who decides to destroy the pesky humans. He sends epidemic, illness, and famine, but each time the humans escape, aided by Enki, their "inventor." Enlil, still enraged, sends a flood, but Enki saves the race by placing one man, Atrahasis, and his family in an unsinkable boat. After the flood, in order to appease Enlil, Enki reduces the life span of each person to the length we know today, and introduces sterility and infant mortality to keep the numbers down.

Clearly, this is an ancient account not just of the origin of the world but of the origin of evil, of human suffering and death, in which the mark of man's rebelliousness is in part his sheer fertility. It is like peering into the crucible of theodicy. Notwithstanding the enormous difference of monotheism, we see something very similar in the early chapters of Genesis (the Israelites would have shared with the Mesopotamian Semites a traditional Semitic culture). In the first chapter of Genesis, God (Elohim) creates man in his own image and charges him to be fruitful and multiply. But in the second chapter—thought to be a different narrative strand—the Lord God (now called Yahweh Elohim) threatens Adam and Eve with death if they eat of the tree of good and evil. They fail the test, and mortality and sin enter the world. Sin is palpable: in Alter's wonderful phrase, God warns the disgruntled Cain that "at the tent flap sin crouches," and in the very next verse Cain rises up and slays his brother. Man "began to multiply over the earth" and to sin, and the Lord repents of his decision to create humans, and sends a flood to eliminate all but Noah and his family. After the Flood, he makes a covenant never to destroy his creation, and human life spans are reduced to 120 years. The stories of the patriarchs now begin, but God cannot cede what seems an anxious desire to control human fertility: men must be circumcised, and the wives of the early patriarchs (Sarah, Rebekah, Rachel) are barren until the Lord chooses to permit them to breed. He will threaten his people again with complete destruction when they follow Aaron's encouragement to worship the golden calf. Promiscuous fertility and polytheism seem to be connected menaces, captured in Yahweh's command in Exodus that the Israelites make no covenant with any of the peoples they vanquish and displace, who "whore after their gods and sacrifice to their gods."

There is an ironic Midrashic commentary, mentioned by Emmanuel Levinas in his book *Nine Talmudic Readings*, in which the Talmudists placed demons—spirits without bodies—inside Noah's Ark. "These are the tempters of postdiluvian civilization," Levinas remarks, "without which, no doubt, the mankind of the future could not be, despite its regeneration, a true mankind." Evil has entered the earth forever and cannot be expunged, even by flood: but how did it get there? What is so fiercely at stake in Genesis and Exodus is the old question best phrased by Boethius in his *Consolation of Philosophy*: "If there be a God, whence cometh so many evils? And if there be no God, whence cometh any good?" Much has been canonically laid at the feet of Adam and Eve, who were, so said the early Christian fathers, created free, and freely chose to rebel, thus inaugurating the calamity of original sin. But this merely pushes on the argument by one easy increment, for God gave them their freedom, and as the seventeenth-century skeptic Pierre Bayle comments in his *Historical and Critical Dictionary*, why would God bestow on mankind a capacity—free will—that he knows in advance man will abuse, even to his eternal doom? Around the biblical writings themselves hovers the heretical notion that evil proceeds from God. An "evil spirit from God" is said to descend upon Saul in 1 Samuel 16:23, and in the book of Isaiah the Lord says: "I form the light, and create darkness: I make peace, and create evil. I the Lord do all these things." Even the early church father Origen, a staunch opponent of such thinking, seems flummoxed by this verse, and casts around for a suitable metaphor:

> Now God has not created evil if by this is understood evil properly so called: but some evils, though really there are few by comparison with the order of the whole universe, followed as a secondary consequence upon his primary work, just as spiral shavings and sawdust follow as a consequence upon the primary activity of a carpenter, and as builders seem to "make" the waste stone and mortar which lie beside their buildings. It may be granted that God sometimes creates some of these "evils" in order that he may correct men by these means.

But this leaves the problem exactly where it was, so that various dualisms, like Gnosticism and Manicheanism—wherein God is opposed by and does battle with a separate, satanic source of evil, or is rivaled by a false god, a demiurge—do indeed seem to be the best explanations of the problem. The Bible itself, of course, uses a kind of dualism to explain Job's suffering: it is Satan who puts God up to the game of testing his righteous servant. Some of the early Jewish commentators were so perturbed by Abraham's various trials—the famine, Sarah's barrenness, his nephew Lot, the command to sacrifice Isaac—that they conjectured that God, as with Job, might have received a challenge from Satan or some other envious angel. In an extraordinary moment in Genesis, Abraham pleads with God to spare the innocent inhabitants of Sodom. Would God wipe out the city and not spare fifty innocents? God agrees to spare the entire city for the sake of fifty. How about forty-five? asks Abraham. God agrees to spare the city for the sake of forty-five. And forty? Yes. And thirty? Yes. And so on, down to ten. What is striking is how openly Abraham cajoles Yahweh: "Far be it from You! Will not the judge of all the earth do justice?" Abraham seems, here, to be holding God accountable to an ethical standard independent of God himself, trying to force his creator to accept the radical idea of sparing even the guilty in order to protect the innocent.

It is interesting to note those cruxes, those moments of stress, when God's ethical incomprehensibility makes the early biblical commentators and rewriters anxious. God's activity in Egypt is one such case. The Lord has promised to lead his people out of Egypt, but first he must teach the Egyptians that "there is none like Me in all the earth . . . so as to show you My power, and so that My name will be told through all the earth." To this end, God says, he will "harden Pharaoh's heart" against releasing the Israelites, and send horrid plagues. Again and again, Moses appeals to Pharaoh to let his people go, yet each time God hardens Pharaoh's heart, and another plague descends. Only when every firstborn of Egypt, from Pharaoh's firstborn to "the first-born of the slave girl who is behind the millstones," has been slaughtered do the Israelites escape. But why would God institute a lengthy stubbornness that only inflicts suffering on those who might freely have avoided it? Ancient writers and annotators conjectured that God had not impelled Pharaoh to resist Moses, but had only kept him in a state of ignorance. Or perhaps, went another line of inquiry, this was proper punishment for all that Egypt had done to the Israelites? Either way, sense had to be made of the impossible.

The best example of the incomprehensible in the Pentateuch is God's command to Abraham that he sacrifice his son Isaac. The brevity of the account is searing, as if the text itself flinches from the unreason, is shocked into wordlessness. Alter's version is terrifying:

> And it happened after these things that God tested Abraham. And He said to him: "Abraham!" And he said: "Here I am." And He said: "Take, pray, your son, your only one, whom you love, Isaac, and go forth to the Land of Moriah and offer him up as a burnt offering on one of the mountains which I shall say to you." And Abraham rose early in the morning and saddled his donkey and took his two lads with him, and Isaac his son, and he split wood for the offering, and rose and went to the place that God had said to him. On the third day Abraham raised his eyes and saw the place from afar.

Auerbach rightly noted that the phrase "On the third day Abraham raised his eyes" is the only indication we have that time has passed: the journey is frozen. One can add to Auerbach that Abraham's gesture, of raising the eyes, though a formulaic one in biblical narrative, takes on here a great power of dread, as if Abraham can hardly bear to look upon the chosen site. Kierkegaard's inspired, appalled rewriting of this scene in *Fear and Trembling* emphasizes its unspeakability. The tragic hero, he says, renounces himself in favor of expressing the universal. He gives up what is certain for what is more certain; he gives up the finite to attain the infinite; and so he can speak publicly about it, he can weep and orate, secure that at least someone will understand his action. But Abraham "gives up the universal in order to grasp something still higher that is not the universal," because what he is obeying, what he is grasping for, is barbarously incomprehensible. So Abraham is utterly alone and cannot speak to anyone of what he is about to do, because no one would understand him.

It is suggestive, then, that one of the major early rewriters of this scene, the first-century Jewish historian Josephus, labors to turn Abraham precisely into a tragic hero. In *Jewish Antiquities*, his enormous history of the Jews from earliest times, Josephus inserts long speeches in which Abraham eloquently apologizes to his son before binding him, and moreover promises him that his death will

not really be death: "Accordingly, you, my son, will not die, not in
any common way of going out of the world, but sent to God, the
Father of all men, beforehand, by your own father, in the nature of
a sacrifice." Isaac, in Josephus's account, is of such a "generous dis-
position" that he willingly offers himself up, and then to cap this
warm little drama, God, intervening to save Isaac, speaks to Isaac
to make clear that "it was not out of a desire of human blood" that
Abraham "was commanded to slay his son . . . but to try the temper
of his mind." Kierkegaard seems admiringly terrified of God's command, but Josephus, ornamenting the unspeakable with explanation, seems merely terrified, and at pains to moisten the hard
ground of God's behavior by ensuring that everyone involved,
human and divine, is at least pleasant.

The Pentateuch ends with Moses's death. On the brink of the
promised land, he addresses his people, and reminds them that they
were chosen not for their righteousness but because other nations
were wickedly following strange gods. Thus "thou shalt love the
Lord thy God with all thine heart, and with all thy soul, and with
all thy might." If they follow the Lord, then blessings will flow; but
if they swerve away from the Lord, then curses will flow. Alter
writes appreciatively in his introduction of the majesty of the Hebrew of Deuteronomy, and his English cascades into foul brilliance,
as Moses, speaking on behalf of the Lord, threatens a hell in which
the Israelites will not even be competent slaves:

> And it shall be, as the Lord exulted over you to do well with
> you and to multiply you, so will the Lord exult over you to
> make you perish, to destroy you, and you will be torn from
> the soil . . . And your life will dangle before you, and you
> will be afraid night and day and will have no faith in your
> life. In the morning you will say, "Would that it were eve-
> ning," and in the evening you will say, "Would that it were
> morning," from your heart's fright with which you will be
> afraid and from the sight of your eye that you will see. And
> the Lord will bring you back to Egypt in ships, on the way

that I said to you, "You shall not see it again," and you will put yourselves up for sale there to your enemies as male slaves and slavegirls, and there will be no buyer.

God takes Moses up a mountain to see the land he himself will not live in: "I have let you see with your own eyes, but you shall not cross over there." Because God several times seems to prepare for Moses's death, the surmise later arose in commentaries that Moses did not want to die; Josephus has him weeping before his death, though the typically terse biblical account makes no mention of such theatrical inflammations. James Kugel, in *The Bible as It Was*, reproduces an extraordinary medieval poem, now in the Bodleian, in which Moses's death marks not the serene triumph of the longed-for possession of Canaan, but the scene of an anguished lament for the great impossible questions of the entire Pentateuch. Why are you afraid to die? God asks of Moses, and Moses goes to Hebron and summons Adam from the grave and cries:

> Tell me why you sinned in the Garden
> [Why] you tasted and ate from the tree of Knowledge.
> You have given your sons over to weeping and wailing!
> The whole garden was before you, yet you were not satisfied.
> Oh why did you rebel against the Lord's commandment?

TOLSTOY'S *WAR AND PEACE*

I.

"Alive, and very much so," Tolstoy's diary entry for November 19, 1889, begins. Yes, reading *War and Peace*, that is how it feels to be caught up in Tolstoy's bright sweep: alive, and very much so. It is to succumb to the contagion of vitality. As his characters infect each other with the high temperature of their existences, so they infect us. Count Rostov dances the "Daniel Cooper" at a ball, and "all who were in the ballroom looked with smiles of joy at the merry old man." His son Nikolai has "that merry brotherly tenderness with which all fine young men treat everyone when they are happy." The Rostov girls are "always smiling at something (probably their own happiness)"; one of them, Natasha, loves to order around the servants, but they "liked carrying out Natasha's orders as they did no one else's." The fat, naive, bumbling hero of the novel, Pierre Bezukhov, is so infectious that footmen "joyfully rushed to help him off with his cloak and take his stick and hat." We cannot resist these people, and they cannot resist themselves: Nikolai goes to war "because he could not resist the wish to go galloping across a level field," and when the French start firing at him, he is amazed that anyone would want to kill him: "To kill me? *Me*, whom everybody loves so?" Likewise, when Pierre is captured by the French, he has a revelation of infinity that is also a revelation of his own infinity. Looking up at the numberless stars, he thinks to himself, joyfully:

"And all this is mine, and all this is in me, and all this is me! . . . And all this they've caught and put in a shed and boarded it up!"

Because this massive sense of self hums its own intoxicating music, these characters cannot play in the milder orchestras of give-and-take, and are often poor at crediting the discrete existence of others. But how vividly Tolstoy communicates their vitality to us! There is the "little princess," Prince Andrei's wife, with her short upper lip and faint mustache; and the soldier Denisov with his "short fingers covered with hair"; and old Prince Bolkonsky, aged but still vigorous, with his "small dry hands"; and a shirtless Napoleon, grunting "Do it hard, keep going," to the valet who is vigorously brushing his fat back and fat, hairy chest; and the wise old Russian general Kutuzov, tired and sagging, who is always yawning through war councils (but who has a swivel eye for the girls, and who corresponded with Madame de Staël); and the smooth Russian diplomat Bilibin, with his pompous habit of gathering the skin over his eyebrows when he is about to produce a bon mot; and three-year-old Natasha, boldly walking on her "blunt little feet" into her father's room, eager to wake him.

Tolstoy is the great novelist of physical involuntariness. The body helplessly confesses itself, and the novelist seems merely to run and catch its spilt emotion. When people talk about Tolstoy's "Homeric" quality, they partly mean this. A friend of the novelist's, the critic Druzhinin, ribbed him about it in a letter: "You are sometimes on the point of saying that so-and-so's thighs showed that he wanted to travel in India!" The old patriarch, Prince Bolkonsky, for instance, loves his son, Andrei, and his daughter, Marya, so fiercely that he cannot express that love in any form except spiteful bullying, yelling at his spinsterish daughter, "If only some fool would marry her!" His firm hands register "the still persistent and much-enduring strength of fresh old age," but his face occasionally betrays suppressed tenderness. As he says farewell to his son, who is going to war, he is his usual self, gruffly shouting, "Off with you!" Yet "something twitched in the lower part of the old prince's face."

In *War and Peace*, more so than in the later *Anna Karenina*, the body is animally legible. The old prince's valet can "read" his master's body; he knows that if the prince is "stepping full on his heels," something is up. When Prince Andrei's wife—the "little princess" with the short lip and faint mustache—dies in childbirth, her dead face seems to say to the living, "Ah, what have you done to me?" Tolstoy feels not only Homeric but also childlike in his simplicity and naturalness, because he is not embarrassed to do the kind of thing beloved of children's and fairy-tale writers, when they read the emotions on the face of a cat or a donkey. Tolstoy does it again and again with his humans (and sometimes with animals, too). At the start of the novel, Pierre has an argument about Napoleon at a salon, and then smiles pacifically at everyone, a smile "which said nothing except perhaps this: 'Opinions are opinions, but you see what a good and nice fellow I am.' And everyone, including Anna Pavlovna, involuntarily felt it." Later, at a ball in St. Petersburg, the sixteen-year-old Natasha Rostov, intoxicated with happiness, has just finished a dance and would like to rest. But someone asks her to dance again, and she agrees, flashing a smile at the man she will eventually become engaged to, Prince Andrei, who has been watching her. Tolstoy explains the smile:

> That smile said: "I'd be glad to rest and sit with you; I'm tired; but you see, I've been asked to dance, and I'm glad of it, and I'm happy, and I love everybody, and you and I understand all that," and much, much more.

Readers always feel that Tolstoy is both an intrusive narrator—breaking in to explain things, telling us what to think, writing essays and sermons—and a miraculously absent one, who simply lets his world narrate itself. As Isaac Babel put it, "If the world could write by itself, it would write like Tolstoy." There is a sense in which Tolstoy is saying to us—to dare a Tolstoyan reading of Tolstoy, for a minute—"I will gladly help you read Natasha's or Pierre's or the little princess's face, but really, anyone could do it. You don't really need me. And you don't really need me because these are the largest, most universal, most natural emotions, not the precious little sweets of the stylish novelist." This is especially true when he is describing physical vitality, since such vitality practically reads itself. The old prince, ignoring his son as Andrei tries to tell him about Napoleon's designs, breaks into croaky song, and "sang in an old man's off-key voice." A few pages later, we see "the old prince in his old man's spectacles and his white smock." An old man with an old man's voice and old man's spectacles: Tolstoy seems to want to push such characterization toward the simplest tautology. What was the old man like? He was like an old man—that is to say, like all old men. What is a young man like? He is like a young man—that is to say, like all young men. What is a happy young woman like? Like all happy young women. The Austrian minister of war is described thus: "He had an intelligent and characteristic head." A character will tend to look characteristic, in both senses of the word—full of character, and somehow typical.

There is a powerful tension in Tolstoy's work between persons and types, the particular and the general, freedom and laws. The quintessential Tolstoyan atmosphere is one in which highly particularized characters, with their hairy fingers and short lips, experience universal emotions that might easily be transferred from one character to another. This is why his minor characters are as alive as his major ones. In the novel's epilogue, Nikolai Rostov's aged mother, the Countess, hears the conversation around her and suddenly perks up. She had finished her tea, writes Tolstoy, "and clearly wished to find a pretext for getting angry after eating." Now that is a very Tolstoyan observation, full of wonderful subtlety, but it is a generalized insight, and does not feel unique to the Countess. Almost anyone of a certain age in this novel might have felt the same way. (Chekhov, who learned so much from Tolstoy, is comparably subtle, but without the urge to generalize.)

Babel's conceit, that Tolstoy's work is so life-filled that he somehow does not seem to write at all, has been the dominant modern tribute paid to the master's animism, from Matthew Arnold's admonition that we should not take *Anna Karenina* as a work of art but as a "piece of life," to A. N Wilson's assertion that *War and Peace*, "for seven-eighths of the time . . . does not feel as if it is being narrated at all." It might be better said that *War and Peace* does not seem unwritten—quite the contrary, for the accumulated drafts amount to five thousand pages, and Tolstoy's wife said that she had written out the equivalent of seven fair copies of the book—so much as written by someone who has never needed to read anybody else's fiction. Tolstoy was a gigantic reader, in fact, of fiction in English, French, and German. He consumed Stifter, Flaubert, Stendhal, Sterne, Dickens, Thackeray (he especially loved another novel set during the Napoleonic Wars, *Vanity Fair*). But he also described *War and Peace* as "not a novel," and claimed that Russian fiction was a flock of black sheep, awkward misfits like Gogol's *Dead Souls* and Dostoevsky's barely fictionalized book about the Siberian prison camp, unconventional books nothing like what he called "European forms."

Tolstoy wrote this enormous not-a-novel from 1862 to 1869, and it is thought that one of his early intentions was to write a domestic saga in the English, Trollopian mode. In his diaries for September 1865, he writes: "Read Trollope, good." A few days later, he is still admiring Trollope, who "overwhelms me with his skill." But by October 3, he writes: "Finished Trollope. Too much that is conventional." That is the key to the restless zeal with which he began to write and rewrite his novel. There is no place in this book for the conscripted conventions that populate the tired familiar fictional army. Though "all of life" may course through the book—birth, death, marriage, warfare—the writing has none of the serial vividness of Thackeray or Dickens, or indeed Dostoevsky; the undulations of "dramatic conflict" are leveled. Cliffhangers become hillwalkers. (One thinks of a chapter in Dostoevsky's *The Devils*, which shamelessly ends with the shout "The suburbs are on fire!") The beginning seems arbitrary (a trivial salon) and the fagged closure still tends to disappoint (the novel's epilogue concerns quiet domestic life seven years after the great events of 1812).

Perhaps Tolstoy did not really know where to start or end. He had originally wanted to write about 1856, and a patrician revolutionary's return from long Siberian exile. He himself had bitter experience of the mood of futility that characterized the years just after the pointless blundering of the Crimean War. He had fought in Crimea, had witnessed the bloody suttee of that campaign, as men willingly sacrificed themselves on the national pyre, and for nothing. His book *The Sebastopol Sketches* lucidly described the opacities of war. In order to write well about 1856, however, he felt that he needed to go back to 1825, when the upper-class rebels known as Decembrists were executed and exiled. But 1825, explained Tolstoy in a note, could not be evoked without the great year of 1812, when Napoleon invaded Russia and occupied Moscow for four weeks. And 1812 would need 1805 as preparation, which is when the novel actually begins—as if to cauterize infinite regression (why not start with the French Revolution?).

Whatever Tolstoy's precise intentions, at some point in 1865 he began to shape the quiet "English" novel—at this point still called *All's Well That Ends Well*—into a Russian epic about Alexander and Napoleon; and by 1867–68, he was writing about the savage national trauma of 1812, and beginning to add the long essays on warfare, freedom and determinism, historiography and the philosophy of history, that increasingly dominate the last six hundred pages of the book. Here was the most flagrant strike against the "pure" European form of the novel. Tolstoy barges into his own work, and unloads his years of reading and thinking about history on the reader, with all the autodidact's sleepless certitude. A fictional description of the battle of Borodino gives way to a military history of the actual battle, complete with a map of the battlefield. *"Il se répete! et il philosophise!!"* commented a shocked Flaubert. Some contemporary Russian critics were appalled by this didactic, philosophical presence, a disdain maintained by popular Western biographers, for whom the essays are just gray clumps of theory fallen very far from the green tree of life that is the novel's proper narrative.

But the essays belong with the fictional narrative, as peace belongs to war. Essentially, *War and Peace* is the story of two families and an outrider: the Rostovs, the Bolkonskys, and Pierre Bezukhov, the large, lofty, comic quester who becomes involved with both families. In the "peace" of the novel's title, people give birth, and die, and marry, and think and talk and dine. However impervious the salons of Petersburg seem to the actualities of war, "peace" is inevitably intertwined with "war." Nikolai Rostov and his brother, Petya, go off to fight Napoleon, as does Prince Andrei Bolkonsky. Having been wounded at Austerlitz in 1805, and having lost his wife in childbirth, Andrei becomes engaged to the irrepressible Natasha Rostov. She breaks off that engagement in a spasm of fickleness, but is haunted by it—literally, because she will nurse the dying Andrei, mortally wounded at Borodino, in 1812. Nikolai, who is all bold charm and youthful high spirits—Tolstoy writes that at Austerlitz, he is momentarily aimless because "there was no one to cut down (as he had always pictured battle to himself)"—survives the war and marries Andrei's sister, Princess Marya. Pierre marries, separates, becomes a Mason, is widowed, and blunders into the theater of war at Borodino, a tall, fat, inquisitive metaphysician dressed in an absurd tall white hat and green trousers. He returns to Moscow as the French are closing in on the city, and imperfectly disguises himself in a coachman's kaftan. He was obviously "a disguised gentleman," writes Tolstoy, perhaps presciently, since this was the kind of costume Tolstoy himself would wear in fierce, prophetic, bearded later life, looking for all the world like a landowner Moses wrapped in an eiderdown. There is a very funny moment, in which kaftaned Pierre is spotted by the Rostovs as they are leaving Moscow. Natasha, characteristically, hangs out of the carriage, exclaiming, "Look, for God's sake, it's Bezukhov!" Pierre is eventually captured by the French, held for a month, and nearly executed. In time, he marries Natasha; the novel's epilogue begins with descriptions of the blissful marriages of these two couples, Nikolai and Marya, and Pierre and Natasha. All's well that ends well.

Or not, because the epilogue actually concludes not with the fictional narrative, but with a final dragonish blast from the flaming, irritable, essay-writing Tolstoy, keen to put us right about freedom and predestination. *War and Peace* is a "not a novel," but a frequently essayistic national epic, and this side of the story also involves two families and an outrider—the two "families" of the French and Russian nations, and Napoleon, who forced them together when he invaded Russia and took Moscow in 1812. *War and Peace* vibrates with anti-Napoleonic anger, and there is thus an interesting contradiction, namely that this great novel about great egotists and solipsists, written by perhaps the greatest egotist ever to put pen to paper, is a cannon aimed directly at the egotism of Napoleon, whom Tolstoy clearly loathes. It is always fascinating, as a result, whenever Tolstoy describes Napoleon dramatically, because his descriptions cannot help crediting the very vitality he most naturally indulges as a novelist but hates in this case as a Russian patriot: Napoleon is infectious in the wrong way, so diabolically contagious that his face launched a thousand battles. "The whole of his stout, short figure, with its broad, fat shoulders and involuntarily thrust-out stomach and chest, had that imposing, stately look which pampered forty-year-old men have."

Tolstoy disliked not just Napoleon's solipsism and vanity ("It was clear that only what went on in *his* soul was of interest to him," he writes) but the egotism of much nineteenth-century historical writing, which essentially agreed with Hegel's Prussian quip that Napoleon was the world-spirit on horseback. The aggression of the narrative descriptions of Napoleon seem to gain their power from the aggression of the historical essays, in which Tolstoy recurringly argues against the cult of the "great man." The writers and philosophers whom Tolstoy had started reading in earnest in 1865 all seemed to agree that in 1812, as Tolstoy puts it, thousands of people went from west to east, slaughtered each other to no purpose, and that they did so because one man told them to. Even those who admitted many and various historical causes never admitted enough. For there are billions of causes of such a bloody migration, says Tolstoy, from Napoleon's war lust to the most humble hussar's need to be fed and paid. And that would be the wrong way to order things anyway, because according to Tolstoy, Napoleon's ambition probably has less to do with historical determinations than the hussar's blind need.

What should absorb our attention as historians is not the singular glory of a Napoleon but the mute, inglorious lives of ordinary people—what Tolstoy calls "the swarmlike life, where man inevitably fulfills the laws prescribed for him." "Kings are the slaves of history. History, that is the unconscious swarmlike life of mankind, uses every moment of a king's life as an instrument for its purposes." Napoleon thought himself royally free, but in fact he was a serf to historical inevitability, since what happened was always going to involve him, and since what happened was always going to happen. Every action of the so-called great men, "which to them seems willed by themselves, in the historical sense is not willed, but happens in connection with the whole course of history and has been destined from before all ages." Tolstoy's conclusion is epistemological skepticism. We know much less than we thought we did. "The more we try to explain sensibly these phenomena of history, the more senseless and incomprehensible they become for us." Only by admitting the most infinitesimal units for observations can we hope to "comprehend the laws of history."

Tolstoy thus has the kind of commitment to rich, ordinary detail that the Annales school would make famous a hundred years later. But he does not seem to believe that any narrative could ever really describe a historical event successfully. He believes that history has laws, and he believes in divine predestination. Of the battle of Borodino, he writes: "And the terrible thing continued to be accomplished, which was accomplished not by the will of men, but by the will of Him who governs people and worlds." But these laws are only partly discoverable, it seems; even if we were accurately to describe all the causes of a historical event, we would still be unable to describe "the one cause of all causes." Tolstoy believes that we are not free but that we have to believe we are in order to live. Reason expresses the laws of necessity, he writes. But consciousness expresses the essence of freedom. Consciousness says: "I am alone, and all that exists is only I." So Tolstoy's "public" history writing is consonant with his "private" novel writing: in war and peace, we feel like persons, but helplessly obey the laws of typology (a young man is like all young men).

There are large contradictions here. One is that the great historiographical skeptic is also the great sermonizing bully, not only telling us what we must think, but clearly writing a form of history himself—or as Viktor Shklovsky succinctly put it, "Tolstoy is history." Second, the novelist who sermonizes about the "swarmlike" life of men is the novelist who, by and large, never writes about ordinary people. Third, theologically speaking, *War and Peace*, for all its radical unconventionality, looks more and more like that characteristically vague growl of nineteenth-century doubt, in which God is no longer describable but impossible to abandon. War, rendered so senseless and evil, and described so painstakingly in all its streaming senselessness, serves only to confirm God's benevolent presence, however spectral. An anti-theodicy is begun, and then fudged. In this respect, Thomas Hardy, say, was a bolder novelist. And isn't there a special tension between the novelist who insists on predestination and the novelist who wants to give his own characters—his own creations—the freedom to break away from him? Tolstoy's radical relaxation of the melodramas of conventional "plot" is certainly a relaxation of authorial tyranny; but his tendency to bully the heroes he most cares about, Andrei and Pierre, Levin and Ivan Ilyich, toward Christian wisdom, always seems coercive. Again, Napoleon is the interesting challenge: Tolstoy must make him vital without making him seem too vital, and thus too free.

II.

There is a famous scene in *War and Peace*, when Prince Andrei visits family estates in Ryazan. On the way, in a forest, he sees a great gnarled oak, surrounded by trees already succumbing to spring. He feels like the oak: it seems to say—here is one of Tolstoy's characters now "reading" a tree!—"spring, love, happiness, what deception!" But on his return in June, he cannot at first identify the oak, because it has bloomed and is uniform with all the other trees. It takes him a moment to realize that he is looking at it:

> The whole day had been hot, there was a thunderstorm gathering somewhere, but only a small cloud had sent a sprinkle over the dust of the road and the juicy leaves. The left side of the woods was dark, in the shade; the right side, wet, glossy, sparkled in the sun, barely swayed by the wind. Everything was in flower; nightingales throbbed and trilled, now near, now far . . . The old oak, quite transformed, spreading out a canopy of juicy, dark greenery, basked, barely swaying, in the rays of the evening sun. Of the gnarled fingers, the scars, the old grief and mistrust—nothing could be seen. Juicy green leaves without branches broke through the stiff, hundred-year-old bark, and it was impossible to believe that this old fellow had produced them. "Yes, it's the same oak," thought Prince Andrei, and suddenly a causeless springtime feeling of joy and renewal came over him.

Richard Pevear and Larissa Volokhonsky, whose translation I have been quoting, follow Tolstoy's repetition of that adjective "juicy"— three times in a short passage. Flaubert, the agonist of style, assassinated repetitions like insects, and today's copy editor, no less than Tolstoy's early translators, is post-Flaubertian in this way. But Tolstoy surely wants the word "juicy" to take the weight of Andrei's renewed optimism; if the passage is written in a loose, free indirect style, we should feel Andrei coming back to this word in his half-articulated thoughts, feel the sap flowing, slowly then faster, through his veins. "Sappy" is indeed the word Constance Garnett uses to translate the Russian "*sochnye*," and, unusually for her, she uses the same word three times, like Tolstoy. Aylmer and Louise Maude use "sappy," too, but simply drop the third iteration, as if it were slightly embarrassing. Anthony Briggs translates the word as "lush," uses it twice, and then substitutes "succulent" for the third "juicy." "Juicy" is a proper translation of the Russian, and "juicy" even sounds more like "*sochnye*" than "lush" or "succulent." But the striking comparison is between the rhythm of Pevear and Volokhonsky and the rhythm of the other translators. Here is Garnett:

> The whole day had been hot; a storm was gathering, but only a small rain-cloud had sprinkled the dust of the road and the sappy leaves. The left side of the forest was dark, lying in shadow. The right side, glistening with the raindrops, gleamed in the sunlight, faintly undulating in the wind.

This sounds like good English, while Pevear and Volokhonsky's version, with its hiccupped run-on, does not: "The whole day had been hot, there was a thunderstorm gathering somewhere, but only a small cloud had sent a sprinkle over the dust of the road and the juicy leaves." Their prose sounds distinctly foreign. It not only sounds more like Tolstoy than the well-mannered scrims put up by the others, it sounds, over the course of the entire scene, like a man working his way toward an apprehension. "Of the gnarled fingers, the scars, the old grief and mistrust—nothing could be seen." This has the dynamic intermittence of actual thought. The Maudes' "Neither gnarled fingers nor old scars nor old doubts and sorrows were any of them in evidence now" sounds like an English lyric poet, Housman perhaps.

Richard Pevear provides a startling example of the ways in which translators do not simply tidy up texts but make things "clear" that they deem obscure. In the novel's epilogue, Marya enters the nursery: "The children were riding to Moscow on chairs and invited her to come with them." That is exactly what Tolstoy writes, because he wants us to experience a little shock of readjustment, as the adult meets the otherwordliness of childish fantasy. But Garnett, the Maudes, and Briggs all insert an explanatory "playing at," to make things easier for the adults: "The children were playing at 'going to Moscow' in a carriage made of chairs, and invited her to go with them" (the Maudes).

This might seems like a small point, but it is in fact a clue to the vision of the whole novel. Tolstoy sees reality as a system of constant adjustments, a long, tricky convoy of surprises, as realities jostle together, and the vital, solipsistic ego is affronted by the otherness of the world. Nikolai Rostov thinks that warfare is a glamorous, pugilistic business of "cutting people down." But warfare is nothing like that, and when he finally has the chance to cut down a Frenchman, he cannot do it, because the soldier's face is not that of an enemy but "a most simple, homelike face." He gets a medal and is even called a hero, but can only think: "So that's all there is to so-called heroism?" By the time Prince Andrei fights at Borodino, he has lost any sense he once had that a battle can be successfully commanded, and applauds the Russian general Kutuzov for at least knowing what to leave well alone. On a trip home, he sees two girls stealing plums from the estate's trees and is comforted, feeling "the existence of other human interests, totally foreign to him and as legitimate as those that concerned him."

One of the great sequences of adjustment involves Pierre's experience as a prisoner of the French, during which he undergoes a colossal moral correction, brought on by witnessing the execution of his fellow captives, and by listening to the wise old peasant, Platon Karataev, who preaches a kind of Christian stoicism. Pierre, dressed in his kaftan and armed with a knife, decides that he must assassinate Napoleon, and is wandering in Moscow, which the French have now occupied. The city is on fire, and in chaos. He is arrested by the invaders, the knife is found, and he is apparently condemned to death. Four men are shot by the French, and then comes the turn of the fifth, a factory worker, a thin boy of eighteen. Pierre will be next. The factory worker is blindfolded, but just before he is killed, he straightens the knot at the back of his head, to make it more comfortable. It is a superb scene, as if lit by lightning, every detail charged with vividness—the pale, frightened faces of the French executioners, the young French soldier who stands by the pit where the bodies are being buried, swaying back and forth like a drunkard, and then the comment of one of the French soldiers: "That'll teach them to set fires." Tolstoy, in his simple, fairy-tale mode, somehow at once both intrusive narrator and absent as air, has Pierre decode this self-defensive muttering—Pierre sees that "it was a soldier who wanted to comfort himself at least somehow for what had been done, but could not." (Again, a universal shame given momentary particularity by a minor character.)

What strikes us nowadays is the mysterious pointlessness of the man fiddling with his blindfold just before death. It was surely with the help of Tolstoy's instruction that George Orwell watched a condemned Burmese man, in his essay "A Hanging," walk toward the gallows and swerve to avoid a puddle on the way. Both Tolstoy and Orwell are making a point about uniqueness and typicality. The human animal will tend to look after its own interests, even when the gesture is so useless that it looks like a decision not typical but radically individual. And Tolstoy the determinist is doubtless interested in the involuntariness of the action: is the condemned man exercising the sweetest gratuity of his free will, or simply helplessly responding to the discomfort of the knot? Either way, the absolute selfishness (in the most basic sense) of another self must be instructive to the self-sufficient Pierre. After his experiences, Pierre's sense of the differences of other people begins to expand. The factory worker adjusted his blindfold, and died; Pierre, figuratively speaking, adjusts his blindfold, and lives.

The adjustment of vision that the condemned man, or even the children riding to Moscow, forces on us is related to a technique for which Tolstoy was praised by the Russian formalist critics of the 1920s and later—estrangement, or the art of making the familiar unfamiliar. Sometimes, this involves seeing the world as a child might. When Natasha goes to the opera, she refuses to see anything but painted cardboard and men and women peculiarly dressed, and finds the whole spectacle false and pretentious. Tolstoy is never greater in this novel than when, like Natasha at the opera, he refuses to make sense of warfare. Again and again, this novel reverses the martial tapestry and shoves the dull clumsy illegible tufts of thread at us. There are the most stunning metaphors. Rostov, standing on the wooden bridge at Austerlitz, hears a rattling "as if someone had spilled nuts," and a man falls beside him. A cannonball whistles past, "as if not finishing all it had to say." A bullet sounds as if it is "complaining about something." In one of the most beautiful of the novel's scenes, young Petya Rostov, Nikolai's younger brother, riding with his friends Denisov and Dolokhov, and with Cossack soldiers, foolishly, boyishly gallops into a storm of French fire, and is felled. His dying is described estrangingly, as if by his friends, who cannot make sense of what is happening: "Petya galloped on his horse along the manor courtyard, and, instead of holding the reins, waved both arms and somehow strangely and quickly, and kept sliding further and further to one side in his saddle." Eventually he falls heavily onto the wet ground. His friend Denisov—he of the short, hairy fingers— approaches the body, and as he looks at Petya, "irrelevantly" recalls him once saying, "I'm used to something sweet. Excellent raisins, take them all." There follows this extraordinarily moving sentence: "And the Cossacks glanced around in surprise at the sounds, similar to a dog's barking, with which Denisov quickly turned away, went to the wattle fence, and caught hold of it."

It is a very modern piece of writing and a very ancient one, as so often in Tolstoy. Stephen Crane learned a great deal from Tolstoy about this kind of writing; in *The Red Badge of Courage*, a man with a shoeful of blood "hopped like a schoolboy in a game." Ian McEwan uses a similar technique in the Dunkirk section of *Atonement*. But if the hacking lament that sounds oddly like the barking of a dog is an example of modern estrangement, then that young man gripping the wattle fence in grief, and those startled Cossacks— especially that transfer of the emotion from the mourner to the Cossacks, from the involved audience to a less involved audience— seem almost biblical (in Genesis, when Joseph, in disguise, meets his brothers, "he wept aloud: and the Egyptians and the house of Pharaoh heard").

Tolstoy seems to write slightingly of women at one moment in the book, when he says: "About the war Princess Marya thought as women think about war. She feared for her brother, who was there;

was horrified, not understanding it." Another generalization: all women think like this. But the novel argues convincingly that no one understands war, indeed that no one understands history. Napoleon says, on the eve of the battle of Borodino, "The chessman are set up," but a few pages earlier Pierre had likened war to a game of chess, only to earn Andrei's scorn: "Yes . . . only with this small difference, that in chess you can think over each move as long as you like, you're outside the conditions of time." It is not, of course, a small difference but an enormous one. It is everything. One is never really outside the conditions of time, least of all in a novel. If no one can understand war, then simply to fear for one's brother, and to be horrified, is precisely to understand what can be understood of war.

So it is perhaps not a banal diminuendo when this novel closes its narrative with scenes, seven years after the epic disasters of 1812, from the domestic lives of Pierre and Natasha, and Nikolai and Marya. These are some of the most serenely lovely passages in the book, not least because typology—which is to say, determinism—is turned on its head. It had always been the women who were talented at "reading" the faces and bodies of the men; the cowed Marya devotedly followed every twitch and spasm of her tyrannical old father, and Natasha, when Pierre first told her about his French captivity, "understood precisely what he meant to convey . . . but also what he could not express in words." Now, at last, it is the men, the vital solipsists, who understand the wordless gestures of their wives. We see Nikolai console his wife, and Tolstoy tells us that likewise, Pierre and Natasha "also talked as only a wife and husband can talk, that is, grasping thoughts and conveying them to each other with extraordinary clarity and quickness, in a way contrary to all the rules of logic." Tolstoy then reproduces a page of this kind of illogical dialogue, one of the tenderest things he ever wrote:

"No, what were you saying? Speak, speak."
"No, you tell me, mine was just something stupid," said Natasha.
". . . And what were you going to say?"

"Just something stupid."

"No, but still."

"It's nothing, trifles," said Natasha, her smile shining brightly.

These are the triumphant "insignificant trifles" of family life. Prince Andrei, the professional soldier, the rising star, the brilliant adjutant to General Kutuzov, died in battle; Napoleon, the genius of world history, failed in battle; but the amateur, unheroic blunderers, Nikolai and Pierre, survived into peace, surrounded by women, who do not understand warfare, and by children, who must not. To live, writes the poet Yehuda Amichai, is to build a ship and a harbor at the same time: "And to finish the harbor / long after the ship has gone down."

MARILYNNE ROBINSON

Growing up in a religious household, I got used to the sight of priests, but always found them fascinating and slightly repellent. The funereal uniform, supposed to obliterate the self in a shroud of colorlessness, also draws enormous attention to the self; humility seems to be made out of the same cloth as pride. Since the ego is irrepressible—since the ego is secular—it tends to bulge in peculiar shapes when religiously depressed. The priests I knew practiced self-abnegation but perfected a quiet dance of ego. They were modest but pompous, gentle but tyrannical—one of them got angry if he was disturbed on a Monday—and pious but knowing. Most were good men, certainly less venal than the average; but the peculiar constrictions of their calling produced peculiar opportunities for unloosing.

This is probably one of the reasons—putting the secular antagonism of novelists aside—that priests are overwhelmingly seen in fiction as comical, hypocritical, improperly worldly, or a little dim. Another reason is that fiction needs egotism, vanity, venality, to produce drama and comedy; we want our sepulchers craftily whited. The seventy-six-year-old Reverend John Ames, who narrates Marilynne Robinson's second novel, *Gilead*, is gentle, modest, loving, and above all, good. He is also a bit boring, and boring in proportion to his curious lack of ego. At home in the Iowa town of

Gilead, in the mid-1950s, aware of his imminent demise, he writes a long letter to his seven-year-old son, which is presented as a series of diary entries. (Georges Bernanos's novel *The Diary of a Country Priest* seems to have been one model.) Mellowly resigned, tired but faithful, he is a man who can serenely exclaim "how I have loved this life," or inform us that he has written two thousand sermons "in the deepest hope and conviction." The reader may roll his eyes at this and think: "*All* two thousand? Not one of them written in boredom or out of obligation?" Yorick, the parson in *Tristram Shandy*, who is so impressed with the eloquence of one of his own eulogies that he can't help writing a self-loving "Bravo!" on his text, seems closer to the human case, and more novelistically vivid.

As if sensitive to the piety of *Gilead*, Robinson subverted this potential traditional objection by making her novel swerve away from the traditionally novelistic. Ames's calm, grave diary entries contain almost no dialogue, shun scenes, seem to smother conflict before it has taken a breath. Very beautifully, *Gilead* becomes less a novel than a species of religious writing, and Reverend Ames's entries a recognizable American form, the Emersonian essay, poised between homily and home, religious exercise and naturalism.

> This morning a splendid dawn passed over our house on its
> way to Kansas. This morning Kansas rolled out of its sleep
> into a sunlight grandly announced, proclaimed throughout
> heaven—one more of the very finite number of days that
> this old prairie has been called Kansas, or Iowa. But it has
> all been one day, that first day. Light is constant, we just turn
> over in it. So every day is in fact the selfsame evening and
> morning. My grandfather's grave turned into the light, and
> the dew on his weedy little mortality patch was glorious.

The result was one of the most unconventional conventionally popular novels of recent times.

Robinson describes herself as a liberal Protestant believer and churchgoer, but her religious sensibility is really far more uncompromising and archaic than this allows. Her essays, selected in *The Death of Adam* (1998), are theologically tense and verbally lush in a manner almost extinct in modern literary discourse, and which often sounds Melvillean or Ruskinian. She is a liberal in the sense that she finds it difficult to write directly about the content of her belief, and shuns the evangelical childishness of gluing human attributes onto God. As a child she "felt God as a presence before I had a name for him," she writes, and adds that she goes to church to experience "moments that do not occur in other settings." In a way that would seem palatable to many Americans, and certainly to her thousands of liberal readers, her Protestantism seems borne out of a love of religious silence—the mystic, quietly at prayer in an unadorned place, indifferent to ecclesiastical mediation.

But she is illiberal and unfashionably fierce in her devotion to this Protestant tradition; she is voluble in defense of silence. She loathes the complacent idleness whereby contemporary Americans dismiss Puritanism and turn John Calvin, the great originator of Puritanism, into an obscure, moralizing bigot. "We are forever drawing up indictments against the past, then refusing to let it testify in its own behalf—it is so very guilty, after all. Such attention as we give to it is usually vindictive and incurious and therefore incompetent." We flinch from Puritanism because it placed sin at the center of life, but then, as she tartly reminds us, "Americans never think of themselves as sharing fully in the human condition, and therefore beset as all humankind is beset." Calvin believed in our "total depravity," our utter fallenness, but this was not necessarily a cruel condemnation: "The belief that we are all sinners gives us excellent grounds for forgiveness and self-forgiveness, and is kindlier than any expectation that we might be saints, even while it affirms the standards all of us fail to attain," she writes in her essay "Puritans and Prigs." Nowadays, she argues, educated Americans are prigs, not Puritans, quick to pour judgment on anyone who fails to toe the right political line. Soft moralizing has replaced hard moralizing, but at least those old hard moralists admitted to being moralists.

I do not always enjoy Robinson's founded ecstasies, but I admire the obdurateness with which she describes the difficult joys of a faith that will please neither evangelicals nor secularists. Above all, I deeply admire the precision and lyrical power of her language, and the way it embodies a struggle—the fight with words, the contemporary writer's fight with the history of words and the presence of literary tradition, the fight to use the best words to describe both the visible and the invisible world. Here, for instance, is how the narrator of *Housekeeping*, Robinson's first novel, describes her dead grandmother, who lies in the bed with her arms flung up and her head flung back: "It was as if, drowning in air, she had leaped toward ether." In the same novel, the narrator imagines her grandmother pinning sheets to a line, on a windy day—"say that when she had pinned three corners to the lines it began to billow and leap in her hands, to flutter and tremble, and to glare with the light, and that the throes of the thing were as gleeful and strong as if a spirit were dancing in its cerements." "Cerements," an old word for burial cloth, is Robinson in her antique, Melvillean mode, and is one of many moments in her earlier work when she sounds like the antiquarian Cormac McCarthy. But stronger than that fancy word is the plain and lovely "the throes of the thing," with its animism and its homemade alliteration.

Her novel *Home* begins simply, eschewing obvious verbal fineness, and slowly grows in luxury—its last fifty pages are magnificently moving, and richly pondered in the way of *Gilead*. *Home* has been presented as a sequel to that novel, but it is more like that novel's brother, since it takes place at the same narrative moment and dovetails with its happenings. In *Gilead*, John Ames's great friend is the Reverend Robert Boughton, the town's Presbyterian minister (Ames is a Congregationalist). The two men grew up together, confide in each other, and share a wry, undogmatic Protestantism. But whereas John Ames has married late and has only one son, Reverend Boughton has five children, one of whom is a very prodigal son, Jack Boughton. In the earlier novel, Ames frets over Jack Boughton (now in his forties), who has been difficult since he was a schoolboy: there has been petty theft, drifting, unemployment, alcoholism, and an illegitimate child, now deceased, with a local woman. One day, Jack walked out of the Boughton home and stayed away for twenty years, not returning even for his mother's funeral. Recently, we learn, Jack has unexpectedly returned after all that time away. In the last part of *Gilead*, Jack comes to Ames for a blessing—for the blessing he cannot get from his own father—and spills a remarkable secret: he has been living with a black woman from Memphis named Della, and has a son with her.

Home is set in the Boughton household at the time of Jack's sudden return, and is an intense study of three people—Reverend Boughton, the old, dying patriarch, his pious daughter, Glory, and prodigal Jack. Glory has her own sadness: she has come back to Gilead after the collapse of what she took to be an engagement, to a man who turned out to be married. Like Princess Marya in *War and Peace*, who does daily battle with her father, the old Prince Bolkonsky, she is the dutiful child who must submit to the demands of her tyrannical old father. She is fearful of Jack—she hardly knows him—and in some ways jealous of the freedom of his rebelliousness. Both children differently resent the facts of their return, and their biological loyalty to their father. Robinson evokes well the drugged shuffle of life in a home dominated by the routines of an old parent: how the two middle-aged children hear the creak of the bedsprings as their father lies down for his nap, and then, later, "a stirring of bedsprings, then the lisp lisp of slippered feet and the pock of the cane." There are the imperious cries from the bedroom—help with bedclothes, a glass of water—and the hours distracted by the radio, card games, Monopoly, meals, pots of coffee. The very furniture is oppressive, immovable. The numerous knickknacks were displayed only "as a courtesy to their givers, most of whom by now would have gone to their reward." For Glory, who is in her late thirties, there is the dread that this will be her final home:

> What does it mean to come home? Glory had always thought home would be a house less cluttered and ungainly than this one, in a town larger than Gilead, or a city, where someone

would be her intimate friend and the father of her children, of whom she would have no more than three . . . She
would not take one stick of furniture from her father's house,
since none of it would be comprehensible in those spare,
sunlit rooms. The walnut furbelows and carved draperies
and pilasters, the inlaid urns and flowers. Who had thought
of putting actual feet on chairs and sideboards, actual paws
and talons?

Much of *Home* is devoted to an attempt to puzzle out the mystery
of Jack Boughton's rebellion, his spiritual homelessness. From earliest years, he had seemed a stranger to his relatives. The family had
been waiting for him to walk out, and he did, and then this story
became their defining narrative: "They were so afraid they would
lose him, and then they had lost him, and that was the story of their
family, no matter how warm and fruitful and robust it might have
appeared to the outside world." Even now, now that he has returned,
reflects Glory, there is "an incandescence of unease about him
whenever he walked out the door, or, for that matter, whenever his
father summoned him to one of those harrowing conversations. Or
while he waited for the mail or watched the news." Over the course
of the book, we discover a little of what he has been doing in the
twenty years away—as in *Gilead*, we learn about the early illegitimate child, and about his eight-year relationship with Della, who is,
ironically enough, a preacher's daughter.

Jack is a suggestive figure—a very literate nonbeliever who
knows his Bible backward, but who finds it hard to do theological
battle with his slippery father. Back home, he dresses formally, putting on his threadbare suit and tie, as if to do his reformed best; but
he has a perpetually wary expression and a studied politesse that
suggest an existential exile. He tries to conform to the habits of the
old home—he tends the garden, does the shopping, fixes up the old
car in the garage—but almost every encounter with his father produces a tiny abrasion that smarts and festers. The novel finely mobi-
lizes, without explicitness, the major biblical stories of father and

son—Esau, denied his birthright, begging for a blessing from his father; Joseph, reunited finally with his father, Jacob; the prodigal son, most loved because most errant.

What propels the book, and makes it finally so powerful, is the Reverend Boughton, precisely because he is not the gentle sage that John Ames is in *Gilead*. He is a fierce, stern, vain old man, who wants to forgive his son and who cannot. He preaches sweetness and light, and is gentle with Jack like a chastened Lear ("Let me look at your face for a minute," he says), only to turn on him angrily like a Timon or Claudius. There are scenes of the most tender pain. Robinson, so theologically obsessed with transfiguration, can transfigure a banal observation. In the attic, for instance, Glory finds a box of her father's shirts, ironed "as if for some formal event, perhaps their interment"; and then the novelist, or poet, notices that the shirts "had changed to a color milder than white." (The cerements, again.) Father and son clash while watching television news reports of the racial unrest in Montgomery. Old Boughton imperiously swats away his son's anger with his bland, milky prophecy—"a color milder than white"— "There's no reason to let that sort of trouble upset you. In six months nobody will remember one thing about it." If we have read *Gilead*, we know, as Jack's father does not, why Jack has a special interest in matters of race.

As the old man palpably declines, an urgency sets in. The funnel of the narrative of imminent death should insist on forgiveness, but this is precisely what the father cannot allow. Nothing will change, and Jack will leave again, as his father always knew he would: "He's going to toss the old gent an assurance or two, and then he's out the door," he complains. Nothing will change because the family situation rests on a series of paradoxes, which interlock to imprison father and son. Jack's soul is homeless, but his soul is his home, for as Jack tells his sister, the soul is "what you can't get rid of." He is condemned to leave and return. If the prodigal son is the most loved because most errant, then his errancy and not his conformity is what is secretly loved, even if no one can admit to that heretical possibility: perhaps a family needs to have its designated sinner? Everyone longs for restoration, for the son to come home and become simply good, just as everyone longs for heaven, but such restoration, like heaven itself, is hard to imagine, and in our lack of imagination we somehow prefer what we can touch and feel—the palpability of our lapses. At least they are palpable, and not otherworldly.

Behind all of Robinson's works is an abiding interest in the question of heavenly restoration. As she puts it in *Housekeeping*, there is a law of completion, that everything "must finally be made comprehensible. What are all these fragments for, if not to be knit up finally?" But will this restoration ever be enough? Can the shape of the healing possibly fit the size of the wound? The mundane version of this in *Home* is the way in which the novel ponders the question of return. The Boughton children come home to this strange, old-fashioned Iowan town, but the return is never the balm it promises to be, for home is too personal, too remembered, too disappointing. Eden is exile, not heaven:

> And then their return to the *pays natal*, where the same old willows swept the same ragged lawns, where the same old prairie arose and bloomed as negligence permitted. Home. What kinder place could there be on earth, and why did it seem to them all like exile? Oh, to be passing anony-mously through an impersonal landscape! Oh, not to know every stump and stone, not to remember how the fields of Queen Anne's lace figured in the childish happiness they had offered to their father's hopes, God bless him.

So as old Boughton is dying, nothing changes, and instead, he petulantly chides his son: "We all loved you—what I'd like to know is why you didn't love us. That is what has always mystified me." He continues a little later: "You see something beautiful in a child, and you almost live for it, you feel as though you would die for it, but it isn't yours to keep or protect. And if the child becomes a man who has no respect for himself, it's just destroyed till you can hardly remember what it was." Early in the novel, the reverend had seemed to want his son to call him something other than his customary, rather estranged "Sir"—Papa, or even Dad. Late in the novel, when Jack calls him Dad, he bursts out: "Don't call me that. I don't like it at all. Dad. It sounds ridiculous. It's not even a word." When he is not rebuking his son, he is complaining about old age: "Jesus never had to be old." He is only calm when asleep: "His hair had been brushed into a soft white cloud, like harmless aspiration, like a mist."

In a final encounter of devastating power, Jack goes to his father to tell him he is going away again. Jack puts out his hand. "The old man drew his own hand into his lap and turned away. 'Tired of it!' he said." They are the last words the Reverend Boughton speaks in this book, an obviously angry inversion of the last, tired words of serene John Ames in *Gilead*: "I'll pray, and then I'll sleep."

So luminous are this book's final scenes, so affecting, that it is all the critic can do not to catch from it, as in this review, the contagion of ceaseless quotation, a fond mumbling.

LYDIA DAVIS

In a small, calm, plain town, a woman spends her days looking after her infant boy. She tells us about her afternoon routine, in which she leaves the house around four o'clock, goes to the post office and the park, does some errands, and always ensures she is home by five thirty, when *The Mary Tyler Moore Show* begins. This woman is somewhat embarrassed to be such a devoted viewer, but has recently consoled herself with the information that the pianist Glenn Gould loved the same show. She is surprised by this. "I see two of my worlds coming together that I had thought were as far apart as they could be." She explains that Glenn Gould was a model for her when she was learning the piano; she imitated the clarity of his fingering, and would practice for four or even six hours at a time. "I did not intend to make a career of music, but I could happily have spent my days working as hard at the piano as any professional, partly to avoid doing other things that were harder, but partly for the pleasure of it."

But she does not seem to play the piano now. What she mainly does, as far as one can tell, is do things that are harder: she looks after her baby, and thinks, and manages, with varying success, her loneliness, and talks, or rather fails to talk, to her husband, when he is home. The unexplained gap between her early ambition and the present banality of her existence hangs mysteriously. The woman

THE FUN STUFF

speaks patiently, intelligently, with a slightly fraught lucidity, and it is only by accident, as it were, that one notices the absolute devastation of her sentences. At dinner, when she and her husband have nothing else to talk about, he asks her about the TV show. "I will tell him something one of the characters said and I can see he is ready to laugh even before I tell it, though so often, in the case of other subjects, he is not terribly interested in what I say to him, especially when he sees that I am becoming enthusiastic." It might be customary enough to have a husband who is not very interested in what you have to say, but it is a harder condition to have a husband who is *especially* uninterested in what you have to say when you become enthusiastic about it. The former can be dealt with, perhaps; the latter seems unbearable. And this is so glancingly disclosed. We are not very surprised when this woman later tells us: "I wish the baby would go to sleep and my husband would not come home for dinner."

This brief monologue is entitled "Glenn Gould," and it is by Lydia Davis. At nine pages, it is longer than most of Davis's works, which are typically between three and four; many are as brief as a paragraph, or a sentence. Most of these pieces, such as "Glenn Gould," are not what most people think of as conventional "stories"— they usually feature people who are unnamed (generally a woman), are often set in unnamed towns or states, and lack the formal comportment of a story that opens, rises, and closes (or fails to close, in the acceptably modernist way). There is no gratuitous bulk in Davis's work, no "realistic" wadding. Her pieces, often narrated by a woman, sometimes apparently by the writer herself, are closer to the soliloquy than the story; they are essayistic poems—quick swipes rather than large framings.

I first heard of Lydia Davis not long after I arrived in the States from London, in 1995. Someone told me that she sounded like the tempestuous Austrian writer Thomas Bernhard (she does and doesn't), and recommended her stories. She was known as a translator of the French autobiographer Michel Leiris, and the philosopher and critic Maurice Blanchot. The Frenchness, the spare forms, and her philosophical rigor, among other things, made her work glamorous in literary circles. It was all too easy to peer down the stretched telescope of the "writer's writer" and see a fashionably limited dot. I greatly enjoyed her stories, intermittently and unsystematically, as their own intermittence seemed to desire and deserve. That was shallow, as several weeks with her *Collected Stories* has taught me. Finally, one can read a large portion of Davis's work, over three decades and more than seven hundred pages, and a grand cumulative achievement comes into view—a body of work probably unique in American writing, in its combination of lucidity, aphoristic brevity, formal originality, sly comedy, metaphysical bleakness, philosophical pressure, and human wisdom. I suspect that her prose will in time be seen as one of the great, strange American literary contributions, distinct and crookedly personal, in the way of the work of Flannery O'Connor, or Donald Barthelme, or J. F. Powers.

We could begin with her sense of humor. Her reputation might be forbidding (bizarrely, she is sometimes called "dour"), but her tone is dancelike, insouciant, and often very funny. Her work contains many piquant details: "My mother and I once carried a piece of coal on a train to Newcastle." In a story about a woman who wanted to marry a cowboy, the narrator meets a man who does resemble a cowboy but does not work as one: "He didn't work as a cowboy but at some kind of job where he glued the bones of chimpanzees together." (This sounds like Thomas McGuane.) Sometimes, her smallest pieces are sweet jeux d'esprit, and resemble the captions you might encounter in a contemporary art installation (i.e., the rare kind that is enchanting and doesn't drive you insane). "Collaboration with Fly," in its entirety, is one sentence: "I put that word on the page, but he added the apostrophe." Likewise, "Idea for a Short Documentary Film": "Representatives of different food products manufacturers try to open their own packaging." Another ditty, titled "Companion," runs, in toto: "We are sitting here together, my digestion and I. I am reading a book and it is working away at the lunch I ate a little while ago." Even when there is less obvious sweetness, there is still real wit. The two lines of "Insomnia" are:

My body aches so—
It must be this heavy bed pressing up against me.

Davis likes playing logical, amusing, and estranging games with familiar phrases. "Special Chair," which is a single paragraph long, teases the pompous academic term for a "named" professorship:

He and I are both teachers in the university system . . . and we would certainly like to be given a special chair at our universities, but what we have gotten so far is the wrong kind of special chair, a special chair belonging to a friend, a chair that swivels and has splayed feet and is special to her for reasons we can't remember.

Or there is the Kafka-like joke (Kafka-like, but also a joke about Kafka-like gloominess) of "The Fellowship": "It is not that you are not qualified to receive the fellowship, it is that each year your application is not good enough. When at last your application is perfect, then you will receive the fellowship." In this mode, Davis is funny in a way that recalls the eighteenth-century aphorist Georg Christoph Lichtenberg, who delighted in such things as: "He marvelled at the fact that cats had two holes cut in their fur at precisely the spot where their eyes were," and meaningful silliness like: "A list of printing errors in the list of printing errors."

What deepens the work, and moves it from game to drama, is that this brisk, insouciant, almost naive tone is often revealed to be a mask, a public fiction, behind which a person is flinching. Take a characteristic story, "Ethics." This single paragraph begins in apparently high spirits, and sounds at first like a good Davis puzzle. A nameless narrator—presumably a woman, or perhaps even the author herself?—tells us that she heard, on an interview program about ethics, that "Do unto others as you would have others do unto you" is the concept that underlies all systems of ethics. "At the time, I was pleased to learn of a simple rule that made such sense." But a moment's reflection complicates matters: "But now, when I try to apply it literally to one person I know, it doesn't seem to work. One of his problems is that he has a lot of hostility toward certain other people and when I imagine how he would have them do unto him I can only think he would in fact want them to be hostile toward him, as he imagines they are, because he is already so very hostile toward them." That the narrator feels no need to identify this man seems significant. Is he a lover, or the unnamed former "husband" who appears so often in this work? All we can guess is that he is important to the narrator, and that one of the people he is hostile toward is the narrator.

In such pieces, what is omitted or suppressed becomes very important, highly charged, and the hunger strike of the spare, lucid words on the page can take on a desperate aspect. The four-page story "Happy Memories" (it, too, is a single long paragraph) also has a deceptively jaunty tone. The narrator tells us that she fears getting old, and being alone. Yet people say that an old woman at least "has her happy memories" to console her. "When her pain is not too bad, she can go over her happy memories and be comforted." What bothers the narrator is that she is not sure how many happy memories she will have, or indeed what makes for a happy memory. "I am happy doing the work I do, alone at a desk. That work is a great part of every day. But when I am old and alone all the time, will it be enough to think about the work I used to do?" Happy memories, she reflects, have to involve relations with other people, but it is striking that the narrator can barely summon anyone who has been close to her. She mentions her mother, briefly, and in the entire story there is this single, and singular, reference to an actual family: "There have been a few times of gardening together as a family that may make a good happy memory." Gardening! And we don't know whether this family is parentally inherited, or created by marriage.

A husband, a lover, is never mentioned. Everyone else the narrator mentions seems to be only slightly known—a man who fixes the dehumidifier, a neighbor who once brought some cake, the librarian down the street. Besides, the narrator continues, for a memory to remain happy, it must not be erased by an unhappy event on the same day. "You have to make sure, somehow, that nothing spoils the thing while it is happening, and then that no later experience erases it." She concludes her brief, shattering inquiry thus: "I should check now and then to make sure I am not alone too much, or unhappy with other people too often. I should add them up, now and then: what are my happy memories so far?" The word "happy," savagely measured out and repeated, is not the only reminder of Beckett here; the relentless control of the piece's tone, grave and comic at once, gives it an implacable Beckettian power.

The woman in "Happy Memories" seems to move between unsatisfactory loneliness and unsatisfactory community. To read *The Collected Stories* is to make a journey around a composite narrator, who at times seems relatively estranged from the author named Lydia Davis, born in 1947 and currently a professor of writing at the University at Albany, SUNY, and at other moments seems confessionally proximate. Stories like "Ethics" and "Happy Memories" acquire an increased resonance from their placement as way stations on this longer personal journey. A nameless hostile man, or the complete absence of a mate, seems more significant on the page when so many of the other stories feature a woman who has quarreled with a lover or husband, or a woman who is separated from a former husband whom she nevertheless insists on calling not "my former husband" but "my husband," or a woman living unhappily alone, or a woman looking after a small boy, without much help from anyone else. In "Therapy," a story early in the collection, a female narrator, estranged from her husband and looking after a son, is struggling to maintain her courage. "In the morning I drank coffee and smoked. In the evening I drank tea and smoked and went to the window and back and from one room into the next room. Sometimes, for a moment, I thought I would be able to do something.

Then that moment would pass and I would want to move and not be able to move." She tells us that her brain is spinning "like a fly." But shame and pride mean that a chin must be kept up. Her "husband" comes around, "and he would sit down and talk to me, breathing into my face until I was exhausted. I wanted to hide from him how difficult my life was." (That phrase, "breathing into my face until I was exhausted," is pungently alive.)

The woman in "What an Old Woman Will Wear" hopes she will have a husband by the time she is old. "She had once had a husband, and she wasn't surprised that she had once had one, didn't have one now, and hoped to have one later in her life." One of the most affecting pieces in the book, "Wife One in Country," barely more than a page long, begins like this: "Wife one calls to speak to son. Wife two answers with impatience, gives phone to son of wife one." It continues, in the same style of battered telex: "After speaking to son, much disturbance in wife one." Wife one imagines her former husband married to a future "wife three," whose job would be to protect her husband "not only from raging wife one but also from troublesome wife two." (As elsewhere, comedy always lines the sadness, a necessarily durable cloth.) The dispatch ends with wife one eating dinner alone while watching television: "Wife one swallows food, swallows pain, swallows food again, swallows pain again, swallows food again."

In more conventional fiction, stuffed with conventional novelistic characters, the reader is allowed to overhear the thoughts of other people. In Davis's soliloquizing work, a narrator is often overhearing herself, and we are then allowed to overhear this painful and funny self-overhearing. More often than not, this narrator does not like what she hears of herself. "If I were not me and overheard me from below, as a neighbor, talking to him, I would say to myself how glad I was not to be her, not to be sounding the way she is sounding," a woman tells us in "From Below, as a Neighbor." (Note again that pregnantly unspecified "him.")

You could say that selfishness, in every sense of the word, is Davis's real theme: the overbearing presence of the self, the insistent

internal volume of the self, the dunning inescapability of being who
one is. The woman who watches *The Mary Tyler Moore Show* in
"Glenn Gould" reflects, with implied envy, on the way that Gould
lived life on his own terms, "and was able to be selfish without hurt-
ing anyone." A typical Lydia Davis narrator has a mind spinning
like a fly, a mind "always so busy, always going around in circles, always having an idea and then an idea about an idea." This interest
in interior obsessiveness resembles Thomas Bernhard's, but whereas
Bernhard's male characters demonically inflict their mental spillage on others and on the reader, Davis's female characters and narrators seem to want to apologize for their spillage, to clear it up, to
reduce the stain. But how would one think less? How would one
be less, achieve lessness? Silence is the Beckettian response, but
silence does not come easily to Davis's narrators. Instead, they grind
themselves into noisy circles, wherein to be thinking (aloud) about
thinking less is just to add to the problem, to add to the mental volume, not to reduce it. Davis is witty with this paradox. The narrator
of "What I Feel" says that she is trying to tell herself that "what I
feel is not very important. I've read this in several books now: what
I feel is important but not the center of everything. Maybe I do see
this, but I do not believe it deeply enough to act on it. I would like
to believe it more deeply."

But how could one not really be the center of everything? As
Jane Austen knew, announcing a desire to be less important is full
of its own self-importance. The woman who narrates "New Year's
Resolution" informs us that she has been studying Zen Buddhism
again, and that her New Year's resolution "is to learn to see myself
as nothing." A friend tells her that *his* resolution is to lose weight.
Comically, she thinks aloud: "Is this competitive? He wants to lose
some weight, I want to learn to see myself as nothing." As with so
much of Davis's writing, the comedy unexpectedly quickens, like
the sudden anger of a flame, and enlarges its intensity: but how does
a person learn to see herself as nothing, she asks, "when she had
already had so much trouble learning to see herself as something in
the first place?" She finds it fairly easy to be "nothing" in the morn-

ings, but "by late afternoon what is in me that is something starts throwing its weight around. This happens many days. By evening, I'm full of something and it's often something nasty and pushy."

One does not need to know anything about the writer named Lydia Davis to feel a confessional pressure in this book. It is something of a hindrance to know that she was married to Paul Auster, had a son with him, was then divorced from him, and married the painter Alan Cote (to whom she is still married, and with whom she has also had a son). The reader will never know at what moments the former husband who appears in these pages is closer to, or farther from, Davis's own former husband, if indeed that person appears at all in these pages. Her work raises no interesting question about the relation of fiction to fact; instead, it raises the more interesting question: how much can a fictional story about a fictional self shed, and still remain a story about a vivid self? The answer is: almost everything, for two reasons: first, because a fictional self needs only to be a voice, or a mouth, to have a presence on the page; and second, because when a fictional self is reduced in this way, an authorial self fills some of the vacated space. Necessarily, the stories, which are sometimes like brief journal entries or aphoristic poems, assemble an intellectual and emotional autobiography; a sensibility is strongly confessed. "We know we are very special," Davis writes in a tiny entry entitled "Special": "Yet we keep trying to find out in what way: not this way, not that way, then what way?" This restless business of "trying to find out" is precisely what constitutes the specialty, in both senses, of this writer.

The autobiographical atmosphere thickens in the last two hundred pages of the book. You could be utterly ignorant of Lydia Davis's personal circumstances and still be pretty sure, on the evidence of the stories, that her parents died in the last ten years or so. Several of the later texts have the ashen pallor of elegy. "Grammar Questions" poses as a piece of philosophical pedantry: if a man is dying in a particular place, the narrator asks, can one still say, "This is where he lives"? And "If someone asks me, 'Where does he live?' should I answer, 'Well, right now he is not living, he is dying'?" The narrator reveals that she is referring to her father; once again, pain and a certain insouciance of tone rub against each other. To say that someone is dying, Davis writes, suggests activity. "But he is not actively dying. The only thing he is still doing is breathing. He looks as if he is breathing on purpose, because he is working hard at it, and frowning slightly. He is working at it, but surely he has no choice . . . I've seen this expression on his face often in my life, though never before combined with these half-open eyes and this open mouth."

Near the end of the collection, there is a peculiarly simple and lovely text, of just three pages, entitled "How Shall I Mourn Them?" The writer—shall we indeed just say, now, "the writer," and sack that convenient factotum, the "narrator"?—has a list of repetitive questions. They begin like this:

> Shall I keep a tidy house, like L.?
> Shall I develop an unsanitary habit, like K.?
> Shall I sway from side to side a little as I walk, like C.?
> Shall I write letters to the editor, like R.?

We infer, from the long, deep journey we have made with this writer, now over hundreds of pages, but especially because of the tender material in several late stories, that the title refers to mourning departed parents. The questions seem to refer to the peculiar habits of friends and acquaintances who, like the writer, have also been in mourning, whose peculiarities are produced by their grief, and whose tics may well be helplessly imitative of their late parents' tics. But as the list of questions continues, you notice that, amid the oddities, the habits described become more ordinary, less peculiar: "Shall I often look up words in my dictionary, like R.?" Or: "Shall I get a little arthritis in my hands, like C.?" Or: "Shall I always read with a pencil in my hand, like R.?" What is being described, one gradually surmises, is not freakishness, but just life itself. So the answer to this beautiful text's question is: "I shall mourn them just by surviving them." A few pages later, a tiny entry, one of the last in the book, entitled "Head, Heart," throbs with pain. "Heart weeps,"

Davis writes, and "Head tries to help heart," by reminding it about loss: "You will lose the ones you love. They will all go." Heart feels better, but not for long.

> Heart is so new to this.
> I want them back, says heart.
> Head is all heart has.
> Help, head. Help heart.

CONTAINMENT: TRAUMA AND MANIPULATION IN IAN McEWAN

In different ways, most of Ian McEwan's novels and stories are about trauma and contingency, and he is now best known as the great contemporary stager of traumatic contingency as it strikes ordinary lives—in *The Child in Time*, a child goes missing at a supermarket, and Stephen and Julie's domestic existence is shattered; in *Enduring Love*, Clarissa and Joe witness the death of John Logan as he falls from a balloon, are changed forever, and spend the rest of the novel trying to absorb the consequences of the spectacle; *Black Dogs* is in part about how Bernard Tremaine, a politician, scientist, and rationalist, drifted away from his wife, June (and vice versa), because of what he deemed her fanciful, emotional, overdetermined reading of the trauma that was meted out to her in 1946 by the black dogs of the title. In *The Innocent*, set in Berlin in the mid-1950s, Leonard Marnham, a telephone communications specialist, is having a passionate affair with Maria Eckdorf, a German. But their relationship cannot survive the traumatic experience of their murder of Maria's ex-husband, and the subsequent dismemberment of his body in her apartment. The central protagonists of *Atonement* have their lives ruined by the traumatic wrongful arrest of Robbie on charges of rape, while the young just-married couple in *On Chesil Beach* do not survive the trauma of their honeymoon night. (It is further intimated that Florence has been traumatized by sexual abuse at the hands of her father.) And then there is Baxter, contingency personified, who enters Henry Perowne's life in *Saturday* through that most random of urban events, the car accident.

Trauma, in McEwan's work, inaugurates a loss of innocence. After the mother's death, the childhood garden is cemented over, in his first novel, and the children, now orphaned, set about creating their own, corrupted version of childhood. The narrator of *Enduring Love* returns to the field where John Logan fell from the balloon and thinks: "I could not quite imagine a route back into that innocence." John Logan's fall is also the narrator's fall from innocence. A strongly Rousseauian narrative marks McEwan's work: the haven of pastoralism is appealed to as the escape from corruption. In *The Child in Time*, Stephen Lewis is a children's writer, but by accident. He originally wrote his first novel—about a summer holiday he spent when he was eleven—as an adult book. But his publisher, Charles Drake, insists that it is a children's book, that children will read it and understand that childhood is finite—"that it won't last, it can't last, that sooner or later they're finished, done for, that their childhood is not forever." Charles Drake subsequently has a kind of nervous breakdown. He and his wife, a physicist working on notions of time, give up the corruptions of London and retire to the countryside, where Charles starts dressing up and playacting as a little boy out of Richmal Crompton, complete with shorts, catapults, and a tree house.

In *Enduring Love*, five men are attempting to stop a hot-air balloon, whose basket contains a small boy, from rising. Hanging on to the ropes that dangle from that basket, they constitute a little Rousseauian natural society, each of them motivated by altruism or sympathy. But one man drops first, and no one will admit it. "Our crew enacted morality's ancient, irresolvable dilemma: us, or me. Someone said *me*, and then there was nothing to be gained by saying *us*." McEwan plays here with recent work in evolutionary biology about the sources of altruism, and may be unaware that Rousseau hovers behind him.

But I suspect he is aware, if only because *The Innocent* makes such knowing implied reference to Rousseau. In the world of postwar Berlin, where Leonard Marnham has come to assist the Americans who are digging a surveillance tunnel to go from their sector to the Soviets', a regime of secrecy and clearance is in operation. Leonard's American handler, Bob Glass, explains that everybody thinks his clearance is the highest there is, everyone thinks he has the final story: "You only hear of a higher level at the moment you're being told about it." Glass then delivers his version of the origins of the self, a curious mixture of Rousseau, evolutionary biology, and rugged individualism:

> Back then we all used to hang out together all day long doing the same thing. We lived in packs. So there was no need for language. If there was a leopard coming, there was no point in saying, "Hey man, what's coming down the track? A leopard!" Everyone could see it, everyone was jumping up and down and screaming, trying to scare it off. But what happens when someone goes off on his own for a moment's privacy? When he sees a leopard coming, he knows something the others don't. And he knows they don't know. He has something they don't, he has a *secret*, and this is the beginning of his individuality, of his consciousness. If he wants to share his secret and run down the track to warn the other guys, then he's going to need to invent language. From there grows the possibility of culture.

This is not very far from Rousseau's theory of how we developed language, with the difference of course that what seemed a fall for Rousseau seems like salvation for the secretive American. McEwan perhaps agrees exactly neither with Rousseau nor with Bob Glass, but the statement seems an important and emblematic one in his work, because his novels so often circle around the idea that a witnessed trauma becomes a corrupting secret whose possession expels one from community—this is the case with Stephen Lewis, nursing his obsessive and in some ways unspeakable grief for his lost daughter, with Leonard Marnham, with June Tremaine, and with Briony in *Atonement*, of whom McEwan writes that she felt she lacked secrets, and could not have an interesting life without them.

"The distortion of a text," says Freud in *Moses and Monotheism*, "is not unlike a murder. The difficulty lies not in the execution of the deed but in doing away with the traces." McEwan's novels follow the traces that trauma makes, and are often smart, in a Freudian way, about how difficult it is to do away with them: the children in *The Cement Garden* cover the corpse of their mother with cement, but botch the job, so that the house begins to smell of her decay and their guilt. But these books also seek, at a formal level, to contain and control the vivid, traumatic happenings that originate their plots. They may be about secrets, but they are themselves highly secretive. McEwan is addicted to the withholding of narrative information, the hoarding of surprises, the deferral of revelations; this manipulation of secrecy, apart from its obvious desire to keep the reader reading, seems to incarnate a desire to repeat the texture of the originating trauma, and in so doing, to master and contain it. Major examples might be the deferred revelation in *The Child in Time* that Stephen's wife has been pregnant for nine months, alone in the countryside, without needing to inform her estranged husband, who is also her impregnator, a secret McEwan hoards until the very end of the book, the better to provide the novel with a rush of harmony, as the bereaved couple finally replace mourning with new life. (This novel, like *Saturday*, formally closes the circle of domestic harmony, and neutralizes trauma with the possibility of a happy ending.) The first chapter of *Enduring Love* silently prepares a secret about John Logan (that he was not with his mistress but with a don and his girlfriend), which it withholds until the end of the book.

This manipulation of surprise is reproduced at the level of McEwan's sentences. He writes excellent prose, but is fond of a kind of thrillerish defamiliarization, in which he lulls the reader into thinking one thing while preparing something else. Here is a characteristic paragraph from *The Child in Time*:

> Stephen was three feet away from this tree when a boy stepped out from behind it and stood and stared . . . It was hard to see clearly, but he knew that this was just the kind of boy who used to fascinate and terrify him at school . . . The look was far too confident, cocky in that familiar way. He had an old-fashioned appearance—a gray flannel short with rolled-up sleeves and loosened tails, baggy shorts supported by a striped elastic belt with a silver snake clasp, bulging pockets from which a handle protruded, and scabby, blood-streaked knees.

It is not a boy, but the regressed Charles Drake, Stephen's former publisher. In *The Innocent*, Leonard and Maria are having sex in her bedroom. He hears her whispering and thinks it is an endearment. This continues for two paragraphs, and then McEwan reveals the content of the whisper. "What at last he heard her say was: 'There's someone in the wardrobe.'" In *Black Dogs*, June Tremaine is walking in the French countryside. "She came to a hairpin bend in the track and turned it. A hundred yards ahead, by the next bend, were two donkeys . . . As she came away from the edge she looked ahead again and realized that the donkeys were dogs, black dogs of an unnatural size." In *Enduring Love*, Joe Rose thinks he glimpses Jed Parry, his stalker, in the London Library. He goes home, makes himself a drink, and hears a creak: "There was someone at my back." It is his wife.

And so on. The middle section of *Atonement* systematically deploys this kind of negative estrangement. Two apparently hostile French brothers approach the English soldiers; one is holding something long and rifle-like in his hand. It is a baguette. Later, after the Germans have started bombing the English forces, Robbie Turner sees, across a field, just the heads of his two fellow soldiers, resting on the soil. McEwan doesn't need to say what we are thinking, that they have been decapitated. As Robbie approaches, he sees that they are not dead, but knee-deep in a grave they are digging for a French boy.

McEwan probably gets some of this from writers like Tolstoy and Stephen Crane. Tolstoy, after all, was praised by the Russian formalists for his talent at defamiliarization. Nikolai Rostov stands on a wooden bridge, in the heat of battle, and there is a sound "as if someone has spilled nuts." A man has fallen down beside him. But Tolstoy's estrangements are often on the order of moral correction or readjustment; they open up a new vein of sympathy, as for instance, when Pierre Bezukhov visits Dolokhov at home, and discovers that the rowdy man-about-town with whom he has just fought a duel is a "most affectionate" son to his old mother and his hunchbacked sister. McEwan's estrangements are, more often than not, visual surprises, designed to keep the reader in his expert grip, and to keep meaning under control. They do not open up but close off. They are secrets, not mysteries. Graham Greene and George Orwell may have been closer models for McEwan. And behind Orwell and McEwan stands a Victorian manipulator like Wilkie Collins. There is the celebrated visual surprise, for instance, when Walter Hartright sees Marian Halcombe, from behind, in *The Woman in White*. She seems to have a fine figure, a "comely shape," until she turns:

She left the window—and I said to myself, The lady is dark. She moved forwards a few inches—and I said to myself, The lady is young. She approached nearer—and I said to myself (with a sense of surprise which words fail me to express), The lady is ugly!

In a recent profile in *The New Yorker*, McEwan said that he wants to "incite a naked hunger in readers." Tastes differ, no doubt (I dislike strong narrative manipulation, and try deliberately to "spoil" plot surprises in my reviews). McEwan's Collins-like surprises "work," I suppose. They retain our narrative hunger, but surely at a cost. His addiction to secrecy has a way of cheaply "playing" us,

and if his withholdings ultimately seek to contain trauma, they also
have the effect of reproducing, in plotted repetitions, the textures
of the larger, originating traumas that are his big subjects. I don't
mean that his books traumatize us—that would be unfair. Just that
we finish them a little guilty, having been exiled from our own
version of innocence by a cunningly knowing authorial manipulator.
The problem is that narrative secrets of this kind (of both the macro
and the micro kind) ultimately exist only to confess themselves—
that is their métier—and when they do, we may find that the novels
have become too easily comprehensible. (One definition of a narrative convention might precisely be: a secret that has finally confessed itself.) *The Innocent*, to select only one novel, too deftly
tightens its little drawstring of thematics around a repeatedly un-
derlined connection between tunneling and sex, rape fantasies and
war conquest, dismemberment of the body and dismemberment of
Berlin into four sectors. Note, also, that many of these narrative
secrets and withholdings are grossly improbable. The woman who
kept her pregnancy a secret for nine months; the fact that the two
dogs that attacked June Tremaine were also used by the Nazis to
rape a woman; the dedicated, daylong fanaticism of Baxter, along
with Perowne's decision, at the end of the book, to perform surgery
on the man who broke into his house and tried to rape his daughter;
the fuse of unlikelihoods that sets fire to the plot of *Atonement*.

For McEwan, I suspect, a story *is* indeed a long string or fuse of
heaped improbabilities, and he delights in the way that, retrospec-
tively, all these improbabilities have been neatly made *sense of*, have
been made hermeneutically legible, turned into necessities: that we
are forced to say to ourselves, "It could not have been any other
way." Leonard Marnham, reflecting on the fact that his engagement
party became a fight, then a murder, then a bloody sawing-up of
body parts, thinks "how all along the way each successive step had
seemed logical enough, consistent with the one before, and how no
one was to blame." But if narrative secrets of this kind—narrative
improbabilities—always become, in the end, narrative predictabili-

ties, then such novels will find it much harder to dramatize meaningfully the impact of contingency on ordinary lives. Contingency is accident, but there is nothing accidental about these highly strung narratives, which in fact attempt to contain and hold accident.

If secrets constitute us as individuals (as Briony Tallis hopes is the case), and secrets are crucial to storytelling, then it must be storytelling itself that expels us from Eden. Storytelling is corrupt and corrupting. This has been one of the themes McEwan has pondered in recent years, and it is hard not to conclude that in so doing he is somewhat anxiously arraigning his own propensity for narrative manipulation. Tellingly, another enormously successful and artistically serious novelist, Graham Greene, did something similar in *The End of the Affair*, using the book, in part, to reflect on storytelling and the "guiltiness" of highly professionalized storytelling. Bendrix, the book's first narrator, is a successful novelist praised for his impeccable craftsmanship. *The End of the Affair* ends with a series of miracles: a book belonging to Bendrix's mistress, Sarah, has healing powers; a man's scarred face is suddenly restored; a stained-glass window in a house that is bombed is the only window not shattered. Greene the Catholic asks, in effect, as McEwan does in *Black Dogs*, when is a coincidence just a coincidence and when is it a narrative miracle (by which I mean authorial manipulation)? In *Black Dogs*, a Marlow-like narrator ponders the unreliabilities and coercions of storytellers. He notes that the remembered trauma of the black dogs has become an originary myth for his mother-in-law, June Tremaine, and he questions the idea that lives have turning points: "Turning points are the inventions of storytellers and dramatists, a necessary mechanism when a life is reduced to, traduced by a plot, when a morality must be distilled from a sequence of actions, when an audience must be sent home with something unforgettable to mark a character's growth . . . June's 'black dogs' . . . I found these almost nonexistent animals too comforting."

This arraignment of fiction is problematic. McEwan, brooding perhaps on his own fictive manipulations, surely exaggerates the

large dastardliness of fiction's manipulations, and conflates his kind
of storytelling with storytelling in general. An extreme and bogus
binarism is thus established, in which the reader is pushed between
an absolute trust in fiction's form-making power and an absolute
skepticism of it. One of Briony's crimes in *Atonement* seems to be
not that she acts like a bad novelist but just that she acts like a novelist at all, imposing form and plot on a story that, properly pursued,
would be limitless. Stories, she reflects, are stories only when they
have endings:

> Only when a story was finished, all fates resolved and the
> whole matter sealed off at both ends so it resembled, at
> least in this one respect, every other finished story in the
> world, could she feel immune, and ready to punch holes in
> the margins, bind the chapters with pieces of string, paint
> or draw the cover, and take the finished work to show to
> her mother, or her father, when he was home.

There has to be a story about Robbie, she thinks,

> and this was the story of a man whom everybody liked, but
> about whom the heroine always had her doubts, and finally
> she was able to reveal that he was the incarnation of evil.
> But wasn't she—that was, Briony, the writer—supposed to
> be so worldly now as to be above such nursery-tale ideas as
> good and evil? There must be some lofty, god-like place
> from which all people could be judged alike, not pitted
> against each other . . . If such a place existed, she was not
> worthy of it. She could never forgive Robbie his disgusting
> mind.

Briony imposes a plot; she makes what she has witnessed mean
something. This is just what Henry Perowne, in *Saturday*, dislikes
about the fiction his daughter gets him to read. On the one hand, he

thinks, fiction is a clumsy, pointless provider of information more efficiently gathered elsewhere, and on the other hand it is too tidy. "Unlike in Daisy's novels, moments of precise reckoning are rare in real life; questions of misinterpretation are not often resolved. Nor do they remain pressingly unresolved. They simply fade."

A second difficulty with McEwan's manipulations is that he seems to want to have it both ways, at once decrying too much pattern and making use of too much pattern. It is all very well for the narrator of *Black Dogs*, or for Henry Perowne, to object to the fakery of "turning points" in fiction, but they are themselves embedded in books devoted to such mechanisms. *Atonement* prosecutes Briony, and by extension a certain kind of fiction, for a compulsive need to tidy up life's limitless messiness with plot, to make loose endings too neat; but *Atonement* is of course itself a very tidy novel, committed to explicitly guiding us through the implications of its own self-conscious fictionality.

And yet *Atonement*, a novel at once manipulative and keen to blame plot making for its manipulative distortions, is a moving and ample story, in a category apart from McEwan's earlier fiction. How does it work? Partly, its multisectioned form allows a little air into McEwan's usual narrative vault; in particular, the first section, set in a country house in 1935, is a brilliant feat of storytelling, whereby McEwan manages to sound both like McEwan and not quite like himself. He must sound a bit more ornate and experimental than usual, so that the section can plausibly be revealed, later on, to have been written by the Virginia Woolf–loving Briony Tallis; yet he must also please those readers who want his usual effects—tight plotting, withheld revelations, dark secrets, turning points. Martin Amis is right to consider this long passage McEwan's best piece of writing: simply at the technical level, it is astonishing to be able to write so well at a slight angle or distance from one's own voice, and yet continue to give readers what they want.

And indeed, knowing what readers want is at the heart of the diabolical success of this book. What is especially interesting about

Atonement in the light of McEwan's status as a popular but serious manipulator is the fairly delicate way it makes readers aware of their own desire to be gratified by serious narrative manipulation. In the fourth section of the book, set in 1999, Briony Tallis is an old and eminent writer who has just been given a diagnosis of dementia. The novel ends with her at her desk, reflecting on the piece of writing she first started in January 1940, and to which she has returned "half a dozen different" times between then and now. But although we comprehend that what we have just read—the text of the entire novel—was written by Briony, we have no great desire to comprehend that what we have just read was *made up*—that is, invented—by Briony; McEwan plays on the complacency of middlebrow readerly expectation, whereby, with the help of detailed verisimilitude, readers tend to turn fiction into fact. If we have just read, in section three, that Briony walked to Clapham and saw Robbie and Cecilia there, this must "really" have happened, yes? On the last two pages of the novel, of course, McEwan lays bear his final secret: it seems that Robbie died at Dunkirk on June 1, 1940, and Cecilia was killed in the same year by a bomb in Balham. The lovers never united. Briony invented their happiness as an act of novelistic atonement for her earlier act of novelistic failure.

Plenty of readers are irritated by this conjuring trick. But perhaps they should go easy on their disdain, because if Briony made it all up, so did they. If the desperation of both her guilt and her wish fulfillment stirs us, it is because, by way of McEwan's delayed revelation, by way of his narrative secret, we have ourselves conspired in Briony's wish fulfillment, not just content but eager to believe, until the very last moment, that Cecilia and Robbie did not actually die. We wanted them to be alive, and the knowledge that we, too, wanted a "happy ending" brings on a kind of atonement for the banality of our own literary impulses. Which is why the ending provokes interestingly divergent responses: it alienates some conventional readers, who dislike what they feel to be a trick, but it alienates some sophisticated readers, who also dislike what they feel to be a trick; and I suspect that the estrangement of both camps has to do with their guilt at having been moved by the novel's conventional romantic power. It shouldn't be possible, but *Atonement* wants to have it both ways, and almost succeeds in having it both ways: it prosecutes and defends—as inevitable—the very impulses that make McEwan such a compellingly manipulative novelist; and it makes us guilty co-conspirators in that machinery of manipulation.

RICHARD YATES

In April 1951, Richard Yates sailed from New York to Paris. He had been there twice before, as a child and later as a soldier, but for him as for so many American writers it was less a place than a laureled idea—the silvery and careless city of Hemingway and Fitzgerald. Careless, but a literary workshop, too: Yates said that he was determined to produce short stories there "at the rate of about one a month." The twenty-five-year-old writer was beginning an indenture that would last until his death, in 1992: he was sentenced to the sentence. Around the compulsion of writing he shaped everything else. There were two other compulsions, smoking and drinking, but they only killed him, while writing plainly kept him alive. (He was an alcoholic, but he never wrote while drunk.) He would live in New York, in Iowa, in Boston, and finally in Alabama, yet his apartments were identical in their shabby discipline of neglect. In each there was a table for writing, a circle of crushed cockroaches around the desk chair, curtains and walls made colorless by nicotine, a few books, and nothing in the kitchen but coffee, bourbon, and beer. Friends and colleagues found these accommodations appallingly bleak; for Yates they were accommodations for writing.

Paris was never the glamorous hubbub for Yates that it had been for an earlier literary generation, but it was there, and in Cannes, and then in London, that the young writer began his career. There is a wonderful moment in Blake Bailey's biography of Richard Yates when, after fourteen unpublished short stories, the fifteenth ("Number 15 off the production line" is how Yates described it) is sent to *The Atlantic*, narrowly rejected, and then narrowly reprieved, and then finally accepted—for two hundred and fifty extremely useful dollars. A cable brought the marvelous news, in unstopped, sky-high capitals. Over the next few years, Yates made only a modest living from his stories, but they brokered his reputation, and secured the interest and encouragement of a publisher who, like all publishers, wanted a novel, not a book of stories. That first novel was *Revolutionary Road* (1961), and it could be said to have dissolved its creator's career even as it founded it, because Yates never published a novel half as good again. Brutally put, he had about ten good years. His later fiction was compulsive but not compelling, necessary to him but not to his readers, who would always chase the fire of his first novel in the embers of its successors.

Yates's early stories are highly disciplined, formally chaste. Because *Revolutionary Road* became the decade's celebrated indictment of suburban surrender, Yates's stories are often likened to John Cheever's, but they are closer to J. F Powers's—there is the same richly restrained prose, luxuriously lined but plain to the touch; there is the same anxious comedy; the same very cold, appraising eye; and the same superb ear for the foolish histrionics of speech. Out of the apparently diplomatic conformity of mid-twentieth-century American realism—the sort of style that made short stories commercially saleable—bursts the monstrous ego of Yates's male characters, smashing all the eggshell niceties. These men are vulnerable, easily provoked by female competition or resistance, and their theatrical, role-playing speech haplessly shrouds and reveals their anxieties, in clouds of unknowing. John Fallon, in "The B.A.R. Man," lives in Sunnyside, Queens, and has been married for ten years to a woman who can't have children and who, tellingly, "earned more money than he did." At lunch with three colleagues, conversation turns to military service, and Fallon is obscurely irritated by the bragging of his friends. None of them, he bets, had to carry a heavy

Browning Automatic Rifle, or B.A.R., like he did. "Every son of a bitch *in* a rifle company's a specialist, if you wanna know something. And I'll tellya *one* thing, Mac—they don't worry about no silk gloves and no tailor-made clothes, you can betcher ass on that." His anger feeds on his inadequacy, because, Yates reveals, in fact he had fired his gun only twice, "at vague areas rather than men, had brought down nothing either time, and had been mildly reprimanded the second time for wasting ammunition." At home, Fallon is cruel to his wife. They are due to go out to a movie, but he picks up the bra she has laid out on the bed—"a white brassiere containing the foam-rubber cups without which her chest was as meager as a boy's"—and waves it in her face, saying, "Why d'ya *wear* these goddamn things?" Fallon tears out of the house, goes drinking, dances at a club, and tries to pick up a woman who isn't interested. He, however, can imagine her body, "undulant and naked, in some ultimate vague bedroom at the end of the night"—one of those moments when a seemingly transparent Yates sentence suddenly takes on riches.

Yates's noticing of the padded foam-rubber bra is typical. These stories share with *Revolutionary Road* a ruthless comprehension, sometimes a little close to cruelty. What impresses is the refusal to let sentiment seep in (though in the later work this toughness, as in Hemingway, can become its own species of sentimentality). "The Best of Everything" is a masterpiece of bleakness, equal to one of Joyce's stories in *Dubliners*. It is the eve of Grace's wedding, and her roommate has discreetly absented herself for the night, so that Grace's fiancé, Ralph, can visit. She prepares for him—she takes from her trousseau a sheer nightgown of white nylon and a matching negligee. But Ralph turns up late in the evening and is wholly involved with his own trivial drama: the boys at work have given him a surprise party, and he is expected back. Does he like what she is wearing? she shyly asks. He feels the slight material between finger and thumb "like a merchant" and asks only: "Wudga pay fa this, honey?" Grace tries to get Ralph to stay, but understands that her appeal—"Can't they wait?"—sounds just like "the whine of a wife." The wholly unappealing Ralph insists on going and says, on the way out: "So I'll see ya, Penn Station, nine o'clock tomorra. Right, Gracie? Only, before I go . . . I'm fulla beer. Mind if I use ya terlet?" As he leaves the house, Grace says wearily, "Don't worry, Ralph . . . I'll be there." And the story ends there, where it has to, at a perfect zero of hope.

On his return from Europe, in September 1953, Yates went back to work, as a freelance copywriter, for the company that had hired him four years earlier, the business machine giant Remington Rand. He found it very dull but said, years later, that "it occupied only about half of my working time and so financed the whole of my first novel." For a year he and his wife and daughter lived in a ranch-style house in Redding, Connecticut. It was this close suburban life, with its dreary drunken rituals and stolid neighbors, along with the Yateses' frequent marital fighting, that provided the material for *Revolutionary Road*, though most of the book was written not there but in the small town of Mahopac, New York, where the Yateses lived in a ramshackle cottage on a genteelly rotting private estate.

Revolutionary Road is a clever and passionate rewriting of *Madame Bovary*, with one signal difference—at the end of Flaubert's novel, both Emma and Charles Bovary lose, because she commits suicide and her dull husband is utterly bereft. In Yates's savage inversion, the wife loses but the dull husband secretly wins: she dies, and he, though deprived of wife and children, prospers at work, and finally secures for himself the safe, unsettled world that his wife died trying to dislodge. In *Revolutionary Road*, mid-twentieth-century American suburban man is so maddening because he is at once a rank escapist and a conservative pragmatist: he is Emma Bovary and Charles Bovary rolled into one; he has arrogated to himself twin rights that ought to be incompatible—to dream of escape and have adulterous affairs, like Emma, while simultaneously dreaming of timid stability, like Charles.

The conservative escapist at the heart of the novel is Frank Wheeler, who lives with his wife, April, in a suburban Connecticut house, at the end of what is called Revolutionary Road (past a new development called Revolutionary Hill Estates). It is 1955. Frank is anything but frank, and springlike April will die in the fall. From the start, the reader senses that Yates will smash open, with a Flaubertian ferocity, the glass case that holds the staged suburban tableau—and show it to be, precisely, staged. The novel begins with a performance, ends with a performance, and courses throughout with performances of one kind or another. As the novel opens, the local amateur dramatic group is presenting a play, *The Petrified Forest*, whose lead player is April Wheeler. The evening is a disaster—the actors lose their nerves and mangle the script—and April and Frank argue violently afterward. She is mortified by the disaster and wants to be left alone; he, wheedling and paternalistic, wants the husbandly right to soothe her, and thus assert a moist control.

Frank works in New York for Knox Business Machines, but prides himself that he takes his job ironically, that he cares nothing for it, and that his real life is elsewhere. Yates was playing a morbid joke on himself when he created Frank Wheeler, because Frank is Yates without the writing: he is saving himself for an invisible "creative" life that he is too unimaginative to envision. When April suggests that he give up his job and the family go to Paris, Frank's bluff is called. Paris had always been the great dream of escape. But seven years ago, when the couple were first together, April had got pregnant, and the Parisian dream had been deferred. This time, they will really do it! As April coaxingly reminds him: "You'll be doing what you should've been allowed to do seven years ago. You'll be finding yourself. You'll be reading and studying and taking long walks and thinking. You'll have *time*." But perhaps there is no Frank to find? The plan for Paris frightens him, though he keeps his fear quiet. For a while, he goes along with April's *Bovarysme*, halfheartedly learns French, and even announces his determination to leave his job in the fall. But when April later tells him that she is unexpectedly pregnant, he gladly seizes the solution. Paris can't now go ahead, or will have to be delayed by several years. Yates comments: "The pressure was off; life had come mercifully back to normal."

Frank is forever rehearsing scenarios in his mind, and in one of them he imagines April asking him what they will do now:

> "Well, but what about you?" April would say. "How are you *ever* going to find yourself now?" But as he firmly shut off the hot-water faucet he knew he would have the answer for her:
> "Suppose we let that be my business."
> And there was a new maturity and manliness in the kindly, resolute face that nodded back at him in the mirror.

But April, determined to go to Paris, and determined not to have a third child, tries to abort it at home, and dies in the bungling of it. Frank's children go to live with his brother and wife. At work, Frank is promoted.

Revolutionary Road anticipates a postmodern critique of authenticity, a critique inaugurated by Flaubert's excoriation of bourgeois cliché. Frank loudly criticizes the suburbs for being insufficiently daring, but his own complaints are blatantly complacent. His ranting has the feel of a performance, no more successful than April Wheeler's *Petrified Forest*. Frank is always playing a role. He is introduced as a man who had "the kind of unemphatic good looks that an advertising photographer might use to portray the discerning customers of well-made but inexpensive merchandise (Why Pay More?)" As a student at Columbia, he played at being an intellectual—he was "a Jean-Paul Sartre sort of man." He plays at being a father, and at being a husband. Later in the book, when he is trying to convince April not to attempt the abortion, he decides that he must impress her as he had once done when they were young. He begins a long attempt to dissuade her, which involves "a form of

masculine flirtation that was as skillful as any girl's." He holds his
head unnaturally erect, and takes care to arrange his features in
"a virile frown" whenever he lights a cigarette. On Revolutionary
Road, life has collapsed into advertising: his attempt to dissuade his
wife from the abortion is described by Yates as "a sales campaign."

Yates's novel is both traditional and radical. Its traditionalism
can be felt in the way it so delightedly flourishes the artisanal virtues of structure and finish. The prose is nicely alert and poised:
"his thin mouth already moving in the curly shape of wit, as if he
were rolling a small, bitter lozenge on his tongue." The book's form
is a solid delight of symmetry and repetition. Just as April's first
pregnancy scuppered the original Paris escape (but didn't really,
because Frank never intended to go), so her third scuppers the later
one (but doesn't really, either, for the same reason). Frank's father
also worked at Knox. A play opens the novel, and a performance ends
it, as the Wheelers' neighbors, the Campbells, tell the new owners of
the Wheelers' house about the tragedy that has vacated their property. In the very last pages, Mrs. Givings, the horridly eager Realtor
who had sold the Wheelers their house, describes, to her husband,
the new owners in the same language she had once used to describe the Wheelers: "She's very sweet and fun to talk to; he's rather
reserved. I think he must do something very brilliant in town"—
suburban life continues without interruption. Frank's children, now
motherless, will have the kind of parentless existence with their
uncle that April Wheeler had as a child, and which, she felt, damaged her. So the horror begins all over again: these repetitions and
circularities overlap to make the novel's heavy plait of determinism.

Nowadays, *Revolutionary Road* perhaps seems more radical
than it did in 1961. It is not merely that it searches out every refuge
of the humanly authentic, and detonates it. It is that a novel about
role-playing is also necessarily a novel that questions its own authenticity. Realism can become the most complacent of narrative
styles, because it is so wary about questioning its own artifice. Yates
is most decidedly a midcentury American realist. But *Revolutionary Road* is, essentially, a novel all about artifice, and thus about

its own artifice. A novel in which characters have become brand names—"a Jean-Paul Sartre sort of man"—is a novel that also raises the question: so what *is* a rounded, a "realistic," literary character? Frank's theatricality is a form of fiction making, after all. When Mrs. Campbell, at the end of the novel, tells the new owners about the "tragedy" of the Wheelers, she does so in a spirit of corrosive and luxurious gossip—her voice, says Yates, had taken on "a voluptuous narrative pleasure." But she is doing, in this sense, no more than the novel itself has done; and if we find Mrs. Campbell's lingering and cruel narrative offensive, then we shall have also to judge Yates's own lingering and cruel narrative, and our ready complicity in it.

Above all, the novel is subtly prismatic. It seems to offer a familiar critique of the suburbs, of the kind we know from movies and books like *American Beauty* and *The Ice Storm*, in which the streets are amok with hysterical housewives and angry soft men. Yates himself said that he intended the novel to function as "an indictment of American life in the nineteen-fifties":

> Because during the Fifties there was a general lust for conformity over this country, by no means only in the suburbs—a kind of blind, desperate clinging to safety and security at any price, as exemplified politically in the Eisenhower administration and the McCarthy witch-hunts . . . I meant the title to suggest that the revolutionary road of 1776 had come to something very much like a dead end in the Fifties.

This is too helpful. Indeed, Yates liked putting big, bright figures in his carpets—controlling symbols and names. Not only do the Wheelers live on Revolutionary Road, but Frank tries, and fails, to build a stone path from his front door to the road! And Knox is a big prison, and Frank isn't frank, and so on. But in fact, the tale is subtler than the teller, because the novel does not allow us an easy point of agreement. Mrs. Givings's son, John, is a former mathematician who has suffered a nervous breakdown and, after a tussle with the state troopers, has been committed to a mental hospital. He is occasionally let out, and twice visits the Wheelers. At one point during his first visit, Frank condemns "the hopeless emptiness of everything in this country," and John Givings eagerly agrees:

> Now you've said it. The hopeless emptiness. Hell, plenty of people are on to the emptiness part; out where I used to work, on the Coast, that's all we ever talked about. We'd sit around talking about emptiness all night. Nobody ever said "hopeless," though; that's where we'd chicken out. Because maybe it does take a certain amount of guts to see the emptiness, but it takes a whole hell of a lot more to see the hopelessness.

This has the ring of an authorial statement, the leathery, hard-won "honesty" for which Yates is praised. (Blake Bailey's biography is titled *A Tragic Honesty*.) And John Givings's status as an outcast, a mental patient who sees through the congealed horror, lends him a seerlike authority. But remember that it was the thoroughly inauthentic Frank Wheeler who supplied the easy Conradian phrase "the hopeless emptiness of everything," and it was the thoroughly inauthentic Frank who, pages earlier, denounced the suburbs for locking up people like John Givings:

> Wasn't this, he asked, a beautifully typical story of these times and this place? A man could rant and smash and grapple with the State Police, and still the sprinklers whirled at dusk on every lawn and the television droned in every living room . . . "Call the Troopers, get him out of sight quick, hustle him off and lock him up before he wakes the neighbors . . . It's as if everybody'd made this tacit agreement to live in a state of total self-deception."

Once again, just as we quickly reach for our own preferred weapon of condemnation—yes, we say to ourselves, how very true is this "beautifully typical story of these times and this place," how right this book is about "the hopeless emptiness of everything"—we find the novel judging our own judgmentalism, qualifying our superiority. And the novel escapes, somehow, to live another, more complicated and mysterious life.

The longer one looks at Richard Yates's work, the more central—and obsessively central—seems the question of gender. (I suspect that this is where *Revolutionary Road* had the greatest influence on the conception and narrative argument of the TV series *Mad Men*.) Yates's stories and novels return repeatedly to the weakness and hysterical anxiety of mid-twentieth-century American masculinity. His fiction, begun in the early 1950s, and written throughout the next four decades, was closely shadowed by the Second World War. For Yates, that war seems to have functioned like an impossibly stern father: no performance would ever suffice. If you fought in it, you never fought bravely enough (Yates was anxious about the bravery of his own conduct in the Seventy-fifth Division, in Europe); if you missed it, the rest of your life would be perforated with inadequacies. In Yates's novel *Disturbing the Peace* (1975), John Wilder, a bipolar alcoholic obsessed with his shortness, angrily recalls that his father would always claim that he fought in the Battle of the Bulge, but that this was not true. Andrew Crawford in *The Easter Parade* (1976) is sexually impotent; perhaps not coincidentally, he had been passed over for war service. The aimless and oafish Evan Shephard in *Cold Spring Harbor* (1986) fails the military exam; it is downhill in his life from there. And there is the violent John Fallon in "The B.A.R. Man."

Yates was, apparently, a relentlessly traditional man, who believed that women should have babies and stay at home. He cleaved to the unreconstructed rigors of alcoholism, Brooks Brothers, and homophobia. His biographer records an incident in which the novelist and his first wife were tussling over how to work the car heater. When she proved to be correct, he exploded: "Well, cut my penis off!" So it is a considerable tribute to his novelistic suppleness that he so ruthlessly dramatized male selfishness and insecurity. His

men operate along a terribly narrow track, squeezed on one side by
patriarchal expectation and on the other by female competition.
Frank Wheeler feels outdone by the surpassing competence of his
father's hands, "and the aura of mastery they imparted to everything Earl Wheeler used." Even on his deathbed, his father's hands
"looked stronger and better than his son's." Yates acutely puts gender
at the center of *Revolutionary Road*, by having April Wheeler propose that in Paris she work to support her ideally free husband. It
could be said that the novel turns less on the question of abortion, or
the stupor of the suburbs, or the timidity of Eisenhower conform-
ists, than on the single question of whether a wife is allowed to
work. Frank nervously pictures this man-eating drone: "When she
came home to the Paris apartment her spike-heeled pumps would
click decisively on the tile floor and her hair would be pulled back
into a neat bun; her face would be drawn with fatigue."

Frank absurdly lectures April about how wanting to have an
abortion is really an expression of her desire to be a man—that
she is trying to open herself up "so that the—you know—so that the
penis could come out and hang down where it belonged." But the
nice joke of the book is that Frank is the traditionally conceived
"woman" of the house: he is hysterical, preening, an effeminate
masquerader always checking in mirrors the proper "impact" of his
face; a parlor soldier. *Mad Men* uses the unfair wisdom of hindsight
to mount an antimasculinist case against the early 1960s that is also
a feminist case: as good postmoderns, we all root for Peggy Olson
(Elisabeth Moss), the secretary at Sterling Cooper, to be given her
chance as a junior copywriter. Yates's work is not feminist, partly
because it is much more interested in men than in women (only
in his novel *The Easter Parade* did he ever explore a systematic
sympathy for a female character), and partly because its fanatical
involvement with male anxiety comes to seem somewhat defensive—
Yates as both critic and victim of his own impacted maleness. But in
a generation of writers deeply invested in maintaining male status,
it is Yates whose work most lucidly lays bear the bitter price of that
investment for both sexes. *Cold Spring Harbor* recounts the useless

and coolly adulterous life of Evan Shephard. In its closing pages, Evan hits his wife, Rachel, and, like John Fallon in "The B.A.R. Man," angrily runs out on her. Rachel consoles herself by looking after their newborn son. "Oh, you little marvel," she tells the baby. "You're a miracle. Because do you know what you're going to be? You're going to be a man." They are the novel's final words.

GEORGE ORWELL'S VERY ENGLISH REVOLUTION

I.

I vividly remember when I first read George Orwell. It was at Eton, Orwell's old school. Not coming from a family with any Eton connections (a portion of my fees was paid by the school), I had refined a test: if a boy's father had gone there, then that boy's grandparents had been rich enough, in the early 1950s, to come up with the money. And if his grandparents had been rich enough, the chances were that his great-grandparents had had enough cash to send Grandpa there in the 1920s—and back and back, in an infinite regression of privilege. There were probably hundreds of boys whose family wealth stretched so far back, into the nineteenth and eighteenth centuries, that to all intents and purposes the origin of their prosperity was invisible, wallpapered over in layers and layers of luck.

It seemed extraordinary to a member of the upwardly mobile bourgeoisie that these boys were incapable of answering two basic questions: How did your family make its money? And how on earth did it hold on to it for so long? They were barely aware of their massive and unearned privilege; and this at a time of recession and Mrs. Thatcher, while English fields became battlegrounds, and policemen on horseback fought armies of striking coal miners. I spent my time at that school alternately grateful for its every expensive blessing and yearning to blow it up. Into those receptive hands fell Orwell's pamphlet, written in 1941, "The Lion and the Unicorn:

Socialism and the English Genius," with its own war cry: "Probably the battle of Waterloo *was* won on the playing-fields of Eton, but the opening of all subsequent wars have been lost there." And also: "England is the most class-ridden country under the sun. It is a land of snobbery and privilege, ruled largely by the old and silly . . . A family with the wrong members in control."

"The Lion and the Unicorn" is a powerfully radical pamphlet, published at a time when Orwell thought that the only way for the British to beat the Nazis was to make the war a revolutionary one. British capitalism had been culpably inefficient. Its lords and captains—the old and silly—had slept through the 1930s, either colluding with or appeasing Hitler. There had been long periods of recession and unemployment. Britain had failed to produce enough armaments; he notes that as late as August 1939, British manufacturers were still trying to sell rubber, shellac, and tin to the Germans. The Fascists, by contrast, stealing what they wanted from socialism and discarding all the noble bits, had shown how efficient a planned economy could be: "However horrible this system may seem to us, it works." Only by shifting to a planned, nationalized economy, and a "classless, ownerless" society could the British prevail. Revolution was not just desirable but necessary. And what was needed was more than just a change of heart but a structural dismantling, "a fundamental shift of power. Whether it happens with or without bloodshed is largely an accident of time and place."

During the 1940s, a social revolution did take place in Britain. Though it would not be Orwell's idea of a fundamental shift of power, Orwell's writing certainly contributed to the quieter change that occurred when the Labour Party won the 1945 election, ousted Winston Churchill, and inaugurated the welfare state. After the war, Orwell became most famous as a left-baiting antitotalitarian, but he did not change his opinion that massive systemic change was necessary in order to make Britain a decent and fair country to live in—he always made the case for nationalization of major industries, tight government regulation of income disparity (he proposed a system whereby the highest income did not exceed the lowest by more than ten to one), the winding up of the empire, the abolition of the House of Lords, the disestablishment of the Church of England, and reform of the great English boarding schools and ancient universities. This revolution, he thought, will be a curious, ragged, English thing: "It will not be doctrinaire, nor even logical. It will abolish the House of Lords, but quite probably will not abolish the Monarchy. It will leave anachronisms and loose ends everywhere . . . It will not set up any explicit class dictatorship." Nowadays, Orwell's imprecision about exactly how this revolution might come about seems telling, because despite the fighting talk ("At some point or other it may be necessary to use violence"), his vagueness seems a kind of wish fulfillment, as if, mimicking his own haziness, a nice muddled revolution might gently and spontaneously emerge from the London fog. "A real shove from below will accomplish it," he writes. A shove—ah, that will do it.

But there is a difference between being revolutionary and being a revolutionary, and journalists aren't required to be tacticians. What is striking, to me, is that Orwell premises the economic viability of his socialistic planned economy on the economic success of the Nazis' planned economy, and, in turn, premises the viability of the planned economy only on its efficiency in wartime. Nazism worked, to use Orwell's verb, because it was good at producing tanks and guns in wartime, but how good would it be at hospitals and universities in peacetime? He doesn't say. So the example of efficient fascism is what inspires the hope of efficient socialism! Orwell seems never to have realized the political contradiction of this, at least explicitly. Unconsciously, he did perhaps realize it, because later works like *Animal Farm* and *1984* worry away at the fascistic temptation inherent in the socialistic, planned, collective economy—or the "classless, ownerless society."

This is not to suggest, as contemporary neoconservatives like Jonah Goldberg absurdly claim, that socialism is just fascism with a bleeding heart. Orwell never thought that. Despite the antitotalitarian books, despite his reputation's later theft at the hands of the right wing and the neoconservatives, he remained revolutionary in spirit. But he never really reconciled his hatred of what he once called "the power instinct" with a candid assessment of the power instinct that would have to be exercised to effect revolution. This was because, as he saw it, the ideal English revolution existed precisely to dismantle power and privilege, so how could it possibly end up replacing one kind of privilege with another? The English just wouldn't do that. An actual revolution, in Russia, with its abuses of power and privilege, necessarily disappointed him, because it contaminated the ideal. Orwell became not so much antirevolutionary as antirevolution. He used an ideal revolution to scourge an actual one—which is a negative form of messianism, really.

When I first read "The Lion and the Unicorn," I was so blinded by flag-waving lines like "And if the rich squeal audibly, so much the better," and "The lady in the Rolls-Royce car is more damaging to morale than a fleet of Goering's bombing planes," that I missed this incoherence. To someone surrounded by alien acres of privilege, Orwell's relentless attack on privilege seemed a necessary, obliterating forest fire: "What is wanted is a conscious open revolt by ordinary people against inefficiency, class privilege and the rule of the old . . . We have got to fight against privilege." Nowadays, I'm struck by the fact that throughout his work, Orwell is much more vocal about the abolition of power and privilege than about equitable redistribution, let alone the means and machinery of that redistribution. There is a fine spirit of optimistic destruction in his work, a sense that if we all just work hard at that crucial, negating "shove from below," then the upper-class toffs will simply fade away, and things will more or less work out in the interests of justice. In "The Lion and the Unicorn," there is a suggestive moment when Orwell writes that collective deprivation may be more necessary than political programs: "In the short run, equality of sacrifice, 'war-Communism,' is even more important than radical economic changes. It is very necessary that industry should be nationalized, but it is more urgently necessary that such monstrosities as butlers and 'private incomes' should disappear forthwith." In other words, let's agree to be a bit vague about the economic stuff, like industrial policy; and let's keep the serious rhetoric for the lady in the Rolls, about whom we can be militantly precise. This is the same Orwell who wrote in his wartime diary, "The first sign that things are really happening in England will be the disappearance of that horrible plummy voice from the radio," and the same Orwell who, dying in an English nursing home, wrote in his notebook about the sound of upper-class English voices: "And what voices! A sort of over-fedness, a fatuous self-confidence, a constant bah-bahing of laughter about nothing, above all a sort of heaviness and richness combined with a fundamental ill-will . . . No wonder everyone hates us so." Getting rid of those accents was more than half the battle for Orwell.

So it is probably fair to say that Orwell was even more consumed by the spectacle of overweening privilege than by the spectacle of overwhelming poverty, despite the two great, committed books he wrote about the poor, *Down and Out in Paris and London* (1933) and *The Road to Wigan Pier* (1937). Again and again, Orwell returns to the abuse of power. In his long essay on Dickens, one of the finest he wrote, he marks Dickens down for not being revolutionary enough (Dickens is "always pointing to a change of spirit rather than a change of structure"), yet applauds his "real hatred of tyranny," and then turns back on himself to repeat the case that a purely moral critique of society is not quite sufficient, since the "central problem—how to prevent power from being abused— remains unsolved."

His nicely pugilistic essay on Tolstoy's hatred of *King Lear* is skeptical about Tolstoy's late, monkish religiosity, and sets up a binarism that is repeated two years later, in his essay on Gandhi. For Orwell, the humanist is committed to this world and its struggles, and knows that "life is suffering." But the religious believer wagers everything on the next life, and though the two sides, religious and secular, may occasionally overlap, there can be no ultimate reconciliation between them. Orwell suspects that when the bullying humanist novelist became a bullying religious writer, he merely exchanged one form of egoism for another. "The distinction that really matters is not between violence and non-violence, but between having and not having the appetite for power." The example he appends to this dictum is an interesting one: when a father threatens his son with "You'll get a thick ear if you do that again," coercion is palpable and transparent. But, writes Orwell, what of the mother who lovingly murmurs, "Now, darling, is it kind to Mummy to do that?" The mother wants to contaminate her son's brain. Tolstoy did not propose that *King Lear* be banned or censored, says Orwell; instead, when he wrote his polemic against Shakespeare, he tried to contaminate our pleasure. For Orwell, "creeds like pacifism and anarchism, which seem on the surface to imply a complete renunciation of power, rather encourage this habit of mind."

Orwell became increasingly obsessed with this kind of manipulative, insidious power; his repeated denunciations of those he thought wielded it—pacifists, anarchists, Communist fellow-travelers, naive leftists—reached a slightly hysterical pitch. But his terror of the tyrannical mother who lovingly murmurs at you while rearranging your brain makes the two novels written under that shadow, *Animal Farm* and *1984*, very powerful—indeed, the only two really fine fictions he ever produced. Reliably, the most appalling moments in *1984* come when the state has already read Winston Smith's mind and abolished his interiority. A man sits in a room and thinks: we expect the traditional realist novel to indulge his free consciousness and represent its movements on the page. When we are told, in effect, that this cannot happen in the usual way, because this man is being watched by the state, that this man fears even to betray himself by speaking aloud in his sleep, the shock, even sixty years after the book's publication, is still great. The all-seeing novelist becomes not the benign author but the dreaded telescreen, or the torturer O'Brien, who seems to know in advance what questions Winston will ask.

Eric Blair (Orwell's real name) was born in 1903, in Bengal, to a father who worked as a minor official in the Indian Civil Service; his mother was the daughter of a French teak merchant who did business in Burma. In a kind of morbid squirm, Orwell wrote that he belonged to the "lower-upper-middle class," a station with prestige but no money. Such families went to the colonies because they could afford to play there at being gentlemen. But this self-description appears in *The Road to Wigan Pier*, where it must have seemed very important to scuff his social polish a bit. In fact, "lower-upper class" would be a more accurate and compact portmanteau: he was the great-great-great-grandson of an earl, the grandson of a clergyman, and in later life kept up with Old Etonian chums such as Cyril Connolly, Anthony Powell, and A. J. Ayer. At St. Cyprian's, a preparatory school he was sent to at the age of eight, the little Eric was inducted into a regime of violence and intimidation. According to his memoir "Such, Such Were the Joys" (not published in Orwell's lifetime, for fear of libel), he was singled out for bullying because he was a poor boy, on reduced fees. There was soft and hard power here—Mummy and Daddy were both at work. The headmaster and his wife used Blair's depressed financial status as manipulative weapons. "You are living on my bounty," the headmaster would say, as he vigorously caned the little boy. His wife comes across as an understudy for O'Brien; she could make young Blair snivel with shame and gratitude, by saying things like "And do you think it's quite fair to us, the way you're behaving? After all we've done for you? You do know what we've done for you, don't you?"

Having crammed for the Eton scholarship, which he won, Orwell then seems to have taken the next five years off, though he read an enormous amount in his own time. Eton was enlightenment itself after St. Cyprian's, and he confessed to having been "relatively happy" there. But he must have been painfully aware, as he had been at St. Cyprian's, of not being able to keep up with wealthier boys. There was probably a more sophisticated version of the inquisition that he remembered from St. Cyprian's, in which "new boys of doubtful social origin" were bombarded with questions like: "What part of London do you live in? Is that Knightsbridge or Kensington? How many bathrooms has your house got? How many servants do your people keep?" (I remember an updated edition of this.) Unable to win a scholarship to Oxford or Cambridge, Orwell joined the Indian Imperial Police, in Burma, in 1922. It was a peculiar decision, but as with the atheist who loves churches, it perhaps represented an unconscious form of rebellious espionage.

School provided Orwell with one of his lifelong obsessions, class; his experience as a colonial policeman provided a tutorial in the other, the abuse of power. The famous essays that come out of the time in Burma, including "A Hanging" and "Shooting an Elephant," are written with cool fire—a banked anger at administered cruelty. In the latter piece, Orwell is ashamed that he must kill a magnificent elephant simply to avoid losing face, as a policeman and white man, before a large Burmese crowd. In "A Hanging," the horror of the execution—"It is curious, but till that moment I had never realized what it means to destroy a healthy, conscious man"—is made more vivid by the triviality that surrounds the event, like trash around the base of a monument: Orwell describes a dog that bounds up and tries to lick the face of the condemned man, and he notices, in a celebrated moment, the prisoner swerve to avoid a puddle as he walks toward the gallows.

Orwell claimed that in a peaceful age he might have been a harmless, ornamental writer, oblivious to political obligation. "As it is," he wrote in 1946, "I have been forced into becoming a sort of pamphleteer. First I spent five years in an unsuitable profession (the Indian Imperial Police, in Burma), and then I underwent poverty and failure." That verb, "underwent," suggests not coercion but voluntary self-mortification. The truth is that Orwell went to Paris in 1928 like hundreds of other poor aspiring artists, to see what he could produce. He did indeed run out of money, and ended up working as a dishwasher, or *plongeur*, in a Paris hotel. He had pneumonia and spent several weeks in a free hospital in Paris, in hideous circumstances, an experience he wrote up in "How the Poor Die." He returned to England, and tramped around London and Kent with the down-and-out, living like the homeless, on bread and butter and cups of tea, and putting up for the night at doss-houses, or "spikes." But he chose to do all this rather than, say, go and live with his parents, because he was scouting for material.

And what material! *Down and Out in Paris and London*, his

first book, which he published in 1933, is in some ways his best
(though *Homage to Catalonia* comes very close). There is a young
man's porousness to impressions and details, a marvelous ear for
speech, and a willingness to let anecdotes play themselves out. Five
years later, he would write again about the poor, this time miners,
steelworkers, and the unemployed in Wigan and Sheffield, but they
are hardly ever allowed to speak in *The Road to Wigan Pier*. As there
are no voices, so there are no stories in the later book, no movement, just the tar of deprivation, which glues his subjects into their
poverty. Orwell has become a pamphleteer, and is now doing rhetorical battle with fellow Socialists. The earlier book, curiously, is a
joyful, dynamic one. There is Boris, the unemployed Russian waiter
and former soldier, who likes to quote Marshal Foch: *"Attaquez!
Attaquez! Attaquez!"* There is the frighteningly precise account of
hunger, and the worldly tips that Orwell enjoys passing on, such as
eating bread with garlic rubbed on it—"the taste lingers and gives
one the illusion of having fed recently." There are the vivid descriptions of the labyrinthine inferno in the bowels of the hotel where he
works: "As we went along, something struck me violently in the back.
It was a hundred-pound block of ice, carried by a blue-aproned
porter. After him came a boy with a great slab of veal on his shoulder,
his cheek pressed into the damp, spongy flesh." And there are characters like Bozo, a London pavement artist, who rattles on:

> "The whole thing with cartoons is being up to date. Once a
> child got its head stuck in the railings of Chelsea Bridge.
> Well, I heard about it, and my cartoon was on the pave-
> ment before they'd got the child's head out of the railings.
> Prompt, I am."

And on:

> "Have you ever seen a corpse burned? I have, in India.
> They put the old chap on the fire, and the next moment I
> almost jumped out of my skin, because he'd started kicking.

It was only his muscles contracting in the heat—still, it give me a turn. Well, he wriggled about for a bit like a kipper on hot coals, and then his belly blew up and went off with a bang you could have heard fifty yards away. It fair put me against cremation."

Bozo, whose collar is always fraying, and who patches it with "bits cut from his shirt tail so that the shirt hardly had any tail left," is both real and heightened. He is pure Dickens, and Orwell almost certainly worked up his speech like a good novelist. Who's to say that Orwell did not come up on his own with that simile, "like a kipper on hot coals"? It perfectly fulfills one of the requests he would make thirteen years later in a well-known essay, "Politics and the English Language," for "a fresh, vivid, home-made turn of speech." His own writing abounds with images of kipperlike pungency: "In the West even the millionaire suffers from a vague sense of guilt, like a dog eating a leg of mutton." In his novel *Coming Up for Air* (1939), the old bucolic town of Lower Binfield has unattractively expanded after the First World War and has "spread like gravy over a tablecloth."

But even if Orwell worked at his journalism like a good novelist, the strange thing is that he could not work at his novels like a good novelist. The very details that sharply pucker the journalism are rolled flat in the fiction. Orwell needed the prompt of the real to get going as a writer. One of the most vivid details in the novel *Keep the Aspidistra Flying* (1936) involves the impoverished hero, about to go to a genteel tea party, inking the skin of his ankles where it peeps through the threadbare sock. You don't forget this: it gives such new meaning to the phrase "down-at-heel." But Orwell saw it in Paris, first recorded it in *Down and Out*, and then recycled it years later in fiction. No one forgets the waiters and tramps and cooks in his first book, inking their heels, stuffing the soles of their shoes with newspaper, or squeezing a dirty dishcloth into the patron's soup as a revenge on the bourgeoisie; nobody forgets Mr. Booker in *The Road to Wigan Pier*, who runs a tripe shop and has filthy fingers,

and "like all people with permanently dirty hands . . . had a peculiarly intimate, lingering manner of handling things." But there is
absolutely nothing memorable in the watery, vaudevillian description
of the urban poor—"the proles"—in *1984*; it is just neutered Gissing.

Orwell is famous for his easy, intimate, frank style, and for his
determination that good prose should be as transparent as a window-
pane. But his style, though superbly colloquial, is much more like a
lens than a window. His narrative journalism directs our attention
pedagogically; he believed, as he put it, that "all art is propaganda."
There is a cunning control of suspense. The dog who bounds up to
the prisoner in "A Hanging" is introduced like this: "Suddenly,
when we had gone ten yards, the procession stopped short without
any order or warning. A dreadful thing had happened—a dog, come
goodness knows whence, had appeared in the yard." Whatever
dreadful thing one has been made to expect at that moment, it is
unlikely to be a dog. The characteristic Orwellian formulation "It is
interesting that" or "Curiously enough" works similarly; it generally
introduces not some penny curiosity but a gold-plated revelation:
"Curiously enough, he was the first dead European I had seen," he
writes in "How the Poor Die." The man swerving to avoid the puddle in "A Hanging" is passed off rather similarly, as a kind of found
object, a triviality noticed by chance. But the essay is carefully structured around two examples of irrelevance, each of them suggestive of
an instinctive solipsism. The dog who bounds up to the condemned
man is living its own joyous, animal life, and this has nothing to do
with the imminent horror; this incursion is then "balanced"—in a
formal sense—by the victim's "irrelevant" swerve, which, among
other things, is suggestive of a body or mind still moving at its own
instinctual rhythm. The piece is highly choreographed.

He almost certainly got this eye for didactic detail from Tolstoy, who is masterful at the apprehension that forces a sudden reappraisal of reality, often a new awareness that another person is as
real to him as you are to yourself. The man swerving around the
puddle has an ancestor in the young Russian, in *War and Peace*,
who is about to be executed by French soldiers, and irrelevantly

fiddles with his blindfold, because it is too tight. Nikolai Rostov, in the same book, finds that he cannot kill a French soldier, because instead of seeing an enemy he sees "a most simple, homelike face." In "Looking Back on the Spanish War," Orwell is about to shoot a fascist soldier, and then cannot, because "he was half-dressed and was holding up his trousers with both hands as he ran."

Orwell is wrongly thought of as the great neutral reporter, immune to the fever of judgment—the cool camera, the unbiased eyeball. He was attacked by Edward Said for propagating "the eye-witness, seemingly opinion-less politics" of Western journalism: "When they are on the rampage, you show Asiatic and African mobs rampaging: an obviously disturbing scene presented by an obviously unconcerned reporter who is beyond Left piety or right-wing cant," wrote Said. I think that almost the opposite is true. Orwell may seem cool, because he does not flinch from violence and poverty and distress, but looks harder at it. Yet he seems to think about horror coolly only to watch it hotly. Henry Mayhew, whose reportage in *London Labour and the London Poor* (1861) is often compared to Orwell's writing about the poor, generally writes a notably detached prose. He goes around the London streets cataloging and recording deprivation, an enlightened anthropologist. But there is nothing detached about Orwell's diction. In *Down and Out* and *The Road to Wigan Pier*, the world of poverty is frequently described as "loathsome," "disgusting," "fetid," "squalid." In the Paris hotel where he works, there is "the warm reek of food" and "the red glare of a fire." He works alongside "a huge excitable Italian" and "a hairy, uncouth animal whom we called the Magyar." Back in England, tramping around the countryside with the homeless, he must share quarters in hostels with people who revolt him: "I shall never forget the reek of dirty feet . . . a stale, fetid stink . . . the passage was full of squalid, grey-shirted figures." In one doss-house, where the sheets "stank so horribly of sweat that I could not bear them near my nose," a man is lying in bed with his trousers wrapped around his head, "a thing which for some reason disgusted me very much." Orwell is woken next morning by a dim impression of some large brown thing coming towards me. I opened my eyes and saw that it was one of the sailor's feet, sticking out of bed close to my face. It was dark brown, quite dark brown like an Indian's, with dirt. The walls were leprous, and the sheets, three weeks from the wash, were almost raw umber colour.

Notice, as ever, the crafty use of suspense ("some large brown thing"), and then the diction—"like an Indian's"—that borrows from a nineteenth-century sensationalist like Wilkie Collins (a contemporary novelist like Ian McEwan has in turn learned quite a lot about narrative stealth and the control of disgust from Orwell).

Perhaps Orwell struck Said as dangerous because though politically didactic, he is rarely obviously sympathetic. On the contrary, he thrashes his subjects with attention. He punishes people with his own transferred masochism. In "How the Poor Die," what stays with the reader is the description of the administration of the mustard poultice:

> I learned later that watching a patient have a mustard poultice was a favourite pastime in the ward. These things are normally applied for a quarter of an hour and certainly they are funny enough if you don't happen to be the person inside. For the first five minutes the pain is severe, but you believe you can bear it. During the second five minutes this belief evaporates, but the poultice is buckled at the back and you can't get it off. This is the period the onlookers most enjoy.

First, there is the apparent coolness ("and certainly they are funny enough if you don't happen to be the person inside"). And then the heat—the leap to that last sentence, with its combination of Grand Guignol and unverifiable self-projection: How can he really know this? Isn't it actually the moment that Orwell might most enjoy as a spectator, even while hating it? Orwell says of Mr. Booker that like all men with dirty hands he handled food in a lingering way, but it is Orwell whose eye cannot stop lingering on those dirty hands. In *Down and Out*, he cannot suppress the relish with which he tells us how many times he has seen the nasty fat pink fingers of the chef touching steak. Then he joyfully drives it home: "Whenever one pays more than, say, ten francs for a dish of meat in Paris, one may be certain that it has been fingered in this manner . . . Roughly speaking, the more one pays for food, the more sweat and spittle one is obliged to eat with it." The effect is both sadistic and masochistic, because Orwell does not exempt himself from the punishment: it is understood that, at some point he, the Old Etonian, will be the diner, not the waiter; and indeed he seems, self-abnegatingly, to want to taste the sweat on the meat, as a salty political reminder. In a similar way, his rhetoric of disgust in *The Road to Wigan Pier* works so well because it involves us in his own difficult struggle to admire the working classes. If I can overcome my repulsion, he seems to say, then you can, too.

There is a long historical connection between revolution and Puritanism (with both a capital and lowercase *p*), and Orwell sings in that stainless choir. In Paris, he exults that all that separates the diners from the filth of the kitchen is a single door: "There sat the customers in all their splendour—and here, just a few feet away, we in our disgusting filth." He is like Jonathan Edwards, reminding his congregation that we are suspended over hell by "a slender thread" and that an angry God can cut it when it pleases him. Throughout the 1930s and early 1940s, as Orwell's radicalism grows, this politics of the slender thread becomes more pronounced. It provides one of the best passages in *Wigan*, when he reminds us that our comfortable existence aboveground is founded on what men do beneath, in hellish conditions:

> Whatever may be happening on the surface, the hacking and shovelling have got to continue without a pause. In order that Hitler may march the goosestep, that the Pope may denounce Bolshevism, that the cricket crowds may

assemble at Lord's, that the Nancy poets may scratch one another's backs, coal has got to be forthcoming.

And it is the same with empire—a stream of dividends "flows from the bodies of Indian coolies to the banking accounts of old ladies in Cheltenham."

II.

It has become a slightly easy commonplace to note that Orwell's radicalism was conservative. He was a Socialist artist but utterly antibohemian, a cosmopolitan who had worked in Paris and fought alongside Trotskyists in Spain but who was glad to get back home to lamb and mint sauce and "beer made with veritable hops." He wanted England to change and stay the same, and he became a great popular journalist in part because he was so good at defending the ordinary virtues of English life, as he saw them, against the menace of change; even when he is attacking something politically disagreeable—like the popular boys' comic *The Magnet*, featuring Billy Bunter, whose tales were set at a posh, Eton-like boarding school—he sounds as if he wants it to last forever. During the war, he wrote a weekly column for the left-wing *Tribune*, as well as squibs for *The Evening Standard*, in which he praised the solid English food he liked—Yorkshire pudding, kippers, Stilton ("I fancy that Stilton is the best cheese of its type in the world"); attacked women's makeup ("It is very unusual to meet a man who does not think painting your fingernails scarlet is a disgusting habit"); asked why people use foreign phrases when "perfectly good English ones exist"; and lamented the disappearance of the warming pan and the rise of the rubber hot-water bottle ("clammy, unsatisfying").

What makes his essays about Donald McGill's seaside postcards, and Dickens, and the decline of the English murder, and Billy Bunter so acute is that he was greatly talented at describing closed worlds, and adumbrating their conventions. If he pioneered what became cultural studies, it is because he could see that these worlds were both real (because they were produced by a living culture) and unreal (because they subsisted on their own peculiar codes). He transferred to the description of these extant fictional worlds precisely the talent he lacked as a novelist for nonexistent worlds; he needed a drystone wall already up, so that he could bring his mortar to it and lovingly fill in the gaps. And he did the same with the greatest closed world, English life, reading the country as if it were a place both real and fictional, with its own narrative conventions. This semifictional England, beautifully described in "The Lion and the Unicorn" and given body in his popular columns, was a rather shabby, stoical, anti-American, ideally classless place, devoted to small English pleasures like marmalade and suet pudding and fishing in country ponds, puritanical about large luxuries like the Ritz Hotel and Rolls-Royces, and suspicious of modern conveniences like aspirins, plate glass, shiny American apples, cars, and radios. There is an undoubted comedy in Orwell's never having realized that what was obviously utopia to him might strike at least half the population as a chaste nightmare.

The biggest convention in this semifictional world is the working class. In *The Road to Wigan Pier*, Orwell says that he knows too much about working-class life to idealize it, and then proceeds to idealize it, like some Victorian genre painter. In the best kind of proletarian home, he says, "you breathe a warm, decent, deeply human atmosphere," and a workingman has a better chance of being happy than an "educated" one. He paints a nice picture: "Especially on winter evenings after tea, when the fire glows in the open range and dances mirrored in the steel fender, when Father, in shirtsleeves, sits in the rocking chair at one side reading the racing finals, and Mother sits on the other with her sewing, and the children are happy with a pen'orth of mint humbugs, and the dog lolls roasting himself on the rag mat." What will that scene be like in two hundred years, he asks, in that utopia where there is no manual labor, and everyone is "educated"? There will be no coal fire, he answers, and no horse racing, and the furniture will be made of rubber, glass, and steel.

Like many radicals, Orwell has strong Rousseauian tendencies: the simpler, apparently more organic life of the countryside seemed a tempting birdsong compared to London's mechanized squawks. He could see that, with or without a revolution, postwar British society would be very different from the bucolic pre-1914 world in which he grew up, and uneasily he returns repeatedly to what lies ahead. For millions of people, he laments, the sound of the radio is more normal than the sound of birds. Modern life should be simpler and harder, he argues, not softer and more complex, and in a healthy world "there would be no demand for tinned foods, aspirins, gramophones, gaspipe chairs, machine guns, daily newspapers, telephones, motor-cars, etc. etc." Note that "etc."—there speaks the puritan, reserving the right to stretch his prohibitions, at cranky whim. In his novel *Coming Up for Air* (1939), the hero returns to the country town he remembers from childhood (based on Orwell's own childhood memories of the Thames Valley) to find that it has become an overdeveloped horror, full of flimsy new houses and orbital roads; it looks just like "those new towns that have suddenly swelled up like balloons in the last few years, Hayes, Slough, Dagenham . . . That kind of chilliness, the bright red brick everywhere, the temporary-looking shop windows full of cut-price chocolates and radio parts." The same new towns recur in "The Lion and the Unicorn," when Orwell admits that life has improved for the working classes since 1918, and that people of an "indeterminate social class" have emerged, in new towns and suburbs around London, places like "Slough, Dagenham, Barnet, Letchworth, Hayes." He acknowledges that this is the future; indeed, he says that this puzzling nonclass will provide the "directing brains" for the postwar Socialist revolution. But he cannot really admire these people:

> It is a rather restless, cultureless life, centring round tinned food, *Picture Post*, the radio and the internal combustion engine . . . To that civilisation belong the people who are most at home in and most definitely *of* the modern world,

the technicians and the higher-paid skilled workers, the air-
men and their mechanics, the radio experts, film producers,
popular journalists and industrial chemists.

Lest one is in any doubt as to what Orwell feels about this "indeterminate class," it is just such people who, in *1984*, have emerged after the war, and who now run the totalitarian apparatus: "The new
aristocracy was made up for the most part of bureaucrats, scientists,
technicians, trade-union organizers . . . These people, whose origins lay in the salaried middle class and the upper grades of the
working class, had been shaped and brought together by the barren
world of monopoly industry and centralized government."

"Monopoly industry and centralized government" sounds pretty
much like capitalism and socialism combined. And perhaps Orwell
had, by the late 1940s, soured on the latter as well as the former. On
the one hand, as Orwell saw it, capitalism produced unemployment
and monopoly and injustice (i.e., England in the 1920s and 1930s);
on the other hand, Socialist collectivism produced totalitarianism
and barren machine-progress (i.e., Soviet Russia). And both political economies seemed to point, willy-nilly, to the loathsome postwar
world of plate glass and industrial chemists and rubber hot-water
bottles. After the war, when Orwell was writing his two most famous
books, he remained faithful to an *ideal* English revolution, while
losing faith in actual socialism because, for all his acute powers of political prophecy, and his general approval of what the Labour Party
stood for, he could not envisage a *realistic* English postwar future.
(In *1984*, when Winston and Julia meet for their first, illicit love-
making, they travel outside soulless London into the unspoiled rural world that Orwell grew up in.)

III.

I sat up when I encountered Orwell's two references to the East
London suburb of Dagenham, because that was where my father

was born, in 1928, into exactly the "indeterminate class" that Orwell cannot bring himself to admire. His father, my grandfather, ended up as a quality-control checker at the Ford factory that came to Dagenham in 1931, and my father's passage out of and up from that rather "cultureless" world was the traditional one for bright working-class boys: he went to the Royal Liberty Grammar School, in Essex, founded in 1921 by the state, to aid boys like him (the drummer Ginger Baker is the best-known alumnus), and then Queen Mary College, at London University, a product of late-Victorian charity, established in the East End to educate workingmen. He was good at science and went on to become a professor of zoology. (An equivalent social movement occurred in America, with the passage of the GI Bill of 1944.) Theoretically, Orwell had to approve of men like my father; practically, he could not, and in *The Road to Wigan Pier*, in perhaps the most scandalous paragraph he ever wrote, he announces that the working-class attitude to education is much sounder than the middle class's—they see through the nonsense of education, "and reject it by a healthy instinct," and sensibly want to leave school as soon as possible. The working-class boy "wants to be doing real work, not wasting his time on ridiculous rubbish like history and geography." He should be bringing home a pound a week for his parents, not stuffing himself into silly uniforms and being caned for neglecting his homework.

"It's a good British feeling to try and raise your family a little," says Mr. Vincy in *Middlemarch*. George Eliot, the estate manager's daughter who ended up living in a grand house on Cheyne Walk, in Chelsea, understood that "good British feeling." But Orwell was suspicious of this indeterminate, petit bourgeois class, because it wanted to change itself first, and society second, if at all. Margaret Thatcher, born in 1925 to a small-town shopkeeper, is the model of this kind of conservative class mobility. Orwell suspected Dickens of the same impulse, noting with displeasure that the novelist sent his eldest son to Eton. Dickens belonged, mentally, to the small urban bourgeoisie, a class that was just out for itself. That is why the great

Dickens novels want to change things, but in fact leave everything in place. "However much Dickens may admire the working classes, he does not wish to resemble them." Orwell means this as a judgment against Dickens. But it is unwittingly comic. Why on earth should Dickens have wanted to resemble the working classes? Why would anyone want to resemble the working classes, least of all the working classes themselves? But Orwell did—at least, somewhat. The upper-class masochist lived frugally, dressed down, and for most of his life, until *Animal Farm* and *1984*, earned very little. His sister said after his death that the kind of person he most admired was a working-class mother of ten children. But if the problem with wanting to get out of the working class is that someone is always left behind, then the problem with "admiring" the working class is that admiration doesn't, on its own, help anyone to get out of it at all. (Tellingly, Orwell reported vividly on extreme poverty, but never reported as vividly on the kind of working-class life he was content to idealize.)

So the question that hangs over Orwell is the one that always hangs over so many well-heeled revolutionaries: did he want to level up society or level it down? The evidence points to the latter. The real struggle for this puritan masochist, the one that was personal— the one that was, ironically enough, *inherited*—was the struggle to obliterate privilege, and thus, in some sense, to obliterate himself. This was, at bottom, a religious impulse, and was not always politically coherent. In *Down and Out in Paris and London*, he pauses to consider the plight of the *plongeur*, working for hours and hours in hotels, so that wealthier people can stay in them. How is this bad situation to be mitigated? Well, says Orwell, hotels are just needless luxuries, so if people stopped going to them, there would be less hard work to do. "Nearly everyone hates hotels. Some restaurants are better than others, but it is impossible to get as good a meal in a restaurant as one can get, for the same expense, in a private house." As Larkin puts it in a poem, useful to get *that* learned. There is a similarly telling moment in Orwell's review of Hayek's *The Road to*

Serfdom. There was much in the book to agree with, he said. (It was also admired by the young Margaret Thatcher.) But Hayek's faith in capitalist competition was overzealous: "The trouble with competitions is that somebody wins them." Not, you notice, that somebody loses them—which would mean raising those people up. Somebody wins them, and that cannot be allowed.

It is hardly fair to claim that Orwell did not earnestly long for the emancipation of the working classes; of course he did. But for all his longing to abolish class distinctions, he could barely credit actual class mobility. For although it may be true that the upwardly mobile working classes do not want fundamentally to change society, their very ascension does change it. (If Orwell had taken any interest in Scotland, he would have seen a relatively socially dynamic culture propelled by a serious stake in education.) Actual class mobility was probably unappealing to Orwell—unconsciously, of course—because he longed for a mystical revolution, a revolution in which England changed and stayed the same; and what seems to have guaranteed England's preservation for him was the idea of a static, semifictional working-class world of decency and good-tempered bus conductors and bad teeth. Change that, and you change England. Yet how can you have revolution and not change that? Thus Orwell stresses, throughout his work, "equality of sacrifice" rather than equality of benefit. The former could be controlled, indeed is control itself; the latter might lead to the Ritz and the Rolls-Royce.

Orwell feared what he most desired: the future. But it is easy to gloat over Orwell's contradictions—to point out that he wrote so well about the drabness and horror of totalitarianism because he himself had a tendency to drab omnipotence; or that the great proponent of urban collectivity liked rural isolation (he wrote *1984* on the Hebridean island of Jura); or more simply, that the hater of private schools put his adopted son down for Westminster, one of the grandest London academies. So Orwell was contradictory: contradictions are what make writers interesting; consistency is for cooking. Instead, one is gratefully struck by how prescient Orwell was, by how much he got right. He was right about how capitalism had failed British society:

subsequent postwar governments did indeed nationalize many of the major industries and utilities (though thankfully, Orwell did not live long enough to see many of them fail). He was right about education: although the private schools kept their autonomy, Oxford and Cambridge opened themselves up to state-aided students, exactly as Orwell had demanded in 1941, and the Butler Act of 1944 universalized free secondary-school education. He was right about colonialism (that he disliked Gandhi seems only to strengthen Orwell's position, by making it disinterested); right about totalitarianism. If his novelistic imagining of totalitarian horror now looks a bit dated, it is partly because his fiction provided the dusty epitaph on a dustier tombstone that he himself helped to carve; and anyway, his coinages, like "Doublethink" and "Newspeak" and "Big Brother," now live an unexpectedly acute second life in the supposedly free West: to see Fox News go after President Obama or Bill Ayers for days on end is to think, simply, "Hate Week."

And Orwell's revolutionary mysticism turned out to be curiously precise: he was right not in spite of, but because of his contradictions. Although an Orwellian revolution never quite came about, an Orwellian victory did. In part, Hitler was defeated by the exercise of a peculiarly English—peculiarly Orwellian—combination of collectivity and individualism. (He marveled, in the summer of 1945, that Britain had won the war without becoming either Socialist or Fascist, and with civil liberties almost intact). This combination of conservatism and radicalism, of political sleepiness and insomnia, this centuries-long brotherhood of gamekeeper and poacher, which Orwell called "the English genius," was also Orwell's genius, finding in English life its own ideological brotherhood. For good and ill, those English contradictions have lasted. If Orwell hammered so noisily at privilege that at times he couldn't hear the working classes eagerly knocking at the door to be admitted, it is because he knew the immense size of the obstacle they would face. To level an Orwellian emphasis, what is remarkable about British society today is not how much bigger the middle class is, but how little the upper classes have given up. The working classes got richer, but the rich got much richer. Britain has now elected its nineteenth Old Etonian prime minister—a Conservative, of course. The Orwell who wrote about the playing fields of Eton would be shocked to discover that, for all the transformations Britain has undergone, the lofty old school is still there, much as it always was, educating the upper classes to govern the country, wreck the City, and have lovely house parties.

"UNFATHOMABLE!"
(MIKHAIL LERMONTOV)

When Samuel Johnson, traveling in the Highlands with James Boswell, reaches Loch Ness, he is impressed by the massiveness of the landscape. The heavy order of his prose is briefly disarrayed. On his right, there are high and steep rocks, and on his left, the deep water laps against the bank in "gentle agitation." The rocks are "towering in horrid nakedness." Occasionally, he sees a little cornfield, which only serves "to impress more strongly the general barrenness." As if to silence these romantic terrors, Johnson plays the calm eighteenth-century surveyor, and in portly periods begins an inquiry into the loch's dimensions:

> Lough Ness is about twenty-four miles long, and from one mile to two miles broad. It is remarkable that Boethius, in his description of Scotland, gives it twelve miles of breadth. When historians or geographers exhibit false accounts of places far distant, they may be forgiven, because they can tell but what they are told . . . but Boethius lived at no great distance; if he never saw the lake, he must have been very incurious, and if he had seen it, his veracity yielded to very slight temptations.

Apparently unable to banish his dread fascination, Johnson can only fixate on the terrible depth of the loch, and what he takes to be the exaggerations of the natives: "We were told, that it is in some places a hundred and forty fathoms deep, a profundity scarcely credible, and which probably those that relate it have never sounded." He scolds the Scots for their lack of knowledge, but the real interest of the passage is Dr. Johnson's obscure knowledge of himself. The Augustan rationalist is pierced by romantic awe, but appears unwilling to admit such "agitation"; and even as he strives to plunge into the nice shallows of data, he is really plunging, against his will, into the loch's transfixing deeps. A good thing he didn't know anything about the resident monster.

Mikhail Lermontov's novel, *A Hero of Our Time*, which first appeared in 1839, opens in a situation and a landscape not dissimilar from Samuel Johnson's. A narrator is traveling through the Caucasus; he explains that he is not a novelist but a travel writer, making notes. For a Russian soldier, the Caucasus was the warm, southern equivalent of Sir Walter Scott's Highlands: an Edward Waverley from Moscow or St. Petersburg might expect adventure, romance, intrigue, death. The mountains of the region were fabled (Noah's Ark was supposed to have passed through the twin peaks of Mount Elbrus). Beyond the natural border of the River Terek was an alluring and dangerous landscape, where Ossetians, Georgians, Tatars, and Chechens harried Russian soldiers and travelers, or offered uncertain alliances. Popular Russian literature delivered cheap bouquets of the same romantic motifs—the rivers, rocks, and chasms, the dark-eyed Circassian girls, the Cossack horsemen. (A hundred years after Lermontov, this *caucasica* was still desirable to the writer Lev Nussimbaum, a Jew from Tiflis who reinvented himself as the Muslim author Kurban Said.)

The narrator of *A Hero of Our Time* seems to have been seduced by this southern Orientalism. "What a glorious place, this valley! On every side there are unassailable mountains and reddish promontories, high with green ivy and crowned with clumps of plane trees." (I am quoting from Natasha Randall's translation.) He marvels at the purity of the mountain air, and the welcome sense of withdrawing from the world and being born anew. But like Dr. Johnson,

Lermontov's narrator seems as alarmed as he is delighted by the landscape. He refers repeatedly to the height of the "somber, mysterious precipices" and the bewildering depth of the valleys: "The horses fell from time to time; a deep fissure gaped to our left in which a stream flowed downhill . . . The wind, digging itself into the ravine, bellowed and whistled like a Nightingale-Robber." He soon meets an old Caucasus hand, a staff captain called Maxim Maximych, who has been in Chechnya for a decade, and warns his new friend about the mysterious ways of the region's inhabitants. "See, nothing is visible here," he tells him, "only mist and snow, and you have to watch or we'll fall into an abyss or get lodged in a hole . . . Such is Asia! Whether its people or its rivers, you can't count on anything in any way!"

Maxim Maximych begins a ravishing tale about a young officer he met five years ago, Grigory Alexandrovich Pechorin, who is now dead. This Pechorin, transferred from Russia, seems to have had a demonic energy, and a changeable temperament: he could spend all day hunting wild boar, yet another time might sit in his room, complaining of the cold and shivering. The year he spent at Maxim Maximych's fort, near the Terek River, was eventful. A local Tatar prince had a daughter, Bela, whose beauty impressed Pechorin. At a party, she casts flirtatious looks at him and sings him a love song. Meanwhile, Pechorin hears that the same prince's young son, Azamat, is desperate to acquire the exquisite horse of a local bandit called Kazbich. For three weeks, Pechorin teases Azamat about his horse lust, singing the animal's praises and watching Azamat gradually pale and wither, "as happens to characters when love strikes in a novel." Pechorin offers Azamat a challenge: if Azamat can deliver his sister to Pechorin, he will steal the horse for Azamat. The exchange is effected: Azamat receives Kazbich's horse, and Pechorin takes Bela captive in the Russian fort, installing her as his wife in his quarters. What did Bela's father, the Tatar prince, do about it? asks the narrator. Kazbich eventually killed him, convinced that the prince had arranged the horse's theft for his son. Kazbich was compensating himself for the loss of his horse, says the narrator. "Of

course, in their terms, he was absolutely right," says Maxim Maximych, which prompts the narrator to the following complacent
eulogy:

> I couldn't help but be struck by the Russian's ability to
> adapt to the customs of the people among whom he finds
> himself living. I don't know if this characteristic of mind
> deserves reprimand or praise, but it does prove his incred-
> ible flexibility and the presence of that clear common sense,
> which forgives evil where it seems unavoidable, or impos-
> sible to destroy.

About the "evil" or lack of "common sense" of the Russian abductor,
Pechorin, the staff captain has nothing to say, except to offer help-
less reverence: "That's what sort of person he was—unfathomable!"
He completes his story by telling us how Kazbich managed finally
to kidnap Bela from Pechorin, how Pechorin and Maxim Maximych
gave chase, how Kazbich stabbed Bela and escaped, and how Bela
died at the fort two days later. But why did Kazbich want to take
Bela? asks the narrator. "These Circassians," says Maxim Maximych,
"are notoriously thieving folk. If anything is lying around, they can't
help but pinch it. Even if they don't need it, they'll steal it anyway."

So ends the first, tremendous section of *A Hero of Our Time*—
with Pechorin, our hero, still no more than a bright smudge on the
page. The reader is quickly aware of two qualities: the twenty-five-
year-old Lermontov is a fabulously gifted storyteller (Pechorin kid-
naps us, as well as Bela) and an extremely sophisticated ironist.
Both Dr. Johnson and Lermontov are writing allegories about the
unfathomable—about readability—but while one is fatly flummoxed
and unknowing, the other is sarcastically omniscient. Johnson re-
presses his fear of the wild landscape and transfers it to questions of
taxonomic accuracy; yet the fear returns in the dread profundity of
Loch Ness. Lermontov, by contrast, deliberately makes his traveler
one of the novel's unreliable narrators, and awards him something

like Johnson's contradictory gestures of control and anxiety. This narrator, and especially the second storyteller, Maxim Maximych, constantly demonize the unpredictable otherness of the Caucasian natives, while passing off as almost familiar the unpredictable otherness of Pechorin. The motives of a bandit like Kazbich are seen as illogical and malevolent, or logical only within a foreign system of honor and vengeance ("Of course, in their terms, he was absolutely right"), while the motives of a Pechorin may be unknowable but are gloriously beyond judgment: "That's what sort of person he was—unfathomable!" And as in Johnson's writing, but this time wittingly, the craggy landscape is summoned to provide its own version of unfathomability, as an analog to the romantic mysteriousness of the novel's hero—later in the book, a group of people will walk to a local chasm, possibly an extinguished crater. In this novel, the ravines are as complex as stories: "The ravines, full of mist and silence, diverge like branches in all directions." A pointless, deadly duel will be fought on a precipice overhanging a menacing gully.

We see a good deal more of Pechorin, this extinguished volcano, but he becomes no less unfathomable, partly because Lermontov cleverly fractures his portrait—the first two sections are narrated by the nameless traveler (and by the blunter second narrator, Maxim Maximych); the last three sections of the novel are narrated by Pechorin, whose diaries have fallen into the hands of Maxim Maximych and are donated to the traveler. There is not a reliable storyteller among them. In varying degrees of sophistication, all three men are victims of romantic grandiosity; a deliberate literariness infests the book, as it does *Eugene Onegin*. Characters take their cues from romantic fashions, and from writers like Scott, Pushkin, Byron, Rousseau, and Marlinsky (the most popular Russian novelist of the 1830s, and a producer of Caucasian adventures). This is how the narrator first sees Pechorin, on our behalf:

> He was of medium height and well-proportioned; his slim waist and broad shoulders indicated a strong physique . . .

His dusty velvet frock coat, fastened only by its two lowest
buttons, allowed a view of his blindingly white linen, indi-
cating the habits of a proper gentleman . . . His gait was
careless and lazy, but I noticed that he didn't swing his
arms—a clear signal of a certain secretiveness of character.
However, these are my own comments, based on my own
observations, and I absolutely do not want to make you take
them on blind faith. When he lowered himself onto the
bench, his straight figure bent as though there wasn't a
bone in his back. He sat the way Balzac's thirty-year-old
coquette would sit, on a chair stuffed with down, after an
exhausting ball . . . His skin had a sort of feminine delicacy
to it; he had blond hair, wavy in nature, which outlined his
pale, noble brow so picturesquely . . . However blond his
hair was, his whiskers and eyebrows were black—the mark
of breeding in a person. To complete the portrait, I will tell
you he had a slightly upturned nose.

So Pechorin, in this account, is both strongly male and slightly effeminate, bold and weak, fair and dark, finely dressed yet dusty from
travel: he smarts into contradiction. On the one hand, the narrator
is a confident nineteenth-century analyst, conventionally reading the
body as a moral map: a man who does not swing his arms is obviously
secretive. On the other, he does not want us to set any store by such
observations! He is also frank about his role as a maker who touches
things up: he is obviously painting a romantic "portrait."

The same narrator praises the candor of Pechorin's diaries—
"this man who so relentlessly displayed his personal weakness and
defects for all to see"—comparing them favorably, in their nakedness, with Rousseau's more wary *Confessions*, which were written
to excite sympathy. Enthrallingly, it does at first seem that Pechorin will confess a good deal. He is a force of pure negation and
disdain—easily bored, he tells us, with an intense desire to contradict: "I have a congenital desire to contradict; my whole life is merely
a chain of sad and unsuccessful contradictions to heart and mind.

When faced with enthusiasm, I am seized by a midwinter freeze."
He arrives at Pyatigorsk, a Caucasian spa town and resort, which
becomes his perfect project, full of mediocrities in search of cheap
excitement. At parties, he affects a complete lack of interest: "She
sang: her voice was not bad, but she sings badly . . . though I wasn't
listening." He has a sharp, disillusioned eye: "I stood behind one fat
lady . . . The biggest wart on her neck was covered by the clasp of
her necklace."

In the spa town, Pechorin befriends a like-minded doctor,
called Werner. The two men, says Pechorin with self-satisfaction,
share a cold egotism: "Sad things are funny to us. Funny things are
sad to us. And in general, to tell the truth, we are indifferent to everything apart from our selves." Pechorin delights in destroying the
weak illusions of this society. All around him, people are manipu-
lating one another but not admitting to it; at least he does so in the
open. "People! They are all the same: they know all the bad aspects
to a deed in advance, and they help you, advise you, even approve of
it, seeing no other way is possible—and then they wash their hands
of it and turn away with indignation from the person who had the
courage to take the whole burden of responsibility onto himself."

Pechorin especially disdains a fellow soldier, Grushnitsky, who
strikes romantic airs, wears a heavy soldier's greatcoat ("a particular
kind of dandyism"), and has already fallen in love with one of the
spa's visitors, the young Princess Mary, the daughter of Princess
Ligovsky. Grushnitsky is a victim of romantic fanaticism, thinks
Pechorin: "His goal is to be the hero of a novel." Before his departure for the Caucausus, says Pechorin sneeringly, Grushnitsky was
probably trying to impress some pretty girl in his village by saying
he was going not just to serve in the army but was "in search of
death." Pechorin observes Grushnitsky's feeble wooing of Princess
Mary and sets himself the task of destroying both players in this
silly romantic love story. The plot is a society version of Pechorin's
abduction of Bela: he must weaken the young man, so that the young
woman is given up. First, Pechorin deliberately alienates Princess Mary by acting insolently in her presence. Then, once he has

secured her angry interest, he switches sides and courts her. Far more attractive and erotically confident than Grushnitsky, he finds it easy to supplant his rival. Finally, just as Princess Mary is his to conquer, Pechorin withdraws his affection, leaving his female victim grief-stricken and bewildered, and his male victim vengeful. The two men eventually fight a duel, one even more pointless than Lensky's and Onegin's fatal dance; Pechorin kills Grushnitsky.

Dostoevsky's great passion for Pushkin seems odd—they are such different writers—until one considers that, literary nationalism aside, what he probably liked about *Eugene Onegin* was its utter absence of rational motive. There is no good reason for Onegin to reject Tatiana, and no good reason for him to flirt with Olga, and no good reason for him to kill Lensky, nor to fall in love, at the end, with Tatiana. The great absences of the poem allowed Dostoevsky, one surmises, to project his own complicated system of egotism and abasement. Pushkin used the brevity of narrative verse to enforce this motivational opacity; Lermontov, enormously influenced by Pushkin, but working in a more capacious and explanatory form, deliberately excised information about his hero. He had originally intended to tell his readers that Pechorin was in the Caucasus as a punishment for fighting a duel, but erased a helpful sentence to this effect from his draft. Pechorin disappears from the narrative as mysteriously as he arrives. The narrator offhandedly informs us, "I learned not long ago that Pechorin had died upon returning from Persia." Again, Lermontov abbreviated what had originally been a description of Pechorin's death in a duel.

Mikhail Lermontov is almost as opaque as Pechorin. He seems to have worked hard at making his brief life a furious enigma, written up by Lermontov. He was born in Moscow, in 1814, into a wealthy and well-connected family. But his mother died when he was three, so his maternal grandmother raised the boy. She had conventional expectations, and her grandson was pushed through the respectable portals of privilege: the Noble Pension school in Moscow, the Junker school in St. Petersburg (for officer cadets), the Life Guards Hussars. But Lermontov was unruly. He became famous for a furi-

ous poem he wrote on the death of Pushkin, in 1837, which bitterly
attacked Pushkin's duelist, Georges d'Anthès. The tsar punished
Lermontov by sending him to a regiment in the Caucasus—a nicely
myopic decision, since the Caucasus had become something of a
tour of duty for radicals: during this happy exile he spent time with
the critic Vissarion Belinsky, and with Dr. Nicholas Maier, a liberal
who was the model for Dr. Werner in *A Hero of Our Time*.

   This was the first of three such punitive sentences. He returned
to St. Petersburg in 1838, where he wrote *A Hero of Our Time* and
his long poem *The Demon*, but was sent back to the Caucasus in
early 1840, after failing to report a duel with the son of the French
ambassador. Once there, he fought with reckless bravery, taking
part in expeditions into Chechnya and Daghestan (his unit was in
search of the Chechen leader Shamil, whose equally notorious lieu-
tenant, Hadji Murad, became the hero of Tolstoy's late novella). He
was granted leave at the beginning of 1841, but in April was ordered
back to the Caucasus, the tsar apparently irritated by the freedom
of Lermontov's movements in Chechnya. On the way back, he
stopped at Pyatigorsk, "our Caucasian Monaco," where, he wrote,
"we are inflamed by women by day and by bed bugs at night." Here
he provoked a man named Martinov, a contemporary he had known
since childhood but who had gone native in the south, wearing kaf-
tans and shaving his head. Lermontov mocked him with tags like
"Monsieur Sauvage Homme." They fought a duel on July 15. Several
accounts suggest that Lermontov's Pechorin-like look of contempt,
and his refusal to fire, goaded Martinov to action. Lermontov was
fatally shot.

   Lermontov's contemporaries found him slippery. His poems
were politically radical—Herzen was very impressed with the poem
"Duma," which struck the proper radical lament: "Sadly I contem-
plate our generation: / Its future is either empty or dark." But its
author seemed to lack political seriousness. He was more interested
in Dada-like pranks and hoaxes than in ideological action—more
Dolokhov, the duelist in *War and Peace*, than Levin. Laurence Kelly,
one of Lermontov's biographers, mentions an incident in which he

appeared on a parade ground with a toy sword, to irritate his commanding officer; and another in which he announced to a group of friends that he would read from a new novel. The reading, he declared, would take four hours. Thirty people turned up, rooms were prepared, doors sealed. Lermontov read for just fifteen minutes— there was no large novel. To provoke one baseless duel seems careless; to provoke two in quick succession seems almost careful, as if the second were morbidly designed to correct the luck of the first. Lermontov lived hurriedly, a bit like the German warrior described by Tacitus, who "thinks it tame and spiritless to accumulate slowly by the sweat of his brow what can be got quickly with the loss of a little blood." He revered Pushkin, and perhaps inherited Pushkin's romantic tendency to see his life as a fatal fragment. He seems always to have been waiting for some kind of defeat or reversal. He wrote to a friend that he loathed society, and went to parties and balls only because the experience would arm him with weapons for use against society when it finally turned against *him*.

So Lermontov may well have been describing himself when he created Pechorin, as Turgenev thought, but this doesn't really get us anywhere. Pechorin, as enigmatic as Lermontov, has been filled with meaning by influential readers. For nineteenth-century radicals, like Belinsky, Pechorin's diappointed nihilism was symptomatic of the drifting despair of a generation that had seen the failure of the December 1825 mutiny against Tsar Nicholas I—whose organizers, by and large liberal Petersburg aristocrats, were efficiently punished, some with death, others with exile to Siberia (from where some were later given the chance to transfer to the Caucasus). Alexander Herzen, in his memoirs, talks about the moral "stagnation that followed the crisis of 1825."

Pechorin, both dehumanized and anguished, can be easily smoothed into this analysis. Less ideologically, others have read Pechorin as the first "superfluous man," a disaffected romantic who sees through everything but who is too aimless and enervated to turn his radical eyesight into radical action; or as a precursor of Flaubert's erotic flâneur, Frédéric Moreau, or of Dostoevsky's more savagely alienated "underground man." Conservative readers excoriated what the radicals most liked, and attacked Pechorin for his "Western" individualism and egocentrism. The tsar read the book in 1840 and thought it full of the "despicable exaggerated characters that one finds in fashionable foreign novels." He had hoped that the old captain, Maxim Maximych, would be the true "hero of our time."

Insofar as Pechorin is now a canonical nineteenth-century romantic antihero, with fragments of Mr. Darcy, Julien Sorel, and Eugene Onegin lodged in him, probably all these different readings have intermittent validity. What is most striking nowadays is the way in which Lermontov cunningly forecloses the possibility of terminal readings. Pechorin is constantly creating himself; he is an act of provisional theater. He is a great analyst of his own twisted motives, but his analysis rarely succeeds in casting any illumination:

> Can it be that my single purpose on this earth is to destroy the hopes of others? Since I have been living and breathing, fate has somehow always led me into the dramatic climaxes of others' lives, as if without me no one would be able to die, or to come to despair! I have been the necessary character of the fifth act; I have played the sorry role of executioner or traitor involuntarily . . . Was I appointed the author of bourgeois tragedies and family novels . . . How could I know?

The man who mocks Grushnitsky for wanting to be the hero of a novel often sees his own role in literary terms—as a novelistic character, or better still, as a controlling author. He boasts of how his greatest pleasure is "to subject everyone around me to my will," but almost in the same breath presents himself as no more than fate's grim servant. He sees through the romantic posturing of Grushnitsky, and his dandyish greatcoat, but praises his own romantic dandyism: "I have actually been told that on horseback, in Circassian costume, I look more Kabardin than most Kabardins. And when it comes to this noble battle attire, I am a perfect dandy."

Of course, if it were just a matter of sorting through Pechorin's most flagrant contradictions, his unreadability would turn out to be legible, just ironically so. But Pechorin is unfathomable because he is really a romantic parodist. He mocks Grushnitsky's dandyism, and then reserves the right to flaunt his own dandyism, because Grushnitsky believes in it while Pechorin does not. He ridicules the idea of Grushnitsky confessing to some village girl that he is going to the Caucasus to seek death, but later in the novel stages his own knowing and bogus "confession," in which he makes Princess Mary cry by prattling on about how difficult his childhood was, and the "despair" that has lodged in his chest. In the course of this piece of theater, it should be noted, Pechorin also thumbs his nose at the earnest and sympathetic political readings of critics like Belinsky and Herzen: "And then despair was born in my breast," he tells Princess Mary, "and not the kind of despair that can be cured by the bullet of a pistol, but a cold, impotent despair, masked by politeness and a good-natured smile. I became a moral cripple: one half of my soul didn't exist; it had dried out, evaporated, died." (Tellingly, on becoming a soldier, Lermontov himself also wrote to a woman, Maria Lopukhina, that he had wanted a literary career but was now becoming "a warrior." Perhaps, he swaggered in his letter, this would be the shortest way to end his life.)

Just before his duel, Pechorin's second asks him if there is someone for whom he would like to leave a memento. His reply is contemptuous: he declares that he has got beyond the romantic habit of those who pronounce the names of their beloved, and bequeath to their friends a lock of their pomaded or unpomaded hair. But this war against romantic affectation is itself affected and romantic, and is anyway being prosecuted amid the antique chivalric machinery of the duel. Parody, as Dostoevsky acutely understood, is an act of admiration as much as of disdain, and perhaps the best way of comprehending Pechorin's distorted histrionics is by way of Dostoevsky's dialectic of assertion and abasement. Dostoevsky persistently suggests that we dislike people—or elements of society—precisely because we so admire them. We often blame people because their blamelessness reminds us of our own sins; we must make them more like us. The old Karamazov patriarch, Fyodor Pavlovich, remembers being asked once why he so hated a certain neighbor, to which he had replied: "He never did anything to me, it's true, but I once played a most shameless nasty trick on him, and the moment I did it, I immediately hated him for it."

Seen in this light, Pechorin is much less powerful than he makes himself out to be, constantly offloading onto others his own weaknesses. In a subtle reading of the novel, A.D.P. Briggs and Andrew Barratt point out that Pechorin is perhaps in love with Princess Mary and desperate to control this unwanted weakness. Near the end of the book he tells Mary that he is leaving town. She pales and sickens before him, and Pechorin says, in an aside to the reader: "This was becoming unbearable—in a minute I would fall to her feet." Pechorin shares Grushnitsky's relentless denigration of women, who are charged by both men (rather as the narrator accuses the Caucasus natives) with being changeable, inconstant, opaque—these being precisely the failings of Pechorin. The novel is, then, a deep exercise in unreliable narration, in which we are encouraged by Lermontov to contest *everything* Pechorin says, and almost to invert the meaning of his statements—his hatred as a kind of love, his strength as really a kind of weakness, his "maleness" as really "femaleness," and so on. This frailty is entirely missed in the playwright Neil LaBute's oafish foreword to the Penguin edition, which stupidly mimics Pechorin's self-deceiving swagger and trumpets male strength: "Writing is not for pussies," declares LaBute. "Anyone who creates a Pechorin doesn't appear to worry much about what society thinks of him . . . Lermontov was shot in a duel . . . Lermontov, like his literary creation before him, took it like a man and said yes."

But Pechorin surely cares not too little but too much about society. He is not to be trusted when he tells Dr. Werner that he is indifferent to everything other than himself: the spider bridegroom drapes society in his web and needs it to survive. In many ways a traditional machinating eighteenth-century French hero, Pechorin looks at once backward to the hero of *Les Liaisons dangereuses* and forward to the predatory, rather eighteenth-century Gilbert Osmond (who is praised by Madame Merle as "unfathomable"). At the same time, his anxious self-deceptions and labile confessions seem modern, too, and prefigure the narrator of Knut Hamsun's *Hunger*, and the unreliable narrator of Thomas Bernhard's great monologue, *The Loser*, whose admiration for his pianist friend, and for the pianist Glenn Gould, is slowly revealed to hide a murderously competitive hatred of both men. Writing may not be for pussies, but writing a swaggering diary about one's supposedly tremendous exploits in a dusty little spa town may well be for pussies—especially when the pussy considers himself a bit of a lion.

THOMAS HARDY

What is this? "Two miles behind it a jet of white steam was travelling from the left to the right of the picture." It is a train, viewed across a valley, in *Jude the Obscure* (1895), and it is the only sentence offered there about this train. Flaubert is always described as the great cinematic novelist, the great novelist of detail, and indeed Flaubert has his own described train steam, too—similarly seen, in *L'Éducation sentimentale*, across fields, but "stretched out in a horizontal line, like a gigantic ostrich feather whose tip kept blowing away." Where Flaubert turns his train steam into writing, flourishing his fine literary simile, Hardy, flirting with the pictorially gnomic, seems to want to resist that conversion; Hardy would like to preserve the visuality of the detail.

Hardy was supremely a man "who used to notice such things," as he describes himself in his poem "Afterwards." Most of his readers thrill to the precision with which he captures the world: the "scarlet handful of fire" in the grate of Gabriel Oak's hut in *Far from the Madding Crowd* (1874), or Bathsheba, in the same book, watching her horses drinking, "the water dribbling from their lips in silver threads." In *The Return of the Native* (1878), the opening of a door during a rainstorm, at night, is described like this: "Thomasin . . . began to discern through the rain a faint blotted radiance, which presently assumed the oblong form of an open door."

But Hardy is at his best when he both sees and feels, when he uses his almost eerie tactility, an animistic ability to enter other things and animals and humans and live their lives. In his literary notebook, he copied out sentences from G. K. Chesterton's book about Robert Browning, published in 1903. Chesterton had written about "the terrible importance of detail" that apparently possessed Browning in an almost demonic way:

> Any room that he was sitting in glared at him with innumerable eyes & mouths gaping with a story . . . If he looked at a porcelain vase, or an old hat, a cabbage, or a puppy at play, each began to be bewitched . . . the vase to send up a smoke of thoughts & shapes; the hat to produce souls as a conjuror's hat produces rabbits.

Hardy comments: "This is true of all poets—not especially of Browning," and double underlines his last four words. The Hardy also possessed by "the terrible importance of detail" is the writer who is not embarrassed to write the scene in which the yearning Jude Fawley lifts his face to the winds, calculates how fast they have traveled from desirable Christminster, speaks to them, "You . . . were in Christminster," and then hears the bells of that city, which seem to call "We are happy here!" This is the poet who likens the silence and speed of a hawk flying at twilight to "an eyelid's soundless blink," who writes a poem to his father's violin and sees "Ten worm-wounds in your neck," who imagines himself a sundial in "The Sundial on a Wet Day" ("I drip, drip here / In Atlantic rain"), and who uses a felled log to remember his dead sister in "Logs on the Hearth":

> The fire advances along the log
> Of the tree we felled,
> Which bloomed and bore striped apples by the peck
> Till its last hour of bearing knelled.

Proust accused Flaubert of not creating even one great metaphor, which is palpably unfair, but Hardy's work has scores of them, a flowing stipend of brilliance. Yet while one is always aware of Flaubert aesthetically shaping his details, squeezing out the chilly gel of their chosenness, Hardy seems to treat simile and metaphor as a mode of quick warmth, a way to bring an alternative life onto the page, without too much thinking about it. Of course, much thought has gone into this impression of less thought: Ezra Pound commented on Hardy's way of keeping his mind on his subject matter, and "how little he cared about manner, which does not in the least mean that he did not care about it or had not a definite aim."

So frosty grass rustles "like paper-shavings" underfoot in *The Woodlanders* (1887), and in the same novel stinging rain is described like this: "The morning had been windy, and little showers had sowed themselves like grain against the walls and window-panes of the Hintock cottages." Yes, we think, hard stabs of rain could be just like grain; but the second metaphor, "sowed," is extraordinary, and goes beyond what most of us could imagine, since like most original metaphors it forces together incompatible media, and is, technically, mixed (you can sow grain but not water). Again, in *Tess of the d'Urbervilles* (1891), Angel and Tess journey on a cart, with the "clucking of the milk in the tall cans behind them": it might seem here as if the writer is going to the wrong part of the farmyard for his likeness, until we try to hear the slopping cluck of milk against a hard pail. Has anyone described the way light changes during the morning better than Hardy does, in his poem "The Going": "while I / Saw morning harden upon the wall." One can see, with the help of these lines, the light becoming more solid, more densely itself; and of course our mornings harden in a different way, too: our days tend to begin loose with possibility, and then harden around us as the lost hours progress and we feel their unfreedom accrete.

Henry James was snooty about Hardy, but I wonder how James would have done if given as a kind of literary test a cow's udder to describe? Admirably, no doubt, with his usual lyrical paradox of oddly precise euphemism, but certainly without the solidity of Hardy's sentence in *Tess*: "Their large-veined udders hung ponderous as sandbags, the teats sticking out like the legs of a gipsy's crock." Again, that likeness to a sandbag is good but ordinary enough; but the teats like the little legs of a common cooking pot is absolutely alive. A lot of rather condescending nonsense used to be written about "the good little Thomas Hardy" (James's phrase, alas) and his modest social origins, those origins somehow explaining both the qualities and the lapses of his writing. Nevertheless, it is hard to escape the conclusion that some of the power of his writing flows from his rural childhood, with its long country walks and immersion in both the natural world and the particular poetry of dialect speech. Again and again, Hardy's images dip into the rural near-at-hand: paper shavings, grain, "clucking" milk, an eyelid's blink, the legs of a pot.

That is why we find in his writing a tendency visible in Dickens, Chekhov, Lawrence, and Henry Green's *Loving*: his own metaphors get very close, in style, to the speech of his least lettered characters, who in turn often use images that Hardy himself might have polished up a bit and used in his descriptive prose: "I were as dry as a lime basket," says Master Coggan in *Far from the Madding Crowd*. "They read that sort of thing as fast as a night-hawk will whir," a traveler says of the busy dons of Christminster. Tess's mother describes her father's unhealthy heart as "clogged like a dripping-pan," while Liza-Lu more simply—but even more vividly—says that it is "growed in." The character's dripping-pan is not far from the author's gypsy's crock, and we see these two styles merge, as it were, in a moment in *The Mayor of Casterbridge* (1886), when Hardy writes about twilight: "It being now what the people call the 'pinking in' of the day, that is, the quarter-hour just before dusk." How Hardy must have relished hearing people talk of the "pinking in." He told Robert Graves that some critic had upbraided him for writing: "his shape smalled in the distance." But how else, Hardy said, laughing, could he have written it? (Lawrence, who took so much from Hardy, has "the dawn is wanly blueing" in *Sea and Sardinia*.)

Probably only the lives of Dickens and Lawrence rival Hardy's, with its rise from the relatively prosperous upper working class into the establishment, its triumphant asymmetries of origin and arrival. The boy whose own father was barely literate ended his life corresponding with Edmund Gosse and Edward Elgar, and lived long enough to scent posterity's massive approval of his work. The boy whose mother in 1833 had watched from the roadside the passage of Princess Victoria hosted the Prince of Wales at his own house in 1923: there is a famous photograph, with Hardy, his second wife, Florence, and the prince sitting awkwardly in the garden at Max Gate, on wicker seats. Florence looks almost asthmatically taut with terror, but Hardy, the only one not looking at the camera, is serenely sunk in himself. The prince confessed that he had not read a word by his host. But what could that matter, really, to Hardy? Imagine the sense of triumph: it was from the prince's grandfather that Hardy had purchased the plot of land on which Max Gate stood, and Hardy's best biographer, Claire Tomalin, speculates that he may have "felt understandably proud that royalty now came to him," which is just what we want her to suggest.

Remove the aspirant mother and half of English literature would disappear. Hardy's father was a builder and his mother, Jemima, had been a servant in several households. Tomalin suggests that Jemima's exposure to literate and genteel families probably encouraged her social aspirations for her children. Unlike her husband, she was a great reader, counting *The Divine Comedy* and *Rasselas* among her favorite books. Perhaps it was Jemima, Tomalin writes, who pushed her son, in successful later life, to go up to London for the summer Season, having herself witnessed the ritual from downstairs as a young woman, when the family she served would transfer itself to London.

Like Lawrence's mother, she used her son's feeble physique as a way to bypass the family calling, and sent him off to Dorchester (a three-mile walk each way), where he attended a good school run by a Nonconformist headmaster, Isaac Last. He read widely, loved animals—cruelty to animals is a recurring theme in his work—and, like Cézanne in this respect, hated to be touched, a characteristic he never lost. At the age of twelve he bought himself a Latin primer; at sixteen, he was articled to a Dorchester architect—the young Hardy's expertise as a sketcher of churches and his knowledge of Gothic building would keep him in such employment for years.

Appropriately, then, the formative intellectual relationship was with an upper-class family. Hardy became close friends with Horace Moule, the rebellious son of a prominent local vicar, whose other children all ended up in impeccably conformist careers, most of them ecclesiastical. Horace Moule committed suicide in Cambridge in 1873, worn down by opium and drink. But in the 1860s, the time of their burgeoning fellowship, he and Hardy exchanged radical books and ideas: the liberal *Essays and Reviews* of 1860 (which defended German biblical criticism, among other things), perhaps *The Origin of Species* of 1859 (it is not clear how early Hardy read this, though he always claimed Darwin as a major influence), Mill, Comte, Marcus Aurelius. A pattern of self-education, ravenous and stringent, had begun. In London for five years from 1862, Hardy attended French classes at King's College, and went daily for a time to the National Gallery to study a selected painter or painting. His *Literary Notebooks*, which have been edited into two large volumes, show how widely he read, painstakingly copying out essays from journals, and summarizing books in English and French—on Russian and French realism, on German philosophy, on evolution, religion, science, music. Late in his life, he made note of Einstein's theory of relativity, and of *Prufrock* and *The Waste Land*.

Claire Tomalin is sensitive to Hardy's class-consciousness, and to the relative perilousness of his social position. She points out that Henry James arrived in London at around the same time, with a bond for a thousand pounds in his pocket and letters of introduction to all the right people. Hardy, meanwhile, poor and relatively friendless, was trying and failing to get published the manuscript of a novel, tellingly titled *The Poor Man and the Lady*. He wrote in his notebook, in October 1870: "Mother's notion, & also mine: That a figure stands in our van with arm uplifted, to knock us back from any pleasant prospect we indulge in as probable." Nowadays, we read this metaphysically, in the stained-glass light of Hardy's theological pessimism. But it might more likely be seen as the expression of a straightforward social fact. He could be knocked back at any moment. Horace Moule, for instance, wrote both warmly and condescendingly about his friend's novel *A Pair of Blue Eyes* (1873): "You understand the woman infinitely better than the lady," and went on to refer to "slips of taste, every now and then." Hardy met Emma Gifford in 1870, and the courtship proceeded fast. But without solid prospects or income, it would be four years before he could marry her, and her father, a solicitor, strongly objected, on grounds of social disparity: Hardy went to Cornwall to ask for her hand, and never spoke to him again. Emma, willful and fiery, was not deterred, but in a horrible irony, as their marriage deteriorated and the two grew alienated, she would snobbishly disdain her husband's origins and his devotion to Dorset. This, then, was the background of the man who in later life went up to London every summer to attend grand parties, who used his Savile Club connections, and who developed an embarrassing tendency to fall in love with well-born ladies: anxious pleasures, no doubt, and easy to forgive.

His cold eye on class and social mobility makes his fiction compelling, a different compulsion from the accelerated grimace of his melodramatic, libretto-like plots. His novels are often fantastical, but about class they are grimly realistic. Eustacia Vye, in *The Return of the Native*, is an English Emma Bovary, looking longingly at Paris as the escape from the provincialism of Egdon Heath. Elizabeth, in *The Mayor of Casterbridge*, occasionally lapses into dialect, "those terrible marks of the beast to the truly genteel," Hardy remarks. Corrected speech is one of the things that sets Tess apart from her impoverished family. Hardy's heroes and heroines are forced to make marriage choices that are sociologically fraught: Will the landed female farmer marry the yeoman or the gentleman farmer (Bathsheba and Gabriel Oak or Farmer Boldwood)? Will the milkmaid marry the clergyman's son or the nouveau riche seducer

(Tess and Angel Clare or Alec d'Urberville)? Will the intellectual stonemason take the plebeian slattern or the sexless idealist and intellectual (Jude and Arabella or Sue Bridehead)?

Sometimes Hardy, like Austen, surrendered to wish fulfillment, and united the yeoman and the middle-class woman: both *Under the Greenwood Tree* (1872) and *Far from the Madding Crowd* end with the happy exhaustion of marriages. But *The Woodlanders* takes the plot of those two earlier novels—a heroine made to choose between suitors—and darkens it. Grace Melbury is wooed by Giles Winterborne, a gentle local man who presses cider for a living. But she is swept away by the higher-born and more seductive Edred Fitzpiers, a doctor new to the area, who is related to a distinguished family. She marries Fitzpiers, only to watch him begin an affair with Mrs. Charmond, a risqué widow and former actress, who lives in the village's big house. Giles dies, and Edred, now estranged from Grace, leaves for the Continent. But Grace and Edred are eventually reunited (he returns from Europe apparently a new man), the novel ending fairly ambiguously: we doubt whether this renovated union will succeed.

What is interesting, in *The Woodlanders*, is the way Hardy contrasts the deep roots of the landscape—the trees that feature so prominently in the book, and which provide a livelihood for many of its characters—with the more fragile roots of the protagonists. Fitzpiers is grand by origin but modest by occupation; Mrs. Charmond is an outsider, who confesses that before she was widowed she had never lived in the country; and Grace, though local, is the well-educated daughter of a self-made timber merchant. Indeed, one of the best things about the book—it brings forth from Hardy a properly complicated mixture of judgment and sympathy—is the presentation of Mr. Melbury, who is bullish and socially anxious, and desperate for his daughter to ignore the lowly Giles in favor of the higher-up Fitzpiers. His daughter is an investment to him: he sent her away to a pricey boarding school and he wants his return. When she chides him for treating her as a "chattel," he is characteristically pleased that she has used such a "dictionary word."

Hardy's position was as shifting as any of his characters', until the great breakthrough late in 1873, when Leslie Stephen offered him four hundred pounds to serialize *Far from the Madding Crowd* in the *Cornhill*. It was a lot of money: a year earlier, Hardy's cousin Tryphena had become headmistress of a primary school at a salary of a hundred pounds a year. Stephen's annual salary at the Cornhill was five hundred pounds. Hardy would soon become well-off; he left an estate of almost one hundred thousand pounds in 1928. *Far from the Madding Crowd* was published in 1874 and sold out in two months. He would write more complicated books, and his prose would get better, too, but there is a joyousness that makes this novel deeply lovable. As in all Hardy, there is coincidence and implausibility, the concertina-pleats of the plot pressing against each other more tightly as the tale speeds toward its melodramatic conclusion. Still, the story also has a beautiful ballad-like purity: Bathsheba and her three suitors, the oaklike Gabriel Oak, the scarlet-uniformed Sergeant Troy (one of the most brilliant namings in English fiction), and the mournful, oppressive, relentless Mr. Boldwood. Henry James reviewed it without mercy, but I think it cast a spell that he would never have admitted: six years later he began *The Portrait of a Lady*, in which a heroine is courted by three men, one of whom, like Boldwood, refuses to accept defeat, and who is called . . . Goodwood.

What one remembers, as so often in Hardy, are the great scenes: Gabriel's young dog excitedly chasing his sheep off the hillside to their deaths; Troy doing his flashy sword exercises for a swooning Bathsheba; Troy returning from his faked suicide to reclaim his wife at Boldwood's Christmas party ("Bathsheba, I come here for you . . . Come, madam"); Boldwood shooting Troy at the same party, and dazedly looking on as Bathsheba presses her hand to Troy's chest to stop the jetting blood. I read the novel at about fourteen, and for a long time it was the only Hardy novel I had read, because I persisted in rereading it rather than beginning a new one. Something I no doubt missed at that age, in my zeal for pure story, was the Shakespearean buoyancy of the speech of the rural characters.

There is a lot of rustic comedy, as for instance when Henery Fray explains to Bathsheba, the mistress of the farm where he works, how Cain Ball, a fellow worker, got his name:

> O you see, mem, his pore mother, not being a Scripture-read woman made a mistake at his christening, thinking 'twas Abel killed Cain, and called en Cain meaning Abel all the time. She didn't find out till 'twas too late, and the chiel was handed back to his godmother . . . She were brought up by a very heathen father and mother who never sent her to church or school, and it shows how the sins of the parents are visited upon the children, mem.

Henery's complacent misappropriation of the biblical curse about the sins of the fathers is sublimely funny, and not unsubtle. Raymond Williams, who did so much to reorient serious study of Hardy, mysteriously declared that his dialect and rustic comedy was one of the least successful aspects of Hardy's work, but Hardy rarely plays these people just for laughs. In *The Return of the Native*, a character bursts into a house to tell Mrs. Yeobright that there has been a commotion at church, and that Eustacia has been stabbed there with a stocking needle, and then can't help adding: "O, and what d'ye think I found out, Mrs Yeobright? The pa'son wears a suit of clothes under his surplice!—I could see his black sleeve when he held up his arm." The little riot of addition, the self's gratuity, the ego's tip to itself, as it were—Hardy has a comedy-cocked ear for it. Here is Master Coggan on the difference between the established church and chapel. Regular church, he says, is cozy and known:

> But to be a dissenter you must go to chapel in all winds and weathers, and make yerself as frantic as a skit. Not but that chapel-members be clever chaps enough in their way. They can lift up beautiful prayers out of their own heads, all about their families and shipwrecks in the newspaper.

That last sentence is not only very funny—there is something so absurd about finding it remarkable that prayer should issue from "their own heads" when prayer is precisely supposed to issue from one's own head—but crystallizes what must have seemed a central difference between established liturgy and dissenting freedom. The zeugma of "families and shipwrecks in the newspaper" is marvelous. Hardy describes a similar character in *The Mayor of Casterbridge* as "bursting into naturalness," which would nicely fit Hardy's own writing here, too.

Far from the Madding Crowd is a cheerful novel—Hardy counted himself a Comtean at this time—but it was followed by much bleaker books. Like Michael Millgate, Tomalin suggests that there was no classic Victorian crisis of faith for Hardy, rather a gradual waning. As a young man he had thought of getting ordained. By the mid-1860s, he was no longer regularly attending church, though he would never entirely cease. *The Return of the Native*, which was published four years after *Far from the Madding Crowd*, expresses the thought that "what the Greeks only suspected we know well; what their Aeschylus imagined our nursery children feel"—that is, "the defects of natural laws." In *The Mayor of Casterbridge*, Hardy declares that Michael Henchard has been brought down by "the ingenious machinery contrived by the gods for reducing human possibilities of amelioration to a minimum."

Much of Hardy's mature writing can be seen as a commentary on John Stuart Mill's essay "Nature," published in 1874. Mill argues that people are always appealing to nature to make moral cases—as, for instance, when acts one disapproves of are deemed unnatural—whereas in fact nature is unmoral, blindly cruel, indifferent. Mill rises to a positively Hardyesque denunciation: "Nature impales men, breaks them as if on the wheel, casts them to be devoured by wild beasts, burns them to death . . . All this, Nature does with the most supercilious disregard both of mercy and of justice, emptying her shafts upon the best and noblest indifferently with the meanest and worst." Mill proceeds from here to mount an attack on theodicy and

the idea of providence, concluding that the only idea of God that
makes any sense is one in which he is beneficent but weak—unable
to stop the suffering he presumably deplores.

Hardy's two last major novels, *Tess of the d'Urbervilles* and
Jude the Obscure, are complex because they both attack nature's
laws and appeal to them. In other words, they share Mill's view of
nature, but often seem not to follow Mill's advice about the un-
wisdom of appealing to nature. On the one hand, this work is full of
characters whose invocation of nature is clearly suspect. When Tess
is raped by Alec, her mother remarks, "'Tis nater after all, and what
do please God," the fatalistic appeal to nature indistinguishable
here from the fatalistic appeal to religion. This is clearly to be rejected. Yet, on the other hand, the same novel makes much reference to "nature's inexorable laws," to the "vulpine slyness of Dame
Nature," and consistently praises Tess as a child of nature. Can nature then be both right and wrong? Similarly, is Tess punished and
finally killed by the absence of providence, or by providence itself?
At the end of the book there is a famously clumsy line: "'Justice' was
done, and the President of the Immortals (in Aeschylean phrase)
had ended his sport with Tess." At this point the novel seems to re-
admit the theologizing it most savagely attacks: Tess is "sacrificed"
on the pagan altar of Stonehenge, going so far as to tell Angel there
that as a pagan she has obviously returned home.

Hardy used to be accused of intellectual confusion on this score.
Postmodern criticism tends to get around these apparent contradictions by praising them, or rather by warmly ironizing them. The
contradictions of these texts are seen as, if not quite intentional on
Hardy's part, then symptomatically inevitable and interesting (the
usual manner in which contemporary criticism elides the question
of authorial intention): these are books that flaunt their own uncer-
tainties and irregularities, that seem to aim to destabilize meaning
and unitary readings.

There is much to be said for this. Hardy has much in common
in this regard with Dostoevsky, another theologically obsessed novelist once accused of bad writing, whose melodramatics and some-

times awkward rapidities have encouraged theorists to see in his texts deliberate, "dialogic" irregularity rather than mere lapses in taste or the presence of oppressive journalistic deadlines. Hardy seems to have had little time for conventional realism, and his manner of loading a huge salad of overdetermined causalities onto the narrative plate certainly looks deliberately ironic. Both *Tess of the d'Urbervilles* and *Jude the Obscure* offer at least four large narrative explanations for the fates of their protagonists: a genealogical explanation (it's "in the blood" of the d'Urberville and Fawley families); a socioeconomic one; a "natural" explanation (nature's cruelty); and a theological one (sometimes merging with the natural explanation, and sometimes pulling away from it, as at the end of *Tess* with the invocation of Aeschylus). Are all these causalities justly blamed, or does each offer only a partial explanation?

And there remains one other form of causality, the one that gives readers most pause: the grinding plots of the novels themselves. Even if one takes postmodernism's proffered exit and happily turns the novels into fascinating melodramatic bricolage, tattooed with a mess of different and contradictory discourses, one is left with the unpalatable paradox that these are deeply coercive novels supposedly fighting against what Sue Bridehead, in *Jude the Obscure*, calls "the common enemy, coercion." True, one cannot show characters trying to fight coercion unless one also represents coercion; but equally, it seems important that the coercion being represented is not overwhelmingly the author's own. "I cannot conceive of God as the arch-plotter against His own creation." Hardy copied these words from Mrs. Humphry Ward's novel *Robert Elsmere* into his notebook. What was he thinking? He had become God himself, plotting against his characters.

My own feeling is that in these last two books Hardy was indeed consumed by a theological bitterness that made the freedom necessary to successful narrative almost impossible, and that he abandoned fiction for poetry after *Jude the Obscure* in part because he could see that he had perforce abandoned narrative itself. What were Hardy's own beliefs? As far as one can tell, he was very close to John Stuart Mill. His position never settled down into a hard cake of despair, and never had the hygienic, disillusioned certainty of Mill's, not least because he could not abandon his nostalgia for Christian belief; his most complexly riven thought appears in poems like "The Oxen," "The Darkling Thrush," and "God's Funeral" (in which he imagines witnessing a cortège carrying the corpse of the deity, and weeps for the absence of the old comfort). But he did indeed begin to think of providence as what he called an Immanent Will, a blind, unsympathetic if not malevolent force. At other times, he argued that this force was striving to express itself and failing to, and was perhaps merely baffled by what it had created. In his last thirty years, he seems to veer from Epicureanism to a very dark Gnosticism, and often to a Sophoclean fatality: better not to have been born. He wrote an uncanny poem, "The Unborn," in which the poet visits the yet-to-be-born, with their excited questions about human existence, and can hardly bear to tell them that the world is terrible. He was consumed with the notion that this Will had botched the original making of the universe, and that the really great punishment was that humans were given consciousness. Animals, after all, suffer less because they cannot reflect on their pain, theologically or otherwise. There is a fascinating notebook entry on this:

> Law has produced in man a child who cannot but constantly reproach its parent for doing much and yet not all, and constantly say to such parent that it would have been better never to have begun doing than to have overdone so indecisively; that is, than to have created so far beyond all apparent first intention (on the emotional side), without mending matters by a second intention and execution, to eliminate the evils of the blunder of overdoing. The emotions have no place in a world of defect, and it is a cruel injustice that they should have developed in it.

It's an extraordinary passage, with that calm implacability characteristic of Hardy in this mood. It was wrong, he seems to say, to have been given human feeling, and this was the first blunder—the aboriginal error of God's "overdoing" things. There should have been a correction of this blunder, just as Genesis seems to offer two accounts of creation. Hardy, of course, is the writer who is always accused of overdoing things, and perhaps his novels strive to mimic, to represent, this theological overdoing? Similarly, Hardy's plots are full of repetition; his characters attempt to mend an original injustice, but the second or third mendings fail: Tess runs from Angel to Alec and then back to Angel, but she is doomed; Jude runs from Arabella to Sue and back to Arabella, but he is doomed. Claire Tomalin quotes a terrible letter Hardy wrote to his friend Rider Haggard, on the loss of Haggard's ten-year-old son. He expressed his condolences, and then added: "Though, to be candid, I think the death of a child is never really to be regretted, when one reflects on what he has escaped." She comments acutely that Haggard, who never replied, "may have understood that Hardy's ability to believe several conflicting things at once meant he sometimes expressed himself strangely." Soon the world would eat the fruit of that strangeness, that terrible honesty, that ironic brutality, in the novel that would make Hardy more complicatedly celebrated than ever: *Tess of the d'Urbervilles* was published later that year.

GEOFF DYER

Walter Benjamin once said that every great work dissolves a genre or founds a new one. But is it only masterpieces that have a monopoly on novelty? What if a writer had written several works that rose to Benjamin's high definition, not all great perhaps, but so different from one another, so peculiar to their author, and so inimitable that each founded its own, immediately self-dissolving genre? The English writer Geoff Dyer delights in producing books that are as unique as door keys. There is nothing anywhere like Dyer's semi-fictional rhapsody about jazz, *But Beautiful*, or his book about the First World War, *The Missing of the Somme*, or his autobiographical essay about D. H. Lawrence, *Out of Sheer Rage*, or his essayistic travelogue, *Yoga for People Who Can't Be Bothered to Do It*. You can spot Dyer's antecedents and influences—Nietzsche, Roland Barthes, Thomas Bernhard, Milan Kundera, John Berger, Martin Amis—but not his literary children, because his work is so restlessly various that it moves somewhere else before it can gather a family. He combines fiction, autobiography, travel writing, cultural criticism, literary theory, and a kind of comic English whining. The result ought to be a mutant mulch, but is almost always a louche and canny delight.

Dyer's sixth book, *Out of Sheer Rage* (1997), established the characteristic voice of his recent work—a loitering investigation, somehow intense and slackerish, the author not quite pursuing but hanging around his subject like a clever, aimless boy on a street corner. Dyer had wanted to write a critical book about D. H. Lawrence, but whenever he tried to begin, he found something to distract him. First, it was his idea of writing a novel:

> Although I had made up my mind to write a book about Lawrence I had also made up my mind to write a novel, and while the decision to write the book about Lawrence was made later it had not entirely superseded that earlier decision. At first I'd had an overwhelming urge to write both books but these two desires had worn each other down to the point where I had no urge to write either.

Then there was the question of where to write—or rather, fail to write—the book on Lawrence: "One of the reasons, in fact, that it was impossible to get started on either the Lawrence book or the novel was because I was so preoccupied with where to live. I could live anywhere, all I had to do was choose—but it was impossible to choose because I could live anywhere."

Dyer goes to Rome, where his girlfriend lives, but it is too hot in Rome to do any work, and the couple absconds to a Greek island. But it is no better there. He gets distracted by Rilke, who at first excites him, but then even reading Rilke is too much. "I had thought that after working on my book about Lawrence in the mornings I would spend the afternoons playing tennis but there were no courts and so, having spent the mornings not writing my book about Lawrence and not reading Rilke, I spent the afternoons not playing tennis." Readers of the Austrian writer Thomas Bernhard will recognize a familiar vaudeville of despair, whereby every possibility is always shadowed by its negation, and nothing can ever be completed because it is always being ceaselessly restarted.

Bernhard is very funny, but despair—particularly the menace of suicide and breakdown—is always present. Dyer is more deliberately funny, and lighter, and *Out of Sheer Rage* represented a seemingly impossible Englishing of the Austrian writer. Like his later books, *Paris Trance* (2000), a novel about two twenty-something English slackers who can't get anything serious done in Paris (one of whom has come to Paris expressly to write his novel, of course), and *Yoga for People Who Can't Be Bothered to Do It* (2003), a series of essays set in Thailand, France, Libya, and Italy, *Out of Sheer Rage* is a work of delicious, stunned truancy. For Thomas Bernhard, obsessive mental activity obstructs work; for Dyer's characters, it is the negative liberty of boredom. It is always easier not to be writing than to be writing, and at least by not writing one is keeping alive the option of at some point writing again. But then, as soon as one is doing absolutely nothing, the intolerability strikes one as not so much a freedom as a prison, walled on every side by limitless possibility—"it was impossible to choose because I could live anywhere." Dyer's is a comic, ruefully self-canceling world, in which even inactivity is a kind of activity, and life becomes a form of "yoga for people who can't be bothered to do it." In Rome, or in Paris, or anywhere really, life dwindles to stasis. "There was less and less to do, which was just as well because I had less and less energy to do anything."

On the one hand, Dyer's work of the last decade seems familiarly postmodern. Grand gestures are futile, and in place of hard work or exacting thought there are sex and drugs and clubbing, and various kinds of mind-bending music. Everything is unfinishable, belated, and philosophically twilit. The Owl of Minerva can barely crank its wings open—no doubt because it has become a fat urban pigeon, toddling between cafés for cultural leftovers. The books turn themselves inside out, like the Centre Pompidou, displaying their inner workings. The book about Lawrence becomes a book about failing to write about Lawrence; a projected work about the ruins of antiquity gets nowhere—"such a book would one day lie in ruins about me" (a typically good Dyer joke). But of course, Dyer's books do get written: interesting books about boredom, successful books about failure, complete books about incompletion. And one can see that, far from enacting an easy ironic resignation, Dyer is really a late romantic, a flâneur out of Barthes and Nietzsche (but with a vinegary English dash of Kingsley Amis), eager to experience as much as possible, to travel and fall in love and meet new people, and wary of writing and reading because, although they preserve such experience, they do so at a mimetic remove. The problem for the romantic is that, in order to have anything to write about, one has to live—that is, not be writing. Not for nothing is D. H. Lawrence, the savage pilgrim, Dyer's great model.

So he has spent much of his life on the move—London, Paris, Rome, Oxford, New Orleans, New York—and much of his best writing has been prompted by travel. He approaches this humorously in *Out of Sheer Rage*, but the English larkiness cannot obscure the intensity of the feeling. Once, he writes there, he found himself walking in a North London street, the road where Julian Barnes lived. "I didn't see him but I knew that in one of those large comfortable houses Julian Barnes was sitting at his desk, working, as he did every day. It seemed an intolerable waste of a life, of a writer's life especially, to sit at a desk in this nice, dull street in north London. It seemed, curiously, a betrayal of the idea of the writer." To spend one's life writing is a betrayal of the writer's life: Dyer knows this is a lunatic paradox, that even romantics have to sit at boring desks and write; but he would rather have his battered paradox than Barnes's clean coherence.

And so he gets up from the desk, and gets on a plane or a boat. He approvingly quotes Rebecca West on how Lawrence would arrive in a place—Florence, say—and immediately start writing about it, even if he knew little about it. "He was writing about the state of his own soul at that moment, which . . . he could render only in symbolic terms; and the city of Florence was as good a symbol as any other." Dyer's book, the impishly titled *Jeff in Venice, Death in Varanasi*, describes itself as a novel, but is two long stories, one set in Venice, and one in the holy Indian city of Varanasi, on the Ganges (also known as Benares or Kashi). These stories have certain fictive connections, and the protagonists of each—a middle-aged English journalist, sent to each city on assignment—are not identical to Geoff Dyer. Geoff is not Jeff. Still, the stories seem to flit in and out of fictionality, in a way that seems intended; they are a Dyer-like combination of essay, travelogue, and invention, and the veronica of the author's soul can be glimpsed behind the two texts. (A note informs us that the author has been to Varanasi, and to three Biennales.)

The character at the center of "Jeff in Venice" is Jeff Atman, a London journalist who covers the art world. He hates his work and indulges in bitter procrastination. "Back home, back at his desk, the perennial question kept cropping up: how much longer could he keep doing this stuff for? For about two minutes at a time, it turned out, but eventually these two-minute increments—punctuated by emails pinging in and out—mounted up. God, what a miserable way to earn a living." He goes to Venice to write about the Biennale, and thus begins a relentlessly funny reply to Thomas Mann's novella. Like Thomas Mann's austere hero, the distinguished writer Gustav von Aschenbach, the very undistinguished Jeff, who at forty-five is going gray, gets his hair dyed black. Like Aschenbach, once in Venice, Jeff Atman (that surname so close to artman, adman, and T. Mann) spies a love object—in his case not an ethereal boy but a beautiful and sexy American named Laura, with a dolphin tattooed on her hipbone. The two get together, have a lot of sex, and snort quantities of coke.

Thomas Mann's august Apollonianism is cynically subverted at every turn of Dyer's story. Venice is a simulacrum of itself, the city no more than a very large art installation. "Every day, for hundreds of years, Venice had woken up and put on this guise of being a real place even though everyone knew it existed only for tourists." The gangs of art critics, artists, and hangers-on are in town not to see art or Venice, apparently, but to go to parties, drink, take drugs, and shag each other. "You came to Venice, you saw a ton of art, you went to parties, you drank up a storm, you talked bollocks for hours on end and went back to London with a cumulative hangover, liver damage, a notebook almost devoid of notes and the first tingle of a cold sore." Maybe the parties themselves are a kind of installation: "Ben said he had it on good authority that later this afternoon, at the Venezuelan pavilion, chocolate-covered cockroaches would be served." Ideally, reflects Jeff, "the perfect installation would be a nightclub, full of people, pumping music, lights, smoke machine and maybe drugs thrown in. You could call it Nightclub, and if you kept it going twenty-four hours a day it would be the big hit of the Biennale."

Essentially, the running joke of "Jeff in Venice" is: what would have happened if Aschenbach had got hold of young Tadzio and had his Dionysian way with him? Wouldn't sex then have triumphed over death? (Mann's novella ends with Tadzio seeming to beckon the aging lecher, who rises from his deck chair, collapses back into it, and dies: he quite literally can't get it up.) The thoroughly postmodern Jeff Atman writes for a magazine called *Kulchur*, but does dirt—to sound Lawrentian for a moment—on Kulchur. The cynicism of Dyer's story would be insupportable if it were not savagely funny, and if there were not Mann's closeted idealism to play off. This, Dyer seems to say, is what we have come to, in the near century since the earlier novella—"when it was impossible to believe that there would come a time when all people cared about was free risotto to mop up all the free bellinis they'd been swilling in the garden."

The moral emptiness of "Jeff in Venice" seems all the more devastating when put into relief by its companion, "Death in Varanasi." The first story is a flowing tide of sex and carnality; the second is dominated by a holy river of life and death, the Ganges. The first gluts itself on fleshly pleasures; the second empties itself of those temptations (there is no sex, and little drinking, though there is a bit of drug taking). The tale is narrated by a nameless middle-aged journalist, who may or may not be Jeff Atman (or Geoff Dyer, for that matter), and who has come to Varanasi, one of the holiest sites of Hindu pilgrimage, to write a piece for a London newspaper. There are links with the book's Venice story, and with Thomas Mann's Venice story. Hindus believe that if you die and are cremated in Varanasi, then you may be absolved of the burden of samsara, reincarnation. So Varanasi, in one guise, is a kind of sublime crematorium, and the Ganges is virtually clogged with the ash of corpses. Aschenbach means, literally, "ash brook." As in Venice, the protagonist is a spectatorial tourist. He lands in town and immediately sets out for the burning river: "That's where I was hurrying, to see bodies being burned. (On arriving at a new place, it's no bad thing to simply do what everyone else does.)" He tries to read up about Hinduism, but can't make head nor tail of it. He is taken, however, with the concept of darshan—the idea that "the more attention paid to a god, the more it was looked at, the greater its power, the more easily it could be seen." Dyer doesn't need to make explicit the connection with Atman's lust for Laura, and Aschenbach's gazing on the godlike Tadzio. And as in Venice, almost anything can seem like an art installation, even a pile of garbage seen from a rickshaw:

> A couple of happy-looking pigs were rooting through a mass of garbage. Some of this rubbish had been compacted down into a dark tar, a sediment of concentrated filth, pure filth, filth with no impurities, devoid of everything that was not filth . . . On top of this was an assortment of browning marigolds, bits of soggy cardboard (not automatically to be discounted as a calorific source) and freshish-looking excrement (ditto). The whole thing was set off with a resilient garnish of blue plastic bags. In its way it was a potential tourist attraction, a contemporary manifestation of the classical ideal of squalor. I was quite excited by it, was tempted to ask the driver to stop so that I could have a better look, perhaps even take a picture.

Whereas Venice provokes Atman's coarse rebellion, Varanasi goads Dyer's deep descriptive talents. There are sharp observations, pungent and funny. A holy man, with a beard "that looked like it was made out of the fur of a long-haired animal, mythical in origin, close to extinction, and completely incontinent." Women "in red and yellow saris flickered by like load-bearing flames." In an amusing scene, the narrator walks down a narrow lane while a cow pushes past him. The cow's tail "was as drenched in shit as an artist's brush in paint. But just because I was me with a nice clean bottom and she was a cow with an ass caked in shit did not mean that I had not been her—or she me—in a previous existence. We could trade places in an instant. The value of your shares in the great Samsara-NASDAQ can go up as well as down." As if thinking the same thought, the cow flicks the narrator in the mouth with its shit-caked tail.

Against the odds, and against the drift of the Venice story, Varanasi has a great impact on the English journalist. Originally booked for five nights there, he moves to a hotel overlooking the Ganges and stays for weeks. Time melts away. He loses his passport. He gets his head and eyebrows shaved, like an Indian mourner, and starts wearing a dhoti. He swims in the ashy Ganges. Earlier, he had seen a terrible dog, so covered with welts and sores that it could only scratch itself all day—"the awful Samsara of itching and scratching, itching and scratching." The reader cannot help but think of "Jeff in Venice," a tale of compulsive scratching and itching. At the end of "Death in Varanasi," the narrator seems to find a religious peace from all that scratching and itching: "I didn't renounce the world; I just became gradually less interested in certain aspects of it, less involved with it."

This religious self-emptying might seem an unexpected turn in Dyer's usually hilarious and worldly work. But in fact, the metaphysics of boredom lead naturally enough to the metaphysics of *shantih*. In the earlier books, Dyer's characters did not fail to write because they were indifferent to writing, but because they wanted too much to write. Negative liberty expresses a fear of completion; if you never start a work, then at least there is no chance of your having finished it. To complete something is in some ways to make it disappear; not starting it is a preemptive strike against loss, a way of elegizing what has not yet disappeared. (Tellingly, Dyer has been repeatedly drawn to writing about epitaphs—ruins, cemeteries, and photographs, which are epitaphs of a frozen moment.) Time is what completes us, and time is what forces us into the endless repetition that is boredom and the tyranny of habit. Travel, sex, and drugs—Dyer's recurrent interests—are ways to cheat time, moments out of time. "For a few moments anything seemed possible," Dyer writes of getting stoned in Rome. Getting high, thinks Jeff Atman, was "like a concentrated version of everything he had ever wanted from life." Getting high might be seen as a maximization of negative liberty, where everything really can be pure potential. "Boredom," writes the philosopher and aphorist E. M. Cioran, "with a bad reputation for frivolity, nonetheless allows us to glimpse the abyss from which issues the need for prayer." That is where Geoff Dyer leaves his narrator, prayerfully bottoming out of boredom.

PAUL AUSTER'S SHALLOWNESS

Roger Phaedo had not spoken to anyone for ten years. He confined himself to his Brooklyn apartment, obsessively translating and re-translating the same short passage from Rousseau's *Confessions*. Ten years ago, a mobster named Charlie Dark had attacked Phaedo and his wife. Phaedo was beaten to within an inch of his life; Mary was set on fire and survived just five days in the ICU. By day, Phaedo translated; at night he worked on a novel about Charlie Dark, who was never convicted. Then he drank himself senseless with scotch. He drank to drown his sorrows, to dull his senses, to forget himself. The phone rang, but he never answered it. Sometimes, Holly Steiner, an attractive woman across the hall, would silently enter his bedroom, and his bed, and expertly rouse him from his stupor. At other times, he made use of the services of Aleesha, a local hooker. Aleesha's eyes were too hard, too cynical, and they bore the look of someone who had already seen too much. But the curious thing was that, despite this hardness, Aleesha looked identical to Holly; it was impossible to tell them apart, as if she were Holly's double. And it was Aleesha who brought Roger Phaedo back from the dead, from the darkness. One afternoon, she was wandering naked through Phaedo's apartment. In his small office, she saw two enormous man-uscripts: two piles, neatly stacked. One, the Rousseau translation, each page covered with almost identical words; the other, the novel about Charlie Dark. She started leafing through the novel. "Charlie Dark!" she exclaimed. "I knew Charlie Dark! He was one tough cookie. That bastard was in the Paul Auster gang. I'd love to read this book, baby, but I was always too lazy to read long books. Why don't you read it to me?" And that is how the ten-year silence was broken. For no good reason, but no bad one either, Phaedo decided to please Aleesha. He sat down and started reading the opening paragraph of his novel, the paragraph you have just read . . .

Yes, that is a parody of Paul Auster's fiction, an attempt to shrink *l'eau d'Auster* into a sardonic sac. It is unfair, but diligently so: it reduces most of the familiar features of his work. A protagonist, almost always male, often a writer or intellectual, certainly a reader, lives monkishly, coddling a loss—a deceased or divorced wife, dead children, a missing brother. Violent accidents perforate the narratives, both as a means of insisting on the contingency of existence and as a means of keeping the reader reading—a woman drawn and quartered in a German concentration camp, a man beheaded in Iraq, a woman severely beaten by a man with whom she is about to have sex, a boy kept in a darkened room for nine years and periodically beaten, a woman accidentally shot in the eye, and so on. The narratives conduct themselves like realistic stories, except for a slight lack of conviction, and a general atmosphere of the B movie. People say things like: "You're one tough cookie, pal," or "Yeah well, my pussy's not for sale," or "It's an old story, pal. You let your dick do your thinking for you, and that's what happens." A visiting text—Chateaubriand, Rousseau, Hawthorne, Poe, Beckett—is elegantly slid into the host book. There are doubles, alter egos, doppelgängers, and appearances by a character named Paul Auster. At the end of the story, the hints that have been punctually scattered like mouse droppings lead us to the postmodern hole in the book where the rodent got in—the revelation that some or all of what we have been reading has probably been imagined by the protagonist. Hey, Roger Phaedo invented Charlie Dark! It was all in his head.

Paul Auster's novel *Invisible*, though it has charm and vitality in places, conforms to the Auster model. It is 1967. Adam Walker, a young poet studying literature at Columbia, mourns the loss of his brother, Andy, who drowned in a lake ten years before the novel opens. At a campus party, Adam meets the flamboyant and sinister Rudolf Born, Swiss by birth, of German-speaking and French-speaking parentage. Born is a visiting professor, teaching the history of the French colonial wars, about which he appears to have decided views. "War is the purest, most vivid expression of the human soul," he tells a startled Adam. He tries to get Adam to sleep with his girlfriend. Later in the book, we learn that he has worked clandestinely for the French government, or possibly as a double agent.

Perhaps because Rudolf Born is so obviously a figure from spy movies—Auster should have called his novel *The Born Supremacy*—he never sounds remotely like a fastidious and well-educated French-speaking European of the 1960s. He says things like "Your ass will be so cooked, you won't be able to sit down again for the rest of your life," or "We're still working on the stew" (about a lamb navarin!), or "Rudolf the First . . . the bright boy with the big dick. All I have to do is pull it out of my pants, piss on the fire, and the problem is solved." He takes an immediate interest in Adam and gives him money to set up a literary magazine: "I see something in you, Walker, something I like," he says, sounding oddly like Burt Lancaster in *Local Hero*, "and for some inexplicable reason I find myself willing to take a gamble on you." For "some inexplicable reason," indeed: Auster anxiously confesses his own creative lack.

This being an Auster novel, accidents attack the narrative like automobiles falling from the sky. Walking one evening along Riverside Drive, Born and Walker are held up by a young black man, Cedric Williams. "The gun was pointed at us, and just like that, with a single tick of the clock, the entire universe had changed," is Walker's banal gloss. Born refuses to hand over his wallet, draws a switch-blade, and ruthlessly stabs the young man (whose gun, it turns out, was unloaded). Walker runs away, returns a little later, but the body is gone. He knows he should call the police, but Born sends a threatening letter the next day: "Not a word, Walker. Remember: I still have the knife, and I'm not afraid to use it." Full of shame, Walker eventually goes to the police, but Born has already left for Paris.

One might tolerate the corny Born, and his cinema-speak, if Adam Walker, who narrates much of the novel in one way or another, were not himself such a bland and slack writer. He is supposed to be a dreamy young poet, but is half in love with easeful cliché. Born "was just thirty-six, but already he was a burnt-out soul, a shattered wreck of a person." Adam has an affair with Born's girlfriend, but "deep down I knew it was finished." Born was "deep in his cups by the time he poured the cognac." "Why? I said, still reeling from the impact of Born's astounding recitation about my family." And so on. At times, the prose seems to be involved in some weird, breathless competition to fit the greatest number of shopworn objects into its basket:

> After torturing myself for close to a week, I finally found the courage to call my sister again, and when I heard myself spewing out the whole sordid business to Gwyn over the course of our two-hour conversation, I realized that I didn't have a choice. I had to step forward. If I didn't talk to the police, I would lose all respect for myself, and the shame of it would go on haunting me for the rest of my life.

There are things to admire in Auster's fiction, but the prose is never one of them, though he is routinely praised for the elegance of his sentences. (A review of *Invisible* in *The New York Times*, likening Auster to Freud, Husserl, and Goethe, called it "contemporary American writing at its best: crisp, elegant, brisk.") The most secondhand sentences in my opening parody, the ones most thickly lacquered with laziness (about being beaten to within an inch of his life, drinking to drown his sorrows, and the prostitute's eyes being too hard and having seen too much) are taken verbatim from Auster's previous work. *Leviathan* (1992), for instance, is supposedly narrated by an American novelist, a stand-in for Paul Auster called

Peter Aaron, who tells us about the doomed life of another writer, a friend named Benjamin Sachs. But Peter Aaron can't be much of a writer. He talks thus about his former wife, Delia: "Guilt is a powerful persuader, and Delia instinctively pushed all the right buttons whenever I was around." He describes Benjamin Sachs's first novel like this: "It's a whirlwind performance, a marathon sprint from the first line to the last, and whatever you might think of the book as a whole, it's impossible not to respect the author's energy, the sheer gustiness of his ambitions." Lest you are tempted to chalk all this up to an unreliable narrator—"that's the point, he's *supposed* to write in clichés"—consider August Brill, the seventy-two-year-old literary critic who narrates Auster's novel *Man in the Dark* (2008). Like Nathan Zuckerman in *The Ghost Writer*, he lies awake in a New England house, inventing fantastic fictions. (He imagines a parallel universe in which America is not at war in Iraq, but engaged in a bitter civil war over the fate of the 2000 election.) But when he thinks about actual America, his language is sodden with cliché. Recalling the Newark riots of 1968, he describes a member of the New Jersey State Police, "a certain Colonel Brand or Brandt, a man of around forty with a razor-sharp crew cut, a square, clenched jaw, and the hard eyes of a marine about to embark on a commando mission." (It is this same Brill who later says to his granddaughter, "You're one tough cookie, kid.")

Clichés, borrowed language, bourgeois bêtises, are intricately bound up with modern and postmodern literature. For Flaubert, the cliché and the received idea are dozy dogs obstructing the difficult path of precision and beauty, beasts to be toyed with, then slain. *Madame Bovary* italicizes examples of foolish or sentimental phrasing, the better to notice them in all their lividness on the page. Charles Bovary's conversation is likened to a pavement, over which many people have walked; twentieth-century literature, violently conscious of mass culture, extends this idea of the self as a kind of borrowed tissue, full of other people's germs. Among modern and postmodern writers, Beckett, Nabokov, Richard Yates, Thomas Bernhard, Muriel Spark, Don DeLillo, Martin Amis, and

David Foster Wallace have all employed and impaled cliché in their work. Wallace's late writing about modern boredom belongs obviously enough to that long Flaubertian tradition. Paul Auster is probably America's best-known postmodern novelist; his *New York Trilogy* must have been read by thousands who do not usually read avant-garde fiction. But while Auster clearly shares some of this interest in mediation and borrowedness—hence, his cinematic plots and rather bogus dialogue—he does nothing with cliché except use it. Cliché is under no significant pressure in his work; it just holds its soft hands with firmer words in the usual way.

This seems bewildering, on its face, but then Auster is a peculiar kind of postmodernist. Or is he actually a postmodernist? Eighty percent of a typical Auster novel proceeds in a manner indistinguishable from American realism; the other 20 percent does a kind of wan postmodern surgery on the 80 percent, often fiddling with the veracity of the plot, so as to cast doubt on its status. Nashe, in *The Music of Chance* (1990), sounds as if he has sprung from a Raymond Carver story (except that Carver would have written more interesting prose):

> He drove for seven straight hours, paused momentarily to fill up the tank with gas, and then continued for another six hours until exhaustion finally got the better of him. He was in north-central Wyoming by then, and dawn was just beginning to lift over the horizon. He checked into a motel, slept solidly for eight or nine hours, and then walked over to the diner next door and put away a meal of steak and eggs from the twenty-four-hour breakfast menu. By late afternoon, he was back in the car, and once again he drove clear through the night, not stopping until he had gone halfway through New Mexico.

One reads Auster's novels very fast, because they are lucidly written, because the grammar of the prose is the grammar of the most familiar realism (i.e., the kind of recognizable "realism" that is in fact comfortingly artificial), and because the plots, full of sneaky turns and surprises and violent irruptions, have what *The New York Times* once called "all the suspense and pace of a best-selling thriller." There are no semantic obstacles, lexical difficulties, or syntactical challenges. The books fairly hum along. But Auster is not a realist writer, of course. Or rather, his local narrative procedures are indeed uninterestingly realist, while his larger narrative games are antirealist or surrealist; which is a fancy way of saying that his sentences and paragraphs are quite conventional, and obey the laws of physics and chemistry, and his larger plots are almost always ridiculous. Nashe, in *The Music of Chance*, inherits money from his father and goes on the road. Eventually, he meets a professional poker player named Jack Pozzi (the name suggestive of jackpot, and also of Pozzo from *Waiting for Godot*). "It was one of those random, accidental encounters that seem to materialize out of thin air." For no very obvious or credible reason, Nashe decides to tag along with Pozzi: "It was as if he finally had no part in what was about to happen to him." The pair end up in the Pennsylvania mansion of two eccentric millionaires, Flower and Stone. Pozzi loses all Nashe's money on a poker game, and the unfortunate duo suddenly owe ten thousand dollars to Flower and Stone, who exact repayment by putting them to work on their estate: their job will be to build, by hand, a huge wall in a field. A trailer is prepared for their quarters. The estate has become a Sisyphean prison yard for Nashe and Pozzi, with Flower and Stone as unreachable gods (Flower's name perhaps gesturing at God's soft side, Stone's at punishment). Nashe gnashes his teeth in this pastoral hell.

Or take what is probably Auster's best novel, *The Book of Illusions* (2002). David Zimmer, a professor of literature, holes up in Vermont, where he mourns the death of his wife and two sons in a plane crash. "For several months, I lived in an alcoholic blur of grief and self-pity." By chance, he sees a silent film starring Hector Mann, a brilliant actor who disappeared in 1929, and who, it was thought, never made a film again. Zimmer decides to write a book about Mann, and the best part of the novel is Auster's painstaking and vivid fictional re-creation of the career of a silent-movie actor of the 1920s. But the story soon hurtles into absurdity. After his book on Hector Mann is published, Zimmer receives a letter from Mann's wife, Frieda: Mann is alive, though dying, in New Mexico; Zimmer must come at once. He does nothing about the letter, and one evening a strange woman named Alma arrives at Zimmer's house. She orders him, at gunpoint, to the New Mexico ranch. Second-rate dialogue is copiously exchanged: "I'm not your friend . . . You're a phantom who wandered in from the night, and now I want you to go back out there and leave me alone," Zimmer tells Alma, in one of those predictable moments of ritual temporary resistance we know so well from bad movies ("Well, buddy, you can count me out of this particular bank heist").

Alma explains to Zimmer that Hector Mann did not die in 1929 but disappeared, to hide the traces of a murder: Mann's fiancée accidentally shot his jealous girlfriend. The rest of the book speeds along like something written by a hipper John Irving—Zimmer goes to the ranch with the mysterious Alma; meets Hector Mann, who then dies almost immediately; Alma kills Hector's wife, and then commits suicide. And at the end, making good on many helpful suggestions throughout the book, we are encouraged to believe that David Zimmer invented everything we have just read: it was the fiction he needed to raise himself from the near death of his mourning.

What is problematic about these books is not their postmodern skepticism about the stability of the narrative, which is standard-issue fare, and amounts, anyway, to little more than weightless fiddling. What is problematic is the gravity and emotional logic that Auster seems to want to extract from the "realist" side of his stories. Auster is always at his most solemn at those moments in his books that are least plausible and most ragingly unaffecting. One never believes in Nashe's bleak solitude, or David Zimmer's alcoholic

grief. In *City of Glass*, Quinn, the protagonist, decides to imperson-
ate a private investigator (who happens to be named Paul Auster).
Though he is a solitary writer, and has never done any detective
work before, he takes on a case that involves protecting a young man
from a potentially violent and insane father, whom he must shadow.
He pursues this lunatic father with desperate fervor throughout the
book. The motive? Quinn's loss of his wife and son, who died several years before the book begins. Quinn, writes Auster, "wanted to
be there to stop him. He knew he could not bring his own son back to
life, but at least he could prevent another from dying. It had suddenly
become possible to do this, and standing there on the street now,
the idea of what lay before him loomed up like a terrible dream. He
thought of the little coffin that held his son's body and how he had
seen it on the day of the funeral being lowered into the ground."

This is the kind of balsa wood backstory that is knocked into
"realist" Hollywood plots every day. Now, a certain kind of comic
postmodernist could play such stuff for laughs, might concede that
the "realistic" material is just as jokey or artificial as the nonrealistic
material—much as, say, the early postmodern Irish writer Flann
O'Brien brilliantly undermines all conventional motive and conse-
quence in his novel *The Third Policeman*. But Auster seems to believe in the actuality of his characters' motives, even if the reader
never does. Thus, while Flann O'Brien is truly funny, Auster is only
ever unwittingly funny. In *The Book of Illusions*, an excruciating
example of this unintended comedy occurs when Alma tells David
Zimmer that Hector Mann and Frieda had a son, Thaddeus, or Tad
for short, who died at the age of three. Imagine the effect it had on
them, she says. Zimmer, who lost Marco and Todd, his two sons, in
the plane crash that also killed his wife, replies that of course he
can imagine such pain. Alma, realizing her mistake, embarrassedly
apologizes. "Don't be sorry," says Zimmer. "It's just that I know what
you're talking about. No mental gymnastics required to understand
the situation. Tad and Todd. It can't get any closer than that, can it?"
The reader has the urge to blow a Flann O'Brien–size raspberry at

Auster's laughable seriousness. Zimmer sounds less like a grieving father than a canny deconstructionist leading a graduate seminar. But Auster is death-suited and thin-lipped here, wanting from the sober scene both the emotional credibility of conventional realism and a frisson of postmodern wordplay (a single letter separates the two names, and *Tod* is German for "death").

What Auster often gets instead is the worst of both worlds: fake realism and shallow skepticism. The two weaknesses are related. Auster is a compelling storyteller, but his stories are assertions rather than persuasions. They assert themselves: they hound the next revelation. Because nothing is persuasively assembled, the inevitable postmodern disassembly leaves one largely untouched. (The disassembly is also grindingly explicit, spelled out in billboard-size type.) Presence fails to turn into significant absence, because presence was not present enough. This is Auster's great difference from postmodern novelists like José Saramago or the Philip Roth of *The Ghost Writer* and *The Counterlife*. Saramago's realism is deeply ironic, and his skepticism feels real. Roth's narrative games emerge naturally out of his consideration of ordinary human ironies; they do not start life as allegories about the relativity of mimesis (though they may become them, and then feed back into the consideration of ordinary human ironies). Saramago and Roth both assemble and disassemble their stories in ways that seem fundamentally grave. They are ironists, and the irony has deep roots.

Despite all the games, Auster is really the most unironic of contemporary writers. Return to Adam Walker's profession of mortification in *Invisible*:

> After torturing myself for close to a week, I finally found the courage to call my sister again, and when I heard myself spewing out the whole sordid business to Gwyn over the course of our two-hour conversation, I realized that I didn't have a choice. I had to step forward. If I didn't talk to the police, I would lose all respect for myself, and the shame of it would go on haunting me for the rest of my life.

A narrator who trades in such banalities is difficult to credit, and the writer who lends him those words seems uninterested in persuading us that they mean anything. But once again, here is an Auster character keen to persuade us, in words of air, of the gravity of his motives, the depths of his anguish: "This failure to act is far and away the most reprehensible thing I have ever done, the low point in my career as a human being." It forced me to "confront my own moral weakness, to recognize that I had never been the person I thought I was." This shame supposedly determines the course of Walker's life. A year later, in Paris, he runs into Born again, and hatches a plan for revenge that will involve informing Born's fiancée of his murderous past. Walker has never been a vengeful person, "has never actively sought to hurt anyone, but Born is in a different category, Born is a killer, Born deserves to be punished, and for the first time in his life Walker is out for blood."

You will notice that the novel's narration has switched from first person to third person—and that the novel's prose has not adjusted its awfulness. The switch in narration is less complex than it seems. An Austerian framing device is in operation. Walker's account of how he met Born in 1967 (the first section of the novel) is revealed, in the novel's second section, to be a manuscript, which he has been working on as an adult, and which he has sent to his old Columbia friend James Freeman, now a well-known writer. Freeman is the only person in possession of this text, which recounts Walker's youthful adventures in New York and Paris, and which moves between first-, second-, and third-person narration. The second section of Walker's narrative contains a scandalous (and quite touching) account of the incestuous affair Walker carried on with his sister, Gwyn, in the summer of 1967, just before he left for Paris. Auster's writing stirs in this passage about taboo breaking, almost as if the radicalism of the content challenges something in his prose: the story has a vividness and pathos largely absent from the rest of the book.

Later in the novel, after the death of Adam Walker, James Freeman sends Walker's manuscript to Gwyn, who denies the incest.

The reader is free to infer, if he so wishes, that Walker invented the relationship with his sister, in part as a way of compensating for the grief of his lost brother. Perhaps he also invented Born's murder of Cedric Williams, and for similar reasons? Unwisely, the novel ends by returning to its least plausible character, Rudolf Born, who is glimpsed, in the present day, now fat and old, and living on a Caribbean island, looked after by servants in expensive isolation like some kind of Dr. No gone to seed. The vitality of the passage about Adam Walker's possible incest is squeezed at either end of the novel by the flamboyantly unreal Born.

The classic formulations of postmodernism, by theorists and philosophers like Maurice Blanchot and Ihab Hassan, emphasize the way that contemporary language abuts silence. For Blanchot, as indeed for Beckett, language is always announcing its invalidity. Texts stutter and fragment, shred themselves around a void. Perhaps the strangest element of Auster's reputation as an American postmodernist is that his language never registers this kind of absence at the level of the sentence. The void is all too speakable in Auster's work. The pleasing, slightly facile books come out almost every year, as tidy and punctual as postage stamps, and the applauding reviewers line up like eager collectors to get the latest issue. Peter Aaron, the narrator of *Leviathan*, whose own prose is so pressureless, claims that "I have always been a plodder, a person who anguishes and struggles over each sentence, and even on my best days I do no more than inch along, crawling on my belly like a man lost in the desert. The smallest word is surrounded by acres of silence for me."

Not enough silence, alas.

"REALITY EXAMINED TO THE POINT OF MADNESS": LÁSZLÓ KRASZNAHORKAI

"Reality examined to the point of madness." What would this look like, in contemporary writing? It might look like the fiction of László Krasznahorkai, the difficult, peculiar, obsessive, visionary Hungarian novelist, the author of six novels, only two of which are presently available in English, *The Melancholy of Resistance* (which appeared in Hungarian in 1989, and in English in 1998) and *War and War* (which appeared in 1999, and was translated in 2006), both published by New Directions. Postwar avant-garde fiction, like postwar conventional fiction, has tended to move between augmentation (abundance, immersion, getting more in) and subtraction (reduction, minimalism, lack, what Samuel Beckett called "lessness"): Beckett started out as an augmenter, and ended his life as a subtractor. But this division is not really a sharp one, because augmentation in the avant-garde novel often looks like a kind of subtraction: augmentation takes the form of an intensification of the sentence rather than an intensification of the things that many people habitually associate with the novel—plots, characters, furniture, objects. A lot has already disappeared from this fictional world, and the writer concentrates on filling the sentence, using it to notate, produce, and reproduce the tiniest qualifications, hesitations, intermittences, affirmations, and negations of existence. This is one reason why very long, breathing, unstopped sentences, at once literary and vocal, are almost inseparable from the progress of experimental fiction since the 1950s. Claude Simon, Thomas Bernhard, José Saramago, W. G. Sebald, Roberto Bolaño, David Foster Wallace, James Kelman, and László Krasznahorkai have used the long sentence to do many different things, but all of them have been, in one way or another, at odds with a merely grammatical realism, whereby the real is made to fall into approved units and packets.

This grammatical antirealism is not necessarily hostile to the real; in fact, all of these writers could be called realists, of a kind. But the reality many of them are interested in is "reality examined to the point of madness." The phrase is László Krasznahorkai's, and of all these novelists, Krasznahorkai is perhaps the strangest. His tireless, tiring sentences—a single one can fill an entire chapter— feel potentially endless, and are presented without paragraph breaks. The poet George Szirtes, Krasznahorkai's brilliant translator, refers to his prose as "a slow lava-flow of narrative, a vast black river of type." It is often hard to know what Krasznahorkai's characters are thinking, because this author's fictional world hangs on the edge of a revelation that never quite comes. In the extraordinary *War and War*, Gyorgy Korin, an archivist and local historian from a provincial Hungarian town, is going mad. For the rest of the novel, he stands "on the threshold of some decisive perception," but we never discover what that perception is. Here is a necessarily long quote from early in the book, as Krasznahorkai introduces Korin's relentless mental distortions:

> because he didn't feel like going home to an empty apartment on his birthday, and it really was extremely sudden, the way it struck him that, good heavens, he understood nothing, nothing at all about anything, for Christ's sake, nothing at all about the world, which was a most terrifying realization, he said, especially in the way it came to him in all its banality, vulgarity, at a sickeningly ridiculous level, but this was the point, he said, the way that he, at the age of forty-four, had become aware of how utterly stupid he

seemed to himself, how empty, how utterly blockheaded he had been in his understanding of the world these last forty-four years, for, as he realized by the river, he had not only misunderstood it, but had not understood anything about anything, the worst part being that for forty-four years he thought he had understood it, while in reality he had failed to do so; and this in fact was the worst thing of all that night of his birthday when he sat alone by the river, the worst because the fact that he now realized that he had not understood it did not mean that he *did* understand it now, because being aware of his lack of knowledge was not in itself some new form of knowledge for which an older one could be traded in, but one that presented itself as a terrifying puzzle the moment he thought about the world, as he most furiously did that evening, all but torturing himself in the effort to understand it and failing, because the puzzle seemed ever more complex and he had begun to feel that this world-puzzle that he was so desperate to understand, that he was torturing himself trying to understand was really the puzzle of himself and the world at once, that they were in effect one and the same thing, which was the conclusion he had so far reached, and he had not yet given up on it, when after a couple of days, he noticed that there was something the matter with his head.

The passage has many of Krasznahorkai's qualities: the relentless ongoingness of the syntax; the way Korin's mind stretches and then turns back on itself, like a lunatic scorpion trying to sting itself; the perfect comic placement of the final phrase ("something the matter with his head"). The prose has about it a kind of self-correcting shuffle, as if something were genuinely being worked out, and yet, painfully and humorously, the self-corrections never result in the correct answer. As in Thomas Bernhard, whose influence is felt on Krasznahorkai's work, a single word or compound ("puzzle," "world-puzzle") is seized and worried at, murdered into unmeaning, so that its repetition begins to seem funny and alarming at once. Whereas the characters in Bernhard's work engage in elegant, even oddly formal, rants—which can be removed from the fictions and performed as bitterly comic set pieces—Krasznahorkai pushes the long sentence to its farthest extreme, miring it in a thick, recalcitrant atmosphere, a kind of dynamic paralysis in which the mind turns over and over to no obvious effect.

In *War and War*—whose epigraph is "Heaven is sad"—Korin has found a manuscript in the archive where he works. He came across the text, which seems to date from the early 1940s, in a box labeled "Family Papers of No Particular Significance." This text is a fictional narrative about four men, named Kasser, Falke, Bengazza, and Toot, who have various adventures, from Crete, to Cologne, to the north of England, and in different periods of history. Korin is overwhelmed by the beauty of this unknown manuscript; at the moment he took it out of its box, "his life changed forever." Already unstable, he decides that the manuscript holds a religious or visionary answer to the "puzzle" of his life. He feels sure that it is really "speaking about the Garden of Eden," and decides that he must go to what he thinks of as *"the very center of the world*, the place where matters were actually decided, where things happened, a place such as Rome had been, ancient Rome, where decisions had been made and events set in motion, to find that place and *then* quit everything." He decides this place is New York. There, he will publish the manuscript by typing it up and putting it on the Internet. Then, he thinks, his life will come to an end.

László Krasznahorkai was born in Gyula, in southeast Hungary, in 1954. He has lived in both Germany and America, but his name is more familiar in Europe than here (in Germany, he is almost canonical, partly because of the amount of time he has spent there, and partly because of his fluent German, and is spoken of as a potential Nobel laureate). He is probably best known through the oeuvre of the director Béla Tarr, who has worked with Krasznahorkai on several movies, including *Damnation*, *Werckmeister Harmonies* (Tarr's version of *The Melancholy of Resistance*), and the massive, overwhelming *Sátántangó*, which lasts for over seven hours. These bleak, cavernous works, which in their spectral black-and-whiteness, sparse dialogue, and reticent scores seem constantly to be wanting to revert to silent pictures, offer a filmmaker's analog of Krasznahorkai's serpentine sentences in their extraordinarily long tracking shots, which can last as long as ten minutes: in *Werckmeister Harmonies*, the camera accompanies for many minutes two characters, Mr. Eszter and Valuska, as they walk through the streets of a gray provincial town; the wordless, stretched ambulation seems almost to occur in real time. Throughout the film, the camera lingers on the blank, illuminated face of Valuska (a naive and troubled visionary) with the devotion of a believer kissing an icon. *Sátántangó* uses a complex tangolike structure (six steps forward, six back) to present the tableau of a collective farm on the brink of collapse. It is famous both for its monumental length and its long, uncut scenes, such as one of villagers drunkenly dancing (an intoxication that, according to Tarr, was not fictional).

These are daring, austere works, but they cannot replicate the peculiar engrossment of Krasznahorkai's prose (nor do they exactly seek to, of course). *Werckmeister Harmonies* considerably simplifies the political machinations of the villagers in *The Melancholy of Resistance*, at the cost of pushing the story toward a Central European magical realism. So readers of English await more of Krasznahorkai's fiction and are, seemingly, reliant on his talented translator, George Szirtes, and on the enlightened largesse—for that's what it necessarily is—of New Directions. His work tends to get passed around like rare currency. I first heard of *The Melancholy of Resistance* because a freakishly well-read Romanian graduate student handed me a copy, convinced I would like it. I opened it, was slightly excited and slightly alienated by the "slow lava-flow of narrative," and then put the book on a shelf, in that resignedly optimistic way that one deals with difficult work—one day, one day . . . The sense of somewhat cultic excitement persists, apparently. While I was taking notes on these books, a Hungarian woman stopped at my table in a café and intensely asked me why I was studying *this particular author.* She knew his work, indeed she knew the author (and had, she said, gone to see *Pulp Fiction* with him in Boston, when it came out), and she would like to talk to me now about *this writer* . . .

The excitement has something to do with Krasznahorkai's literary mysteriousness. Thomas Bernhard's world, by comparison, is at once reasonable and insane: a pianist and writer, say, recalls a friend who committed suicide and their interaction wth Glenn Gould. This book—Bernhard's *The Loser*—is an extreme form of unreliable first-person narration but at least conforms to a basic generic conventionality. Even if the sentences are difficult, such a world is comprehensible, even desperately logical. But the abysses in Krasznahorkai are bottomless and not logical. Krasznahorkai often deliberately obscures the referent, so that we have no idea what is motivating the fictions: reading him is a little like seeing a group of people standing in a circle in a town square, apparently warming their hands at a fire, only to discover, as one gets closer, that there is no fire, and that they are gathered around nothing at all.

In *War and War*, Korin is convinced of the transcendent importance of his discovered manuscript. He travels to New York, finds lodgings with a Hungarian interpreter, Mr. Sárváry, gets a computer, and begins to type up the text. But the desperation of his attachment to this text is equaled only by his inability to describe its actual import:

> It took no more than the first three sentences to convince
> him that he was in the presence of an extraordinary docu-
> ment, something so out of the ordinary, Korin informed
> Mr. Sárváry, that he would go so far as to say that it, that is
> to say the work that had come into his possession, was a
> work of astonishing, foundation-shaking, cosmic genius, and,
> thinking so, he continued to read and reread the sentences
> till dawn and beyond, and no sooner had the sun risen but
> it was dark again, about six in the evening, and he knew,
> absolutely knew, that he had to *do something* about the vast

thoughts forming in his head, thoughts that involved making major decisions about life and death, about not returning the manuscript to the archive but ensuring its immortality in some appropriate place . . . for he had to make this knowledge the basis of the rest of his life, and Mr. Sárváry should understand that this should be understood in its strictest sense, because by dawn he had really decided that, given the fact that he wanted to die in any case, and that he had stumbled on the truth, there was nothing to do but, in the strictest sense, to stake his life on immortality.

It is not just that this "truth" upon which Korin has stumbled is not defined; it is also that Krasznahorkai recesses Korin himself: this passage is third-person description, but notice the strange, unstable way in which it veers between the report of a present activity ("he continued to read and reread the sentences till dawn"), the description of a mental state ("he had to *do something* about the vast thoughts forming in his head"), and an account of an unstoppable monologue that Korin is apparently delivering to Mr. Sárváry ("something so out of the ordinary, Korin informed Mr. Sárváry"). The result is that the entire passage, even those elements that seem anchored in objective fact, has the quality of hallucination. One senses that Korin spends his entire time either manically talking to other people or manically talking to himself, and that there may not be an important difference between the two. Both Bernhard and Sebald similarly recess their characters, so that a character's stories and impressions are often told to someone else before being told to the reader, and everything gets, as it were, an extra layer of fictionality. As in Sebald, almost every page of *War and War* contains the phrase "said Korin," or some variation thereon ("It was Hermes, said Korin, Hermes lay at the heart of everything"). At one moment we get this sublime confusion: "believe me when I say, as I said before, he said, that the whole thing is unreadable, insane!!!"

In New York, Korin starts to tell first Mr. Sárváry, and then

Sárváry's partner, about the manuscript. Day after day, he sits in the kitchen, retelling the stories about Kasser, Falke, Bengazza, and Toot. Krazsnahorkai reproduces these strange and beautiful fictions—there are remarkable passages about Cologne Cathedral and Hadrian's Wall. Korin tells Sárváry's partner that as he reads the manuscript and types it up, he can "see" these characters, because the text is so miraculously powerful: "he could see their faces and expressions from the moment he started reading as clearly as anything . . . faces you see once and never forget, said Korin." And slowly the reader confirms what he has suspected since the start, that Korin found no manuscript but is writing his own in New York; that "the manuscript" is a mental fiction, a madman's transcendent vision. The "said Korin" tag inevitably slips into the implied "wrote Korin." Reading, saying, writing, thinking, and inventing are all mixed up in this novel, and inevitably get mixed up in the reader's mind, too.

Which is a way of suggesting that this is one of the most profoundly unsettling experiences I have had as a reader. By the end of the novel I felt that I had got as close as literature could possibly take me to the inhabiting of another person, and in particular the inhabiting of a mind in the grip of "war and war"—a mind not without visions of beauty, but also utterly lost in its own boiling, incommunicable fictions, its own grotesquely fertile pain ("Heaven is sad"). This pain is gravely inscribed into the pages of *War and War* much as Korin feels that pain is inscribed into the pages of his own manuscript:

> the manuscript was interested in one thing only, and that was *reality examined to the point of madness*, and the experience of all those intense mad details, the *engraving* by sheer manic repetition of the matter into the imagination, was, and he meant this literally, Korin explained, as if the writer had written the text not with pen and words but with his nails, scratching the paper into the paper and into the mind.

Since *War and War*, Krasznahorkai has also published, in English, a small collection of linked texts—not a novel, but a collaboration between the writer and the German artist Max Neumann. *Animalinside* (translated by Ottilie Mulzet, and published jointly by New Directions, Sylph Editions of London, and the Center for Writers and Translators at the American University in Paris) is a series of fourteen exquisite and enigmatic paintings, with short, paragraph-length texts by Krasznahorkai. In a brief introduction, Colm Tóibín explains that Krasznahorkai first worked from one of Neumann's images, "and then Neumann, spurred in turn by the words, made the rest of the images to which Krasznahorkai, his mind let loose by the captured visuals, responded by writing the other thirteen texts." Neumann's images feature black dogs, pasted in dense silhouette into the pictures, sometimes menacing and wolfish, sometimes playful and even cartoonish. In the first, a dog (or wolf) seems poised to jump, but appears to be imprisoned in a small room, its head almost hitting the ceiling. In the fourth, the black dog, again leaping, is trapped within a gridlike rectangle. In the fifth, a man calmly reads a newspaper—he looks like a contented, professorial gent—while the black dog leaps at his head from the left of the picture.

Resembling, in form, Beckett's *Texts for Nothing*, Krasznahorkai's words often seem like a kind of commentary on late Beckett—there is a steady emphasis on nothingness, entrapment, going on and being unable to go on. These beautiful fragments have the packed intensity of Krasznahorkai's longer fiction, in particular its control of repetition and echo. In the first text, for instance, Krasznahorkai sees the dog as a boxed victim, desperate to escape its cage, and condemned to "howl with one howl." He takes two words, "tautening" and "nothing," and makes "one howl" of them, by using them again and again:

I want to stretch open the walls, but they have tautened me here, and here I remain in this tautening, in this constraint,

and there is nothing else for me to do but howl, and now
and forever I shall be nothing but my own tautening and
my own howling, everything that there was for me has become nothing . . . I have nothing in common with this
space, in the entire God-given world I have nothing in
common with this structure . . . so that I don't exist, I only
howl, and howling is not identical with existence, on the
contrary howling is despair.

The reader might think of Beckett's *The Unnamable*, and the narrator's cry at being "a wordless thing in an empty place, a hard shut
dry cold black place, where nothing stirs, nothing speaks . . . like a
caged beast born of caged beasts born of caged beasts born of caged
beasts born in a cage and dead in a cage, born and then dead."
Krasznahorkai is a more political writer than Beckett, and inevitably this caged beast accrues political and moral implication. This
dog is both victim and aggressor; aggressor because it is victim. If it
could, it would "jump up to sink my teeth into your throat." In the
fifth text, which accompanies the picture of the dog leaping at
the man contentedly reading a newspaper, the beast seems to have
become the Other, everything that threatens that bourgeois con-
tentment—an immigrant perhaps, a terrorist, a revolutionary, or
just the feared stranger: "I shall rear up and tear apart your face
and then what good will all your expectations spent in horror, in
anguish, in dread turn out to be." The dog promises to come like
the apocalypse, like a thief in the night, and shatter every consoling
structure: "because in reality I will be there so quickly that it will
be impossible at all to measure it . . . because before me there is no
past, after me there will be no need of the future, because there
will be no future, because my existence is not measured by time . . .
you raise your head from today's newspaper, or you just happen to
look up, and there I am in front of you." By the end of this relentless
text, the dog has passed through the political and become metaphysical or theological. The dog is now everyone's secret dread,
everyone's inevitable fate: it might be suffering, pain, death, evil,

what Norman Rush in his novel *Mortals* calls "hellmouth": "the opening up of the mouth of hell right in front of you, without warning." And though Krasznahorkai's dog seems to be thinking its savage thoughts and threats and aiming them at the human in a terrible monologue, the subtle suggestion is that this may be nothing more than the recitation of human fear, a projection of savagery *onto* the Other, by the man mildly reading his newspaper.

Krasznahorkai is clearly fascinated by apocalypse, by broken revelation, indecipherable messages. To be always "on the threshold of some decisive perception" is as natural to a Krasznahorkai character as thinking about God is to a Dostoevsky character; the Krasznahorkai world is a Dostoevskian one from which God has been removed. His novel *The Melancholy of Resistance* is a kind of comedy of apocalypse, a book about a God that not only failed but didn't even turn up for the exam. Less manic, less entrapped than *War and War*, it has elements of a traditional social novel; it is set in a provincial Hungarian town and features a range of vivid characters—the wicked, quasi-fascist Mrs. Eszter, who is plotting to take over the town and appoint herself head of a committee for moral and social renewal; her sickly, philosophical husband, a musician who long ago resigned from his directorship of the town orchestra and spends his days on a chaise longue, thinking bitter and refined thoughts; János Valuska, a postman and visionary dreamer, who walks all day through the town "considering the purity of the cosmos," and is mocked by people who think him simple or odd; and the kind of supporting cast you want in Central European comic novels (the drunken police chief, the hapless mayor).

But this kind of summary does no justice to the unfathomable strangeness of this novel. The town is in a state of decline and uncertainty: the streetlights are out, rubbish is piling up uncollected. A traveling circus arrives, whose only attraction is an enormous whale, mounted in a curious, doorless truck, and some pickled embryos. The circus has been moving through the region, accompanied by a group of apparently aimless but oddly menacing onlookers, men who hang around the town's main square near the whale, waiting for something to happen. Everything is full of vague and doomy im-minence, and Mrs. Eszter sees her opportunity: if she can foment (or even manage) some kind of anarchy, blame the unrest on un-named "sinister forces," and then successfully quash that unrest, she may attain her desire, to head the "tidy yard and orderly house movement." The men do eventually go on the rampage, smashing up things and people, burning buildings. But why? We are never told. One of them states that "we could not find a fit object for our disgust and despair, and so we attacked everything in our way with an equal and infinite passion." The army is called in, and Mrs. Eszter triumphs. Within fourteen days of taking charge, she has "swept away the old and established the new."

It is unclear whether the whale really had anything to do with the irruption of violence; Krasznahorkai mischievously dangles the possibility that the circus is a difficult artwork, that it was simply misread by everyone as an agent of apocalypse, in the way that all revolutionary and obscure artworks are misread (by implication, this novel included). Obviously, the whale is some kind of funny, gloomy allusion to Melville, and perhaps Hobbes: like the levia-than, like Moby-Dick, it is vast, inscrutable, terrifying, capable of generating multiple readings. But it is static, dead, immobile, and the Puritan God who makes Melville's theology comprehensible (however incomprehensible Melville's white whale is) has long van-ished from this nightmarish town in the shadow of the Carpathians. Meaning scrambles for traction, and the sinister doorless truck that sits silently in the middle of the town square is also a joke about the Trojan horse: naturally, in Krasznahorkai's world, the Trojan horse is empty. No one gets out of it.

The Melancholy of Resistance is a difficult book, and a pessi-mistic one, too, since it seems to take repeated ironic shots at the possibility of revolution. The only resistance offered to Mrs. Eszter comes in the form of Valuska (who is arrested and put in a mental asylum) and Mrs. Eszter's husband, who is a feeble, isolated foe. The pleasure of the book, and a kind of resistance also, flows from its extraordinary, stretched, self-recoiling sentences, which are marvels of loosely punctuated stream-of-consciousness. These are used with particular brilliance to capture the visionary gropings of Valuska, who wanders through the town thinking cosmic thoughts, and of Mr. Eszter: for years, he has been obsessed with tuning his piano to Werckmeister's old harmonic system, and then with choosing one suite of music to play for the rest of his life.

Krasznahorkai can be a comic writer, and comic justice is meted out on Mr. Eszter, who finally tunes his piano, sits down to play, and is horrified by the hideous sounds he makes. Eszter thinks of music as a kind of resistance to reality:

> Faith, thought Eszter . . . is not a matter of believing something, but believing that somehow things could be different; in the same way, music was not the articulation of some better part of ourselves, or a reference to some notion of a better world, but a disguising of the fact of our irredeemable selves and the sorry state of the world, but no, not merely a disguising but a complete, twisted denial of such facts: it was a cure that did not work, a barbiturate that functioned as an opiate.

Mental fictions may enrage us, and may lead to madness, but they may also provide the only "resistance" available. Korin, Valuska, and Mr. Eszter are, in their different ways, all demented seekers after purity. Alas, though, they are suspended between their "irredeemable selves and the sorry state of the world," and the "twisted denial of such facts" that their private paradises constitute. That they cannot exactly describe or enact their private Edens makes those internal worlds not less but more beautiful. Inevitably, as for all of us but perhaps more acutely for them, "heaven is sad." And so the rage goes on, can't go on, must go on.

ISMAIL KADARE

I.

Like Trieste or Lvov, the ancient city of Gjirokastër, in southern Albania, has passed its history beneath a sign perpetually rewritten, in different hands, but always with the same words: "Under New Management." It enters the historical record in 1336, as a Byzantine possession, but in 1418 was incorporated into the Ottoman Empire. The Greeks occupied it in 1912, yet a year later it became part of the newly independent Albania. During the Second World War, it was taken by the Italians, taken back by the Greeks, and then seized by the Germans: "At dusk the city, which through the centuries had appeared on maps as a possession of the Romans, the Normans, the Byzantines, the Turks, the Greeks and the Italians, now watched darkness fall as a part of the German empire. Utterly exhausted, dazed by the battle, it showed no sign of life."

The novelist Ismail Kadare was born in Gjirokastër, in 1936, and those words are from *Chronicle in Stone*, the great novel he drew out of his boyhood experiences of the Second World War. It was published in Albanian in 1971, and in English in 1987. (The first translation was by the Albanian intellectual and scholar Arshi Pipa; the latest version has been revised by David Bellos, who has added new passages that Kadare first included in the French edition of his *Complete Works*, published in 1997.) Despite the many horrors it describes, *Chronicle in Stone* is a joyful, often comic piece of work, in which that concentrated irony for which Kadare would become famous—most notably in his later political parables and allegories of communism, like *The Concert* and *The Successor*—is already visible. In this early novel the irony has a more generous, truant warmth. A teenage boy narrates the events, at once wide-eyed and sophisticated: he lives in a large, rambling house, surrounded by relatives, in what appears to be the Albanian Muslim section of a city notable for its Ottoman and Christian influences. War arrives, in the form of Italian bombing, British bombing, and finally the dark rondo whereby Greek and Italian occupiers arrive and depart from the stage like vicars in an English farce: "At ten in the morning on Thursday the Italians came back, marching in under freezing rain. They stayed only thirty hours. Six hours later the Greeks were back. The same thing happened all over again in the second week of November."

But in some ways Kadare is more interested in the kinds of stories that the town might have thrown up at any time in the last thousand years. Townspeople talk of spells, witches, ghosts, and legends. Our young narrator discovers *Macbeth* and reads it obsessively, seeing parallels between medieval Scotland and modern Gjirokastër. A group of old women discuss a neighbor's son, who has started wearing spectacles, an occurrence that is treated superstitiously, as an ominous disaster. One of the women, Aunt Xhexho, says: "How I kept from bursting into tears, I'm sure I don't know. He walked over to the cabinet, flipped through a few books, then went over to the window, stopped, and took off his glasses . . . I reached out, picked up the glasses, and put them on. What can I tell you, my friends? My head was spinning. These glasses must be cursed. The world whirled like the circles of hell. Everything shook, rolled, and swayed as if possessed by the devil." Her interlocutors all agree that a terrible fate has befallen the bespectacled boy's family. "It's the end of the world," intones one of the women, regularly. Throughout the novel, these and other neighbors and relatives comment on ordinary events, and this commentary forms a stubborn resistance to the novelty of the occupation. As a mark of how beautifully Kadare blends this atmosphere of the city's traditional antiquity with the rapidity of wartime development, consider something this same woman, Xhexho, says when she first hears an air-raid siren: "Now we have a mourner who will wail for us all."

In this novel, Kadare does something very interesting with narrative: he alternates between the first-person "I" of the young boy who tells the story, and a technique that could be called unidentified free indirect style, whereby he regularly hands off third-person narrative to an implied community, or village chorus, who replace both the boy's perspective and the omniscient perspective of the novelist. On the one hand, the boy is constantly seeing things with the strange, and estranging, perspective of a young writer-to-be (and this is very much a writer's bildungsroman, among other genres). The whole town is anthropomorphized by the narrator—the stones seem to speak, the raindrops are alive, the buildings are like people: "The fortress was indeed very old. It had given birth to the city, and our houses resembled the citadel the way children look like their mothers." A villager's house is seen thus: "It was a somewhat unusual-looking house, with many gable-ends and overhanging eaves. It seemed to me to be dripping with sleep." But the storytelling also switches from the boy to a diffused third person, the voice of the community itself: "We've never seen anything like this, said old women who knew the ways of the world and had even been to Turkey." In the little provincial comic flick of that phrase, "and had even been to Turkey," we can read, if we want to, the limited viewpoint of the boyish narrator. But I think we are meant to hear, instead, the limits of the town instead, as if, say, a group of mothers were speaking among themselves, and agreeing that the wisest women in Gjirokastër "know everything—after all some of them have even been to Turkey!" This is how Kadare can reproduce a good deal of speech in this book without needing to attribute it to any particular source; it is merely interested commentary from the town:

"What about our anti-aircraft gun? Why doesn't it
come on?"

"You're right, we do have an anti-aircraft gun. Why don't
we ever hear it?"

The gap between the provincialism of "and had even been to Turkey" and the cosmopolitanism of the author who is able to see the
provincialism of the phrase is ironic, and it is the fond, rueful ironic
gap that opens up when an author, raised in a small, relatively pe-
ripheral place, leaves it and writes from a larger, relatively more
central place: we find this gap, and this kind of ironic-comic "community" narration, in the Sicilian fiction of Giovanni Verga, in Ce-
sare Pavese's *The Moon and the Bonfires* (narrated by a man who
has returned to the rural village of his boyhood), in V. S. Naipaul's
A House for Mr. Biswas, and in some of José Saramago's fiction. Like
Naipaul's novel, *Chronicle in Stone* recalls a community that can be
remembered by the author but that cannot, practically speaking,
be returned to by the author. For the author has grown up and grown
away, and the old city will rise up to remind him, in famous, more
"sophisticated" places like Paris or Moscow, of that old childhood:
"Often," writes Kadare in a touching postscript, "striding along wide
lighted boulevards in foreign cities, I somehow stumble in places
where no one ever trips. Passersby turn in surprise, but I always
know it's you. You emerge from the asphalt all of a sudden and then
sink back down straight away."

Kadare, thankfully, lacks the weight of Naipaul's postcolonial
baggage, and his novel has none of the savagery of critique that
makes *A House for Mr. Biswas* sometimes uncomfortable to read.
Whereas Naipaul is both proud and ashamed of Trinidad, seeing it
from the viewpoint of metropolitan London, Kadare celebrates his
old town, and celebrates its resistance to foreign occupation, its way-
ward, singular longevity. When, for instance, Kadare describes the
old women known as the "old crones," he essentially praises them for
making *all* forms of rule or government, *all* forms of historical im-
position or occupation, alien and foreign:

These were aged women who could never be surprised
or frightened by anything any more. They had long since
stopped going out of their houses, for they found the world
boring. To them even major events like epidemics, floods
and wars were only repetitions of what they had seen before. They had already been old ladies in the thirties, under
the monarchy, and even before, under the republic in the
mid-twenties. In fact, they were old during the First World
War and even before, at the turn of the century. Granny
Hadje had not been out of her house in twenty-two years.
One old woman of the Zeka family had been inside for
twenty-three years. Granny Neslihan had last gone out thirteen years before, to bury her last grandson. Granny Shano
spent thirty-one years inside until one day she went out into
the street a few yards in front of her house to assault an Italian officer who was making eyes at her great-granddaughter.
These crones were very robust, all nerve and bone, even
though they ate very little and smoked and drank coffee all
day long . . . The crones had very little flesh on their bones,
and few vulnerable spots. Their bodies were like corpses
ready for embalming, from which all innards likely to rot
had already been removed. Superfluous emotions like curiosity, fear and lust for gossip or excitement had been shed
along with useless flesh and excess fat.

It is this affection, which can only be called love, that animates
much of the comedy of the novel. One thinks of this exchange, for
instance, about Stalin:

> "They say there's a man called Yusuf, a man with a red
> beard, Yusuf Stalin his name is, who's going to smash them
> [the Fascists] all to pieces."
> "Is he a Muslim?" Nazo asked.
> Xhexho hesitated a moment, then said confidently, "Yes.
> A Muslim."

Or there is the way the townspeople start orienting their lives around the British bombing raids, as if they were in one of Donald Barthelme's surrealist fictions: "The English planes paid us regular visits every day. They would loom in the sky almost to a schedule, and people seemed to get used to the bombings as a disagreeable part of a daily routine. 'See you tomorrow at the coffee house, right after the bombing,' 'I'll be up at dawn tomorrow; that way I think I'll have the house cleaned before the bombing.' 'Come on, let's go down to the cellar, it's almost time.'"

And yet, if this novel is certainly a loving tribute to a childhood town, that tribute is never uncomplicated. In an emphasis characteristic of Kadare's wit, the memory of the town's past is regularly burlesqued, too:

> I had heard that the First Crusade had passed this way a thousand years before. Old Xixo Gavo, they said, had related this in his chronicle. The crusaders had marched down the road in an endless stream, brandishing their arms and crosses and ceaselessly asking, "Where is the Holy Sepulchre?" They had pressed on south in search of that tomb without stopping in the city, fading away in the same direction the military convoys were now taking.

There is something Monty Python–ish about the Crusaders, miles off course, demanding to see the Holy Sepulchre, and the link to the hopelessness of the modern soldiers is deftly made. One enjoys the comedy while wondering, as one is surely meant to, about the accuracy of Xixo Gavo's chronicle. The novel's complexity has to do with the fact that its comedy is tinged with ruefulness: the city outlives its occupiers, but it cannot fight back and gets bombed anyway. The community dreams fruitlessly of revenge. Dino works on his homemade plane, the plane that is going to vanquish the British or Italian bombers, but when the narrator sees it, he is sad—it is just a few bits of wood in a man's living room. Likewise, the city's old aircraft gun excites everyone, but never shoots down anything. Kadare seems to suggest that one has pride, even nationalistic pride, about being Albanian, but it is necessarily tempered—not by Naipaulian shame but by practical irony, an ironic awareness of Albania's littleness and dispensability in the world:

> "In Smyrna one time," the old artilleryman said, "a dervish asked me, 'Which do you love more, your family or Albania?' Albania, of course, I told him. A family you can make overnight. You walk out of a coffee house, run into a woman on the corner, take her to a hotel, and boom—wife and children. But you can't make Albania overnight after a quick drink in a coffee house, can you? No, not in one night, and not in a thousand and one nights, either." . . .
>
> "Yes, sir," another old man added. "Albania is a complicated business all right."
>
> "*Ex-treme-ly* complicated. It sure is."

That "extreme complication" is given voice in many of Kadare's later works—as near farce in his wonderful, boisterous Evelyn Waugh–like novel, *The File on H.*, and as fiercely political allegory in works like *The Successor* and *Agamemnon's Daughter*. Nothing is more complicated in *Chronicle of Stone* than the fact that, in Gjirokastër, foreign war is beginning to veer toward civil war. The Greeks and Italians come and go, the British run their bombing raids, and the Germans arrive as occupiers at the end of the book. But there is a way in which all of these conquerors are ephemeral, and seen almost lightly, from a comic distance. Yet when the Communist partisans start rounding up characters we have known for two hundred or so pages, and executing them in the street, the horror is immediate, local, and potentially limitless, and seems to draw a different kind of attention from the author: one is reminded that this book was written in the 1960s and 1970s, when the Communist regime may well have seemed to Kadare to be agonizingly invulnerable. The novel mentions that one day a notice is posted on a ruined house: "*Wanted: the dangerous Communist Enver Hoxha. Aged about 30.*"

Enver Hoxha, the Communist leader who kept a ruthless and paranoid grip on Albania for forty years until his death in 1985, was also born in Gjirokastër, in 1908. The novel does not mention Hoxha again, but his shadow, and the shadow of the regime he would build after the war, falls heavily on the last eighty pages of the book. In one scene, some of the townspeople are deported by the Italians. As a crowd watches, a passerby asks what they have done. Someone else replies: "They spoke against." "What does that mean? Against what?" asks the passerby. "I'm telling you, they spoke against." The absent, suppressed referent—"against what?"—is garish in its silence, and Kadare would become a master analyst of this sinister logic of lunacy, in its Communist totalitarian form. Later, one of the partisans shoots a girl by mistake, in a scene that illustrates all of Kadare's power. He has come for the girl's father, Mak Karllashi, whom he calls "an enemy of the people":

> "I'm no enemy of the people," Mak Karllashi protested. "I'm a simple tanner. I make people's shoes, I make *opingas*."
> The partisan looked down at his own tattered moccasins.
> "Get out of the way, girl," he shouted, aiming his gun at the man. The girl screamed . . . The gun of the one-armed partisan fired. Mak Karllashi went down first. The partisan tried to miss the girl, but in vain. She writhed tight against her father as if the bullets had stitched her body to his.

There is the humble detail of the partisan looking down at his (doubtless worn through) moccasins, and the way this detail is picked up and repeated by the extraordinary image of the bullet "stitching" the daughter to her father (the bullets like needles, but also a beautiful image of how much the daughter wanted to attach herself, sew herself, to her father)—though many great books lay ahead of Kadare when he wrote these words, he has never written better than this.

A page or two later, the same partisan is sentenced to death by fellow partisans for killing the girl (he is accused of "the misuse of revolutionary violence"). With nice political absurdism, he raises his arm and cries: "Long live Communism!" and is immediately shot dead. Though *Chronicle in Stone* ends with the German occupation of the city, it gapes, forebodingly, at the postwar Albanian world.

II.

At the end of the war, though the nine-year-old Ismail Kadare did not know it of course, he and the thirty-seven-year-old Enver Hoxha were approaching each other like two dark dots on a snowy landscape, still miles apart but steadily converging on the same frozen lake. *Chronicle in Stone* represents an act of political resistance, of the cunning, subtle kind that allowed Kadare to survive Hoxha's regime, even as some of his books were banned. *The Palace of Dreams*, published in 1981, and more obviously antagonistic, is one of those censored novels. Like many of Kadare's books, it is set in an imprecise past shaded by myth, but lit by the glare of totalitarian thought control. The Palace of Dreams is the most important government ministry in the Balkan Empire, where bureaucrats sift and decode the dreams of the empire's citizens, all of them working to find the Master-Dreams that will help the sultan in his rule. The novel's hero, from a prominent political family, rises up the ranks of the ministry; yet he cannot save his own family from—indeed, he unwittingly precipitates—their political persecution. Enver Hoxha must have known at once that this surreal dystopia vividly conjured up, in carefully deflected form, the secret police apparatus of modern Albania.

The censoring of *The Palace of Dreams* seems to have pushed Kadare beyond the boundaries of suggestion, allegory, implication, and indirection. Certainly, the novella *Agamemnon's Daughter*, which Kadare wrote in the mid-1980s, around the time of Hoxha's death, is laceratingly direct and bitterly lucid. It is perhaps his greatest book, and, along with its sequel, *The Successor* (2003), surely one of the most devastating accounts ever written of the mental and spiritual contamination wreaked on the individual by the totalitarian state. Kadare's French publisher, Claude Durand, has told of how Kadare smuggled some of his writings out of Albania, in 1986, and handed them to Durand, camouflaging them by changing the Albanian names and places to German and Austrian ones, and attributing the writing to the West German novelist Siegfried Lenz. Durand collected the rest of this work, on two trips to Tirana, and the manuscripts were deposited in a safe at a Paris bank. As unaware as anyone else that Albanian communism had only five years left to run, Kadare envisaged this deposit as an insurance policy, *d'outre-tombe*. In the event of his death, by natural or unnatural causes, the publication of these works would make it "harder," in Durand's words, "for the Communist propaganda machine to bend Kadare's work and posthumous image to its own ends."

That is a considerable understatement. I'm not sure any regime could bend *Agamemnon's Daughter* to is own ends. It is a terrifying work, relentless in its critique. It is set in Tirana in the early 1980s, during the May Day Parade. The narrator is a young man who works in radio broadcasting, and who has been unexpectedly invited to attend the festivities from inside the Party grandstand. The formal invitation is unexpected, because the narrator is a passionate liberal, strongly (though privately) opposed to the regime, and because he has recently survived a purge at his radio station, resulting in the relegation of two colleagues. On the day of the parade, he cannot stop thinking about his lover, Suzana, who has broken off their relationship because her father is about to be chosen as the supreme leader's designated successor. He has asked his daughter not to jeopardize his career by consorting with an unsuitable man. Chillingly, she tells her lover that when her father explained the situation to her, "I saw his point of view."

The novella confines itself to the day of the parade, and is essentially a portfolio of sketches of human ruination; a brief *Inferno*, in which victims of the regime are serially encountered by our narrator, as he walks to the stands and takes his seat. There is the neighbor who watches him from his balcony, "looking as sickly as ever . . . He was reputed to have laughed out loud on the day Stalin died, which brought his career as a brilliant young scientist to a shuddering halt." There is Leka B., a former journalist who displeased the authorities and got transferred to the provinces, to run amateur theatricals. He tells the narrator that he put on a play that turned out to have "no less than thirty-two ideological errors!" Kadare's comment is withering: "It was as if he were delighted with the whole business and held it in secret admiration." There is G.Z., another former colleague, who has survived a purge, though no one knows quite how: "his whole personality and history corresponded in sum to what in relatively polite language is called a pile of shit." Kadare likens him to the Bald Man in the Albanian folktale, who is rescued from hell by an eagle—"but on one condition. Throughout the flight, the raptor would need to consume raw meat." Eventually, since the journey takes several days, the Bald Man has to offer his own flesh to feed the bird, and by the time he makes it to the upper world, he is no more than a bag of bones.

At the center of *Agamemnon's Daughter* is an icy reinterpretation of the Iphigenia story. The narrator reflects on Euripides's play, and on Iphigenia's apparently willing self-sacrifice, in order to help her father's military ambitions. He turns around the Greek tale in his mind and blends it with the remembered pain of Suzana's departure. Hadn't Stalin, he thinks, sacrificed his son Yakov, so as to be able to claim that he was sharing in the common lot of the Russian soldier? But what if the story of Agamemnon is really the story of Comrade Agamemnon—the first great account of absolute political tyranny? What if Agamemnon, in "a tyrant's cynical ploy," had merely used his daughter, so as to legitimate warfare? As, surely, Yakov, "may he rest in peace, had not been sacrificed so as to suffer the same fate as any other Russian soldier, as the dictator had claimed, but to give Stalin the right to demand the life of anyone else." The narrator realizes, as he watches Suzana's father standing next to the Supreme Guide on the grandstand, that the Supreme Guide must have asked his deputy to initiate his daughter's sacrifice. *Agamemnon's Daughter* ends with this dark, spare, aphoristically alert declamation: "Nothing now stands in the way of the final shriveling of our lives."

Kadare is inevitably likened to Orwell and Kundera, but he is a deeper ironist than the first, and a better storyteller than the second. He is a compellingly ironic storyteller because he so brilliantly summons details that are able to explode with symbolic reality. Anyone who has read *The Successor* cannot forget the moment when the Hoxha figure, called simply the Guide, visits the newly renovated home of his designated successor. The Successor's wife offers to show the Guide around, despite the anxiety felt by others that the lavishness of the renovation may have been a huge political blunder. The Guide stops to examine a new living room light switch, a dimmer that is the first of its kind in the country.

> Silence had fallen all around, but when he managed to turn on the light and make it brighter, he laughed out loud. He turned the switch further, until the light was at maximum strength, then laughed again, ha-ha-ha, as if he'd just found a toy that pleased him. Everyone laughed with him, and the game went on until he began to turn the dimmer down. As the brightness dwindled, little by little everything began to freeze, to go lifeless, until all the many lamps in the room went dark.

In its concentrated ferocity, this seems like something very ancient: we could almost be reading Tacitus on Tiberius.

III.

Alas, there is nothing quite of this high order in Kadare's novel *The Accident* (translated from the Albanian by John Hodgson). The new book is spare and often powerful, but it is a bit too spare, so that the ribs of allegory show through, in painful obviousness. Many of Kadare's familiar procedures and themes are in evidence, beginning with the positing of an enigma that needs decoding. One morning in Vienna, sometime not long after the end of the war in Kosovo, a

young Albanian couple is killed in a car accident. The taxi that had
been taking them from their hotel to the airport suddenly veers off
the autobahn and crashes. The taxi driver, who survives, can give
no reasonable account of why he left the road, except to say that he
had been looking in his rearview mirror at the couple, who had
been "trying to kiss," when a bright light distracted him. The accident is suspicious enough to attract various investigators, not least
the intelligence services of Serbia, Montenegro, and Albania. The
dead man, known as Besfort Y., appears to have been an Albanian
diplomat, working at the Council of Europe, and may have been
involved in NATO's decision to bomb Serbia. Perhaps the woman
who died in the car, who was Besfort's girlfriend, and is known in
the reports as Rovena St., knew too much, and Besfort tried to kill
her, in a botched plan? But why did Besfort seem to refer to Rovena
as "a call girl"? A few months before the accident, he had taken her
to an Albanian motel and she had been "frightened for her life." So
a friend of Rovena's tells investigators. Rovena, says the friend,
"knew the most appalling things . . . She knew the precise hour
when Yugoslavia would be bombed, days in advance."

The security services give up, in the face of the usual Balkan
incomprehensibility, and a mysterious, nameless "researcher" takes
over. This authorial stand-in, who works "without funds or re-
sources or powers of constraint," decides to reconstruct the last forty
weeks of the couple's lives, using diaries, letters, phone calls, and
the testimonies of friends.

> Everywhere in the world events flow noisily on the sur-
> face, while their deep currents pull silently, but nowhere is
> this contrast so striking as in the Balkans. Gales sweep the
> mountains, lashing the tall firs and mighty oaks, and the
> whole peninsula appears demented.

Kadare feeds off Balkan incomprehensibility: he likes to tease
it and tease at it, while simultaneously making fun of people who
talk about "Balkan incomprehensibility." He is deeply interested in

misreading, yet his prose has a classical lucidity, so that much of his power as a storyteller has to do with his ability to provide an extraordinarily lucid analysis of incomprehensibility. This analysis veers between the comic and the tragic, and never finally settles in one mode. In both *The Accident* and *The Successor*, we begin with an apparent accident—in the earlier novel, the country's designated successor has been found in his bedroom, shot dead—that allows Kadare to work through rival explanations. (*The Successor* is based on the "mysterious" death, reported as suicide, of the Albanian prime minister, Mehmet Shehu, in 1981. He had been Hoxha's closest political ally for decades, but after his death he was denounced as a traitor and enemy of the people, and his family arrested and imprisoned.) A question that haunts both novels is: When did it begin? When was "the accident" inevitable? When did the tide first turn against the Successor? Was it when the Guide failed to come to the Successor's birthday party, for instance? The deconstructive, blackly surreal answer, of course, is that it has always begun; the tide was turning against the Successor even as he was rising up the Party ranks.

Likewise, in *The Accident*, one can see that Besfort and Rovena were always doomed, and that the reason, as in *The Successor*, is murkily ideological. The nameless "researcher" discovers that Besfort and Rovena have been together for twelve years. Rovena was a student when she met Besfort, who was older than she, and had come to the university at Tirana to teach international law. From the start, the relationship appears to have been electrically erotic, with Besfort as the seducer and dominant partner. The novel hints at very rough sex. They agree to part, but soon reunite. The couple meets in various European cities and expensive hotels, exercising a freedom unthinkable before the collapse of communism, their itinerary largely determined by Besfort's diplomatic travel (where "diplomat" probably also means "spy"). But in Graz, for the first time, Rovena feels that Besfort is suffocating her, a feeling that will mount as the relationship progresses. "You're preventing me from living," she tells him, and elsewhere she complains that "he has me in chains . . . he is the prince and I am only a slave." "He wanted her entirely for himself, like every tyrant." To these charges, he replies that she "took this yoke up yourself, and now you blame me?" He had been her liberator, writes Kadare, "but this is not the first time in history that a liberator had been taken for a tyrant, just as many a tyrant had been taken for a liberator." Partly as a game, and partly as an admission of the terminality of their relationship, the couple start speaking of themselves as client and call girl. Besfort thinks of killing her.

The Accident is a difficult novel. It has a very interrupted form, continually looping back on itself, so that dates and place-names seem almost scrambled and the reader must work a kind of hermeneutic espionage on the text. Unlike in Agamemnon's Daughter and The Successor, the analysis of incomprehensibility seems not lucid but opaque. Yet at the same time, the symbolic pressure seems a little too transparent, not suggestively or richly related to the human narrative. One gathers that Kadare is presenting a kind of allegory about the lures and imprisonments of that new post-Communist tyranny, liberty, and he has Besfort bang home this decoding: "Until yesterday," he tells Rovena, "you were complaining that it was my fault that you aren't free. And now you say you have too much freedom. But somehow it's always my fault." Besfort is the new liberty that Rovena cannot do without, and to which she is willing to be enslaved, and this freedom is dangerous and frequently squalid.

The Accident thus offers an interesting reply to the question with which Kadare closes Agamemnon's Daughter. At the end of that novella, the young narrator thinks of the Communist slogan "Let us revolutionize everything" and asks, rhetorically, "How the hell can you revolutionize a woman's sex? That's where you'd have to start if you were going to tackle the basics—you had to start with the source of life. You would have to correct its appearance, the black triangle above it, and the glistening line of the labia." He means that totalitarianism will always be thwarted by some nonideological privacy, or surplus, beyond its reach. Kundera has repeatedly explored the same question, with regard to a libidinous erotics of resistance. Yet The Accident grimly suggests that it is indeed possible to "revolutionize" a woman's sex, and that capitalism can do it perhaps more easily than communism. After all, the point about Besfort and Rovena, if I am reading the novel right, is that their relationship is thoroughly contaminated by ideology and politics; their very postures of submission and domination are overdetermined.

In a long speech that is surely at the emotional and ideological heart of the book, Besfort tells Rovena, who was only thirteen at the end of the dictatorship, about the kind of madness that prevailed under Hoxha. He describes a world of crazy inversion, reminiscent of Dostoevsky's universe, in which citizens willingly pretended to be conspirators, so as to confess their love for the leader while being simultaneously punished for crimes they had not committed. Each plotter, says Besfort, turned out to be more abject than the last:

> The conspirators' letters from prison became more and more ingratiating. Some requested Albanian dictionaries, because they were stuck for words to express their adoration of the leader. Others complained of not being tortured properly. The protocols sent back from firing squads on the barren sandbank by the river told the same story: their victims shouted, "Long live the leader!," and as they conveyed their last wishes some felt such a burden of guilt that they asked to be killed not by the usual weapons but by anti-tank guns or flamethrowers. Others asked to be bombarded from the air, so that no trace of them would remain . . . Nobody could distinguish truth from fiction in these reports, just as it was impossible to discern what the purpose of the conspirators, or even the leader himself, might be. Sometimes the leader's mind was easier to read. He had enslaved the entire nation, and now the adoration of the conspirators would crown his triumph. Some people guessed that he was sated with the love of his loyal followers, and that he now wanted something new and apparently impossible—the love of traitors.

We are back in the world of Leka B., who was oddly proud of his thirty-two ideological errors, and in the world of *A Chronicle of Stone*, and the partisan who dies shouting "Long live Communism!" Kadare also subtly suggests that this dense, overwrought speech might itself be evidence that Besfort is a victim of the totalitarianism he so despises—that he cannot escape its deformations, its legacies, the memory of its hysteria. But a melancholy thought also casts its shadow. Might this be true of Kadare, too? It seems poignant that easily the most powerful section in the novel returns to old ground and old obsessions, and it seems poignant that this allegory of the tyranny of liberty is less effective, as a novel, than Kadare's earlier allegories of the tyranny of tyranny. Perhaps it is in the nature of freedom, still after all a transitional event in the history of postwar Albania, that a novelist even of Kadare's great powers will seem, when trying to allegorize it, to grasp at amorphousness, will seem to stab at clouds; whereas the old Kadare, who worked within and against totalitarianism, was sustained by the great subject of the Hoxha regime, like a man sitting on a huge statue. Kadare would not be the only novelist who has found, with the collapse of communism, that his world has disappeared, however much he also longed for the destruction of that world. These are early days yet.

ENGLISH MUDDLE:
ALAN HOLLINGHURST

Most of the prose writers acclaimed for "writing beautifully" do no
such thing; such praise is sent comprehensively, like the rain on the
just and the unjust. The English novelist Alan Hollinghurst is one of
the few contemporary writers who deserve the adverb. His prose
has the power of re-description, whereby we are made to notice
something previously neglected. Yet unlike a good deal of modern
writing, this re-description is not achieved only by inventing brilliant metaphors, or by flourishing some sparkling detail, or by lay-
ing down a line of clever commentary. Instead, Hollinghurst works
quietly, like a poet, goading all his words—nouns, verbs, adjectives,
and adverbs—into a stealthy equality in his sentences. I mean something like this, from his novel *The Line of Beauty*: "Above the trees
and rooftops the dingy glare of the London sky faded upwards into
weak violet heights." We can suddenly see the twilit sky of a big city
afresh, and the literary genius is obviously centered in the unexpected strength of that adjective "weak," which brings alive the di-
minishing strata of the urban night sky, overpowered by the bright
lights on the ground. The effect is unexpectedly paradoxical, because we don't usually associate heights with weakness, but with
power or command. And the poetry lies not just in what the sentence paints, but in how it sounds: there is something mysteriously

lovely about the rhythm of "weak violet heights," and the way the two adjectives turn into a noun that is really just another adjective but pluralized into a noun; the sentence does indeed seem to drift away into the far distance: weak violet heights, weak violet heights . . .

At its best, this musicality in Hollinghurst's prose is self-conscious without being self-regarding: his language attends both to itself and to the world. In his second novel, *The Folding Star*, Hollinghurst described the experience of watching the Wimbledon tennis tournament on TV on a warm summer's day, with the windows open. Occasionally, a plane can be heard outside: "the sonic wallow of a plane distancing in slow gusts above." Again, the power comes from nouns and adjectives placed in unusual combinations—the paradox of "slow gusts" (a gust is usually rapid) and the almost onomatopeic "sonic wallow," which truly slows the sentence down. Or again from *The Line of Beauty* comes this fantastically precise description of the hero's trousered erection: "buttoned away in a hard diagonal." We would not normally think of an abstract "diagonal" as having properties of hardness or softness. Yet once the phrase is encountered, it seems exact and inevitable: a "hard diagonal" sounds both firm (the obvious meaning) and difficult (the difficulty of keeping that diagonal buttoned up).

When a writer has an ear as good as Hollinghurst's, the danger is a lush antiquarianism, with all the English ancestors—in particular, Shakespeare, Keats, Hardy, Edward Thomas, Philip Larkin—ripening the sentences to bursting. In addition, Hollinghurst has an appealing love of Henry James, whose presence could be strongly felt in *The Line of Beauty*. But James is a perilous model for a twenty-first-century novelist because his own refinements come so close to self-parody: the contemporary James mimic runs the risk, essentially, of pastiching a parodist. When, for instance, a grand London house, in *The Line of Beauty*, is described as having stone stairs that, on the top flight, give way to the "confidential creak of oak," the reader delights in the phrase, and forgivingly looks the other way at the notably Jamesian alliteration. But in Hollinghurst's latest novel, *The Stranger's Child*, it is harder to ignore this absurdly Jamesian sentence: "This large claim seemed rather to evaporate in its later clauses." Or this: "This was exactly Dudley's version too, though the cool nerve of 'improving' made Daphne laugh." In the new novel, we also find that "Cecil made a low disparaging murmur"; another character says something "with a brave little quiver"; the same character says something "with a little stricken look"; someone else says something "with an air of momentary concession"; and the Augustinian sadness after sex is described as "the bleak little minute of irrational sadness." Sex itself—specifically, gay sex—is feared and anticipated by one character as "the unimagined and vaguely dreaded thing" (compare James's fabled, perhaps apocryphal, premonition of his death: "So here it is at last, the distinguished thing"). This sounds like Max Beerbohm's famous parody of late James. It does a writer as talented as Hollinghurst few favors to be fossicking in fustian in this way; I spent too much time, while reading this often beautiful novel, itching to write a parody of Hollinghurst's Jamesianism. ("Ralph's cock was small but sincere; in the afternoon's fading light, thinned by winter's quick transit, it seemed to Hugh almost shyly noble. The two men could hear Lady Soames's little lacquered laugh, somewhere downstairs . . ." And so on.)

This stylistic antiquarianism might seem a minor failing, were it not that *The Stranger's Child* is itself an exercise in literary antiquarianism. It is about a Rupert Brooke–like poet called Cecil Valance (Hollinghurst's fictional invention), who dies heroically in the First World War. In the section that opens the novel, it is 1913 and Cecil Valance is visiting the family house of his Cambridge chum George Sawle. Cecil, it seems, is bisexual: he flirts with George's sister, Daphne, while frolicking more emphatically with George, who is infatuated with the glamorous and aristocratic poet. During the visit, the two young men struggle to explore a shared erotic life away from society, but they seem to be constantly watched by George's suspicious mother, Freda (it is she who later discovers "the unimagined and vaguely dreaded thing," and who destroys her son's amorous correspondence with Cecil); by George's conventional and not very intelligent brother, Hubert; and by Daphne, a clever, impressionable teenager. Cecil Valance only stays three days at Two Acres, the Sawle family house on the edge of north London, but the house party becomes a piece of literary history, because it is here that Cecil writes a poem for Daphne, which memorializes the house and its garden. It is titled "Two Acres," and after Cecil Valance's death in France, in 1916, it is quoted by Churchill in an obituary of the poet that appears in the *The Times*, and quickly taken up and anthologized as the great English war poem, part bombast and part elegy for a lost English pastoral innocence. This is exactly what happened to the Rupert Brooke poem that begins, "If I should die, think only this of me: / That there's some corner of a foreign field / That is forever England," and Hollinghurst suggests throughout the novel that "Two Acres" is roughly on a par with Brooke's sentimental nationalism ("Two blessèd acres of English ground," runs one of Valance's lines).

The Stranger's Child tracks the afterlife of this poem by following the twentieth-century vicissitudes of the two families, the Valances and the Sawles. A second section, set in 1926, reveals that both Cecil Valance and Hubert Sawle died in the war—although Hubert died in relative obscurity, while Cecil's aristocratic family built a beautiful marble tomb for him in the chapel of the great family house, Corley Court. We learn that the Valance poem is already canonical. The mistress of Corley Court is now Daphne Sawle, who married Cecil's brother, Dudley. George Sawle, it appears, has officially corrected his youthful homosexuality by marrying a rather hideous bluestocking, Madeleine; they are both academics. A third section—the best in the book—jumps ahead to 1967, to a small town near Oxford, where we meet Paul Bryant, a lowly bank clerk. Bryant is gay, with literary aspirations (he reads Angus Wilson), and his connection to Cecil Valance is oblique: the bank's manager, Mr. Keeping, is married to Daphne's daughter Corinna; Cecil Valance was her uncle.

The Valance connection is cemented when Paul meets Peter Rowe, who teaches at a local boys' school: housed in Corley Court, which is no longer inhabited by the Valance family. (Though what is now the school chapel still contains, of course, Cecil Valance's mausoleum.) Paul and Peter become lovers. A fourth section, which takes place in 1980, shows Paul Bryant, now a minor man of letters, working on his biography of Cecil Valance. He assiduously interviews the old survivors—Daphne, who is now in her eighties; George Sawle; and Jonah Trickett, who briefly worked as Cecil's young manservant during the Two Acres visit in 1913. The real subject of Paul's biography, as it is the real subject of Hollinghurst's novel, is the hidden homosexuality of this now idealized literary representative.

This is a big, spacious novel, and Hollinghurst uses the history of the Valance and Sawle families to effect a subtle and moving commentary on English decline. But before giving that complexity its proper due, it seems important to register some dismay at the literariness of the subject, and the quiet politesse of its execution. *The Line of Beauty* was a very Jamesian book, both in theme and style, but it stropped its edges on the hard concerns of contemporary English society. The gorgeous prose did not seem anachronistic when being used to examine Nick Guest's rise in the London of Mrs. Thatcher's 1980s. A steady current of satire kept the writing energetic, alert, devastating. In that novel, the 1980s were not merely a discrete historical period—and so the book was not a historical novel—because the fictional material (love of money, excess of all kinds, fashionable drug abuse, political opportunism, the scythe of AIDS) so easily spilled beyond its temporal borders. Hollinghurst may have seemed at times to be secretly in love with the world of Gerald Fedden, the posh Tory MP whose household Nick gatecrashes, as Evelyn Waugh was in love with the Marchmains; but Nick's lower-middle-class alienation from that privileged world stiffened the book's moral fibers so that it read like some impossible and previously unimagined merging of *Brideshead Revisited* with the watchful, critical postwar avariciousness of middle-class writers like Kingsley Amis and John Braine.

Only about a third of *The Stranger's Child* is set before the
Second World War, but the apparently modern sections are so turned
back toward the subject of Cecil Valance, in a posture of retrospec-
tive literary whodunit, that the novel struggles to escape an old-
fashioned, period feel troublingly akin to, if better written than,
A. S. Byatt's historical novel *The Children's Book*. Here, as in Byatt's
historical reconstruction, there is talk of King's College, Cambridge,
and the Apostles, and Lytton Strachey ("'We do see Lytton from
time to time,' Cecil said, with an air of discretion"), and Rupert
Brooke:

> "Oh, Rupert Brooke," said Freda, "what an Adonis!"
> Cecil gave a snuffly smile as if at some rather basic mis-
> apprehension. "Oh, yes, I know Brooke," he said. "We used
> to see a lot of him in College, but now of course rather less."
> "My mother thinks Rupert's work rather advanced,"
> said George.
> "Really, my dear?" said Elspeth, with twinkling concern.

Most American readers may not be aware of just how thickly traf-
ficked this corridor of English literary history has been in recent
years. A writer like Hollinghurst can spin yards of this soft stuff
practically in his sleep. I found myself reading much of the book trying to waken Hollinghurst from this diligent slumber by muttering
into his ear one of Wyndham Lewis's revolutionary modernist max-
ims, designed to stir England up in the early twentieth century:
"Kill John Bull with Art." For in addition to spinning his nice soft
yards, Hollinghurst, perhaps in deference to the deference of his
material, pulls in the elbows of his prose and too often produces a
kind of polite professionalized filler. He develops a bad habit of pinning tidy little tails onto his characters' exclamations:

> said Clara, with the slight asperity that gave even her
> nicest remarks an air of sarcasm.

said Freda, and frowned at her own sharp tone.

said Clara, with a vague shake of the head.

said Cecil, with the delighted firmness that conceals a measure of uncertainty.

said Mrs Riley, and she made a little grimace of reluctance.

A character says something "drily," only to be followed by another character, less than ten pages later, also saying something "drily." I lost count of how many times people look "levelly" or "narrowly":

John looked at him narrowly.

Rob looked at the last letter more narrowly.

Bryant said, glancing narrowly at Rob.

She looked narrowly towards it.

looked him in the face, levelly but sweetly.

said Daphne, as levelly as she could.

Paul cleared his throat and looked at her more narrowly than before.

A character's blush is even described in that quaint register last encountered in popular writing like the Hardy Boys books: "Rob raised an eyebrow, too, coloured slightly." A conversation is interrupted by a hoary technique: "But at that moment the door was opened by Wilkes and her mother came in." Three pages later, the same conversation is interrupted in exactly the same way: "But at that moment the door flew open, and there was Nanny." And there is a great deal of repetitive muddling:

And a muddled sense of protest.

His heart quickening for a moment in a muddle of protest and shame.

And so the boys carried on into puberty, in a colourful muddle of hearsay and experiment.

> In the usual muddle of gloom and relief.
> Peering forward over the wheel into the muddled glare
> on the edge of Worcester.
> Puzzled for a moment by his own muddled feelings of
> affection and irritation.

These relics—flecks of aspic—are, in themselves, hardly hei-
nous, but cumulatively they suggest an overindulgent hospitality toward the material, a comfort level that the prose persistently locates
and secures. Hollinghurst seems too ready to enjoy a fond English
elegy he should be examining rather than perpetuating. "Muddle,"
for instance, is the quintessential postwar English word: for decades now, the country has been "muddling along" in its own post-
imperial wake. It rather prides itself, in its bashful way, for its ability
"to muddle through." (The historian Peter Hennessy once titled a
book about postwar Britain *Muddling Through*.) Hollinghurst himself appears to link Englishness and muddle in his novel *The Folding Star* when he describes the experience of watching Wimbledon
with the curtains closed as "an English limbo of light and shade,
near and far, subtly muddled and displaced."

But could it be that the word "muddle" offers a nice English
blur where a nasty clarity might be preferable? At one level, *The
Stranger's Child* can seem an exercise in fairly conservative pastoral
elegy centered on two English family houses, both of which are lost
by their declining families. While Corley Court becomes a school,
the Sawle house, Two Acres, is neglected. In a long, moving passage, Paul Bryant tries to find the subject of Cecil's poem, and almost fails. In Stanmore, now in north London, no one has heard of
Two Acres (neither of the house nor of the poem). Even the old
station was closed in 1956. Paul stops a dog walker and asks for
help. "*Two* Acres? No . . . I don't know it. Are you sure it's round
here? . . . We have a third of an acre, and believe me that takes a
good deal of work." Paul does eventually find the house, bleakly
abandoned and showing signs of having been divided into flats—

"like almost every house in London." This shell of former glory is still protected by a burglar alarm bearing the telling name Albion Security:

> You could strip all the romance from a place if you were determined enough, even the romance of decay. He'd had the idea that he would find things more or less as they had been in 1913—more deeply settled in, of course, discreetly modernized, tastefully adapted, but the rockery still there, the "glinting spinney" a beautiful wood, and the trees where the hammock had been slung still bearing the ridges of the ropes in their bark. He thought other resourceful people would have come, over the years, to look at it, and that the house would wear its own mild frown of self-regard, a certain half-friendly awareness of being admired. It would live up to its fame. But really there was nothing to see. The upstairs windows seemed to ponder blankly on the reflections of clouds.

It is a scene that gathers in its easy rhythms a tradition of English pastoral, from poems like Larkin's "MCMXIV" ("Never such innocence, / Never before or since, / As changed itself to past / Without a word") and "Cut Grass" ("Lost lanes of Queen Anne's lace") to novels like *Howards End*, William Golding's *The Pyramid*, and Sebald's Anglophilic *The Rings of Saturn*. Centrally behind it is *Brideshead Revisited*, and where, for Waugh, the plebeian horror of the postwar years is exemplified by the lower-middle-class soldier Hooper, to whom the great house of Brideshead is irrelevant, it could be said that for Hollinghurst the decline from greatness is exemplified by the lower-middle-class Paul Bryant, who tramps around the grounds of the neglected house, at once sleuth and vandal: "He turned his back on the house, put down his briefcase, and had a short fierce piss into the long grass." (An action oddly akin to the poet's in Larkin's "Church Going," who enters the empty church, removes his bicycle clips, and mounts the church's lectern, mockingly miming the words "Here endeth," more loudly than he had meant to.)

Of course, Hollinghurst's analysis is more complicated than Waugh's, because Paul Bryant treasures Two Acres, and is in some ways the keeper of the Valance literary flame. Yet Hollinghurst also unforgivingly prosecutes Bryant in this novel: by the time we encounter him in the 1980s, he is a minor literary schemer, relentless, intrusive, and duplicitous. In the novel's last section, set in 2008, the young man from the provinces, who optimistically read Angus Wilson, has become Paul Bryant "who writes all those biographies—there was that one that caused all the fuss about the Bishop of Durham." Bryant's first book, we learn, was his biography of Cecil Valance, which outed the poet as a gay writer, and which, for good measure, claimed that his brother, Daphne Sawle's husband, was also gay, along with plenty of other family revelations. Bryant may once have treasured Corley Court and Two Acres, but his appreciation seems to have been narrowly political and careerist. Even if Bryant had been, say, a Michael Holroyd (whose biography of Lytton Strachey is mentioned in the novel), full of the right literary love, this biographical custodianship seems a poor substitute for the real thing—a house still alive and properly peopled. Literary flame-keeping, Hollinghurst seems to suggest, is closer to the British "Heritage" industry than we at first imagine.

Fortunately, *The Stranger's Child* also works against its own mild conservatism. Bryant's outing of Cecil Valance is not merely muckraking and a sign of implacable decline, because Hollinghurst's own project in this novel is a similar kind of outing—the retrieval of a buried and largely secretive erotic life. Hollinghurst's best, most delicate writing in this book circles around repressed and suppressed gay experience. Behind Valance's official literary renown is another much more fugitive existence, and both Hollinghurst and Bryant, in their different ways, want to track it down. In this sense, his novel offers, really, an unofficial history of twentieth-century

gay life: there is George's achingly incommunicable love for Cecil
(wonderfully evoked in a few swift scenes); there is the bisexual artist Revel Ralph, who sleeps with Daphne and eventually marries
her; there is the lengthily played out flirtation and consummation of
Paul Bryant and Peter Rowe; there is the revelation that a friend of
the Sawle family, Harry Hewitt, thought of as straight, was in love
with George's brother, Hubert, killed in the First World War. And
there is the sadness of George Sawle's lifelong struggle as an uncon-
vincing heterosexual. The scene when Paul Bryant, in his role as
Valance biographer, goes to the aged George's house to try to coax
him into confession about his relationship with Cecil is both painful
and comic. While George's suspicious wife, Madeleine, lurks outside the room, George shows Paul a photograph—it is of George
and Cecil as young men. Cecil's shirt is off, and George's is half
undone. Later, Paul writes up the moment in his diary (with "C" for
Cecil, and "GFS" for George Sawle):

> It gave me my first real idea of C's body, and because the
> camera was like an intruder I suddenly felt what it must
> have been like to come into his presence—my subject! Very
> odd, and even a bit of a turn-on—as GFS seemed to feel,
> too: "I look positively debauched there, don't I?" he said. I
> said, "And were you?" and felt his hand, rubbing my back
> encouragingly, move down not quite absent-mindedly to
> just above my waist. He said, "I'm afraid I probably was, you
> know."
>
> The atmosphere was now rather tense, and I glanced at
> him to see how conscious he was of it himself. "In what
> way, would you say?" (shifting away a bit, but not wanting
> to startle him). He kept looking at the picture, breathing
> slowly but heavily, as if undecided: "Well, you know, in the
> normal ways," which I suppose was quite a good answer. I
> said something like, "Well, I don't blame you!" "Awful, isn't
> it? I was quite a dish back then! And look at me now"—

turning his face to mine with a jut of his bearded chin
while his hand moved down again in a determined little
rubbing motion on to my bum.

It is one of the achievements of the novel that it systematically vali-
dates the prohibited wisdom of George's "Well, you know, in all the
normal ways" through the depiction of a variety of different gay re-
lationships.

Unfortunately, perhaps because Hollinghurst is so intent on un-
covering the machinery of decorous repression, his own writing
about this buried homosexuality is full of decorous repression—it
inescapably recalls Kazuo Ishiguro's fiction, especially *The Remains
of the Day*, and Hollinghurst can seem to be treading once again
over English ground that has been well worked. After all, it is hardly
a revelation that the young men of the Rupert Brooke era were often
more drawn to each other than to women, and that this attraction
had to be delicately negotiated in a wider world that did not always
indulge it. The velvety fumblings and occlusions of George and
Cecil, or of Harry and Hubert, are fairly tame, and tame by the standards of Hollinghurst's own previous fiction, which has often been
breathtakingly carnal. In particular, there is a mysterious way in
which the novel, even as it paces steadily toward its late revelations,
gets flatter and less interesting. Far too much time is spent on Paul
Bryant's circular, sidelong interviews with George, Daphne, and
Jonah the servant; and Hollinghurst makes the error of filling the
last two hundred pages of the book with what amounts to literary
gossip—a portrait of *The Times Literary Supplement* in the early
1980s, a book party, a scene in a secondhand bookshop, a funeral
"celebration," and a Cecil Valance conference at Oxford, where we
get to meet Paul Fussell and Jon Stallworthy ("He realized that the
man standing near him was Professor Stallworthy, whose life of Wil-
fred Owen had fought rather shy of Owen's feelings for other men.")

The Stranger's Child is a frustrating book, both a large and a
curiously small novel—it trembles for a time on the verge of moving
beyond the parochialism of its familiar literary setting, and is then

finally happy to fall back into the comfy and the known. Reading it, I was put in mind of a phrase from Larkin's "Church Going," which envisages a certain kind of latter-day, fogeyish, antiquarian church visitor—"some ruin-bibber, randy for antique." This novel is randy for antique; I hope its successor, like its predecessor, is randy for the present.

LIFE'S WHITE MACHINE:
BEN LERNER

In his autobiography *My Past and Thoughts*, the nineteenth-century Russian writer Alexander Herzen discussed the moral stagnation that followed the crisis of December 1825, when an optimistic rebellion, led by liberal aristocrats and army officers in St. Petersburg, was easily crushed by Nicholas I, the new tsar. Young radicals, Herzen wrote, discovered a "complete contradiction of the *words* they were taught with the *facts* of life around them." Their books and peers spoke one language, the language of reform and radicalism, but their parents spoke another, that of the dominant political and financial interests. The young man was thrown into a quandary: he could turn away from this chasm and "dehumanize himself" or suffer the heart pain of ideological arrest: "After that there followed for some, the weaker and more impatient, the idle existence of a cornet on the retired list, the sloth of the country, the dressing-gown, eccentricities, cards, wine; for others a time of ordeal and inner travail." From this historical paralysis arose, during the next forty years, the drifting, weak, amoral, angry heroes of Russian literature: Eugene Onegin, Lermontov's Pechorin, Turgenev's Superfluous Man, and Dostoevsky's Underground Man.

Adam Gordon, the narrator of Ben Lerner's subtle, sinuous, and very funny novel *Leaving the Atocha Station*, is a direct descendant of those frustrated Russian antiheroes. He is a young

American poet who, in 2004, is spending a fellowship year in Madrid; his announced project is "a long, research-driven poem" exploring the legacy of the Spanish Civil War. If that "research" sounds like the boxed-up confection that people present in order to get fellowships abroad, that's because it is: Adam knows little about the Civil War and not much about Spanish poetry. In Madrid, like one of Herzen's young men in a dressing gown, he spends his time reading Tolstoy, Ashbery, and Cervantes; going to parties; downing tranquilizers; smoking spliffs; trying and largely failing to love and be loved by two Spanish women, Teresa and Isabel; and dodging the head of the foundation that has funded his sojourn.

At once ideological and post-ideological, vaguely engaged and profoundly spectatorial, charming and loathsome, Adam is a convincing representative of twenty-first-century American *Homo literatus*—a creature of privilege and lassitude, living through a time of inflamed political certainty, yet certain only of his own uncertainty and thus always more easily defined by negation than by affirmation, clearly dedicated to poetry but unable to define or defend it (except to intone emptily that poetry isn't *about* anything) and implicitly nostalgic for earlier, mythical eras of greater strength and surety. He has long worried, for instance, that he is incapable of having "a profound experience of art and I had trouble believing that anyone had, at least anyone I knew." Insofar as he is interested in the arts, he tells us, he is

> interested in the disconnect between my experience of actual artworks and the claims made on their behalf; the closest I'd come to having a profound experience of art was probably the experience of this distance, a profound experience of the absence of profundity.

Adam Gordon may be aimless, but he has a poised intelligence, hospitable to paradox and dialectic, so that his "profound experience of the absence of profundity" becomes, for the reader, an engrossing enquiry into a man's shallow depths; this short novel in which, essentially, nothing much happens never feels like a longer one. Lerner nicely combines the Superfluous Man tradition with the flâneur tradition: Adam is both a thoughtful voyeur and a wicked immoralist, receptive to his new sensations yet thwarted by his old sensibility. As in Lermontov's *A Hero of Our Time* (and as in Fernando Pessoa's *Book of Disquiet*, which might well be this novel's model in the flâneur tradition), the narrator is condemned to wander the darkened corridors of his own authenticity, so that the reader can no longer see him clearly, no longer easily knows what is authentic and what is inauthentic. Like Pechorin, Adam is sometimes bizarrely emotionless, but is also abruptly changeable—sometimes oddly histrionic, and at other moments chronically passive.

He is a cauldron of immiscible liquids. Yet "cauldron" is too violent; Adam's chief vices are his distance from things and his softly defeated temperament. Before he can start anything, he is already measuring his failure and fraudulence. To combat this weakness, he has developed the arts of deception. So as to seem busy when he is in fact idle, he rarely responds to emails, "as I thought this would create the impression I was offline, busy accumulating experience, while in fact I spent a good amount of time online, especially in the late afternoon and early evening, looking at videos of terrible things." At a Madrid party, he is sure that he is not attractive enough for his surroundings, and thus "sets" his face into an interesting rictus: "Luckily I had a strategy for such situations, one I had developed over many visits to New York . . . I opened my eyes a little more widely than normal, opened them to a very specific point, raising my eyebrows and also allowing my mouth to curl up into the implication of a smile. I held this look steady once it had obtained, a look that communicated incredulity cut with familiarity." In order to hide his awkwardness, and also in order to impress Teresa, whom he has just met at this party, he surreptitiously rubs spit on his cheeks (fake tears) and tells her that his mother (alive and well in Kansas) has died. Far from disbelieving him, Teresa responds with stories of her own grief—except that Adam's Spanish is not good enough for him to understand her:

> She described the death of her father when she was a little
> girl, or how the death of her father turns her back into a
> little girl whenever she thinks of it; he had been young
> when he died but seemed old to her now, or he had been
> old when he died but in her memories grew younger. She
> began to quote the clichés people had offered her about
> what time would do, how he was in a better place, or maybe
> she was just offering these clichés to me without irony . . .
> The father had been either a famous painter or collector of
> paintings and she had either become a painter to impress
> him or quit painting because she couldn't deal with the pres-
> sure of his example or because he was such an asshole, al-
> though here I was basically guessing . . .

This gag about losing things in translation, a version of which recurs
throughout the book, is funny, but it is not just comically inert.
Leaving the Atocha Station is, centrally, about communication and
translation, about what can be truthfully expressed, not just in a
foreign tongue, but in one's native language. Lerner, a poet in his
early thirties who has already written three books of verse, is interested in whether words truly belong to us. In that exchange between Adam and Teresa, for instance, Adam's inability to understand
Teresa may be a real inability, or it may be an unwillingness to understand her (because my fake grief is more real than your real grief);
either way, it threatens to make Teresa as inauthentic, as unreal, as
Adam—she may be quoting clichés ironically or just quoting clichés,
who can tell? As the book develops, Adam exaggerates his weakness
with Spanish in order to evade revealing himself. As he jokes about
his relationship with his other girlfriend, Isabel:

> My Spanish was getting better, despite myself, and I expe-
> rienced, with the force of revelation, an obvious realization:
> our relationship largely depended upon my never becom-
> ing fluent, on my having an excuse to speak in enigmatic
> fragments or koans . . . I wondered, as we walked past the

convents and gift shops, how long I could remain in Madrid without crossing whatever invisible threshold of proficiency would render me devoid of interest.

Again, this is funny and wily, but beneath it runs dread, the dread of nullity. For the book's persistent question is: If Adam Gordon were able to summon himself into authenticity, would there be anything to see? Are we in fact constituted by our inauthenticities? When Adam appears on a panel to discuss literature and politics, he has nothing to say, and trots out platitudes that he learns by heart, along with a quotation from Ortega y Gasset ("who I had at one time thought was two people, like Deleuze and Guattari, Calvin and Hobbes"). Initially he is inclined to skip the obligation altogether, because he has nothing to say, because literature isn't politics (so he believes), and because his Spanish isn't good enough. Teresa reminds him that his Spanish is fine, and asks: "When are you going to admit that you can live in this language?" And then asks him, even more acutely, "When are you going to stop pretending that you're only pretending to be a poet?"

But if Adam stopped pretending that he was only pretending to be a poet, he would have to write some poems and confront questions of talent and vocation, let alone the larger difficulty of what it means to write poetry. (Is poetry really never *about* anything?) He is in Madrid when al-Qaeda bombs trains at the Atocha station, yet his detached attitude contrasts painfully with the engagement of his Spanish friends. At one moment, Adam seems to offer a telling confession to the reader. He has always known himself to be a fraud, he says. Who isn't a fraud?

Who wasn't squatting in one of the handful of prefabricated subject positions proffered by capital or whatever you wanted to call it, lying every time she said "I"; who wasn't a bit player in a looped infomercial for the damaged life? If I was a poet, I had become one because poetry, more intensely than any other practice, could not evade its anachronism and marginality and so constituted a kind of acknowledgment of my own preposterousness, admitting my bad faith in good faith, so to speak.

It is a characteristic passage, both in its slipperiness and in its elegant acuity. Adam seems to be offering a fairly familiar postmodern defense of poetry: We are all trapped in modes of inauthenticity, all of us mediated by discourses more powerful than the mere individual's ("capital or whatever you wanted to call it"); the poet cannot evade this mass imprisonment, but can at least write from a position of self-conscious marginality—"admitting my bad faith in good faith, so to speak." It seems a very American, very privileged kind of impotence, and Lerner, I think, deliberately contrasts Adam's expensive weakness with the fervor and political ardency of the Spanish artists and poets whom Adam befriends, a fervor that can seem both naive and courageous alongside Adam's aimless knowingness.

But this is a novel full of deception and self-deception. And, in this larger context, what makes Adam's confession here authentic or believable? Is this a heartfelt admission of impotence, or is it just another stage in the greater inauthenticity? Isn't there something a bit flippant about that formulation "capital or whatever you wanted to call it"? The reader inevitably suspects that this is a confession that deconstructs itself, rendering the confessor not more knowable but less. Adam talks grandly about admitting his bad faith in good faith, but perhaps this is an example of apparently good faith admitting itself in bad faith?

This kind of discussion can make Ben Lerner's novel sound more like heavy going than it is; in fact, like his verse, it has a beguiling mixture of lightness and weight. There are wonderful sentences and jokes on almost every page. Lerner plays a nice game at the expense of W. G. Sebald, for instance, by using grainy photographs with obscure or teasing captions. An aerial picture of a bombed-out Guernica has the caption "I tried hard to imagine my poems or any poems as machines that could make things happen." The effect is less Sebald than the cartoons of Glen Baxter. Throughout the novel,

Adam refers, ironically, to the various stages of his "project," stages that clearly have nothing to do with his official research project. (The third phase of his project seems to be "boredom.") These bogus references culminate, near the end of the book, in the sublime comedy of "I took one of the longer showers of my project."

Nor should the book's own "project," unlike its narrator's, be characterized only in negative terms—by what it refuses or mocks or evades. Lerner is attempting to capture something that most conventional novels, with their cumbersome caravans of plot and scene and "conflict," fail to do: the drift of thought, the unmomentous passage of undramatic life; what he calls several times in the book "life's white machine": "*that other thing*, the sound-absorbent screen, life's white machine, shadows massing in the middle distance . . . the texture of et cetera itself." Reading Tolstoy, Adam reflects that even that great Russian master of the texture of et cetera itself was too dramatic, too tidy, too momentous, too formal: "Not the little lyric miracles and luminous branching injuries, but the other thing, whatever it was, was life, and was falsified by any way of talking or writing or thinking that emphasized sharply localized occurrences in time." This antinarrative, this deliberate avoidance of the conventional grammar of "realism," this reaching for what cannot be disclosed or confessed in narrative, is exactly how *Leaving the Atocha Station* proceeds. Of course, this self-description sounds as much like Virginia Woolf as John Ashbery. But then it is one of the paradoxes of this cunning book that what might seem a skeptically postmodern comedy is also an earnestly old-fashioned seeker of the real—*that other thing*, life's white machine.

PACKING MY
FATHER-IN-LAW'S LIBRARY

"Yet, he said, it is often our mightiest projects that most obviously
betray the degree of our insecurity."   —W. G. Sebald, *Austerlitz*

Route 12D, north of Utica, New York, south of Fort Drum and Car-
thage, runs through poor, shabby countryside. In the unraveled
townships, there are trailers and collapsed farmhouses. Here and
there, a new silo, shining like a chrome torpedo, suggests a fresh
start, or maybe just the arrival of agribusiness. The pall of lost prosperity hangs heavily. Heavily? No, to the skimming driver aiming
elsewhere, it only falls vaguely, or vaguely guiltily.

In Talcottville, an example of that lost prosperity can be seen
from the road—a grand, fine limestone house with a white double-
storied porch. The house is anomalous, both in its size and in its
proximity to the road. But for a long time it must have been the
house's contents that were truly anomalous: a careful, distinguished
library of thousands of volumes. For this was Edmund Wilson's family home, built at the end of the eighteenth century by the Talcotts,
one of whom married Wilson's great-grandfather. It was the place
the literary critic most happily returned to in later life, though
never uncomplicatedly. In his journal of life in Talcottville, *Upstate*,
Wilson expresses his love for the region while grumbling, in an old

man's crooked jabs, about the bad restaurants and intellectually modest company. "In a sense, it has always been stranded," he once wrote of the property. It was here that he died, one morning in June 1972.

I used to drive past Edmund Wilson's house on my way to Canada, where my wife's parents lived after my father-in-law's retirement. Though in apparently reasonable shape, the Wilson home always seemed closed up, forgotten, and in some ways it is the condition of such a house, ignored by a newer road, to seem chronically forgotten. In my mind, I could see into the library, see those shelves and shelves of eloquent, mute books, sunk in themselves like a rotting paper harvest, the ancient, classical authors gesturing in puzzlement to the classical, New World place-names of New York state: Rome, Troy, Ithaca, Syracuse.

My father-in-law died last year, and my mother-in-law is ailing, so this summer we drove up to my parents-in-law's house, to empty it for sale. Again we passed the Wilson house, and again I thought about the silent longevity of his books, and the strange incommunicability of that defunct library, so uselessly posthumous, sleeping by the side of this provincial road. I knew that what awaited us in Canada was the puzzle of how to dispose of my father-in-law's library, a collection of about four thousand books, similarly asleep in a large Victorian house in the flat, open fields of rural Ontario. We would take perhaps a hundred back to Boston, but had no room in our house for more. And then what?

François-Michel Messud, my father-in-law, was a complicated, difficult, brilliant man. He was born in France but spent his early childhood in Algiers, and then, nomadically, in Beirut, Istanbul, and Salonica. In the early 1950s, he came to America, as one of the first Fulbright Scholars, and stayed on to do graduate work in Middle Eastern studies. He started a PhD on Turkish politics, but abandoned it and went into business, a decision probably born of academic anxiety and patriarchal masochism. He was, in fact, not a very engaged businessman, and retained the instincts of a fine scholar and curious traveler. His mind was worldly, with little hospitality toward literature or music or philosophy. What interested him were societies, tribes, roots, exile, journeys, languages. I found him easier to admire than to love, and rather feared him. Educated in an austere French environment, a child of the deprivations of the 1930s and 1940s (he remembered that Jacques Derrida was in the same class as he in junior school in Algiers: "not then a very good pupil"), he could be captious, censorious, bullying. After six in the evening, when cocktails made everything hazardous, one learned to tread carefully, for fear of splashing into an error that might be roughly corrected. Not to know precisely who the Phoenicians were (not to know where they came from and when they flourished); not to know the names of the two most famous mosques in Istanbul, or the history of the civil war in Lebanon, or the ethnic composition of the Albanians; not to recall exactly who said "Beware of Greeks bearing gifts," or to flub a French phrase; not to recall why the Sephardim are called the Sephardim, or to praise something by Bruce Chatwin, was to court swift disdain.

I was grateful not to be his son; his anxious male authority was so different from my reticent father's that I was alternately impressed and alienated by it. Once, early in my marriage, when I had been living in France for a few months and my ability with the language was improving, we were at dinner, and someone at the table praised me for my increased fluency. Everyone else piously agreed. "I don't see why I should praise you yet," my father-in-law broke in; "it's a very small improvement and you have a long way to go." I knew he would say it, hated him for it, agreed with him. He himself liked to recount the story of arriving from France, at Amherst College in 1954, and being told by his American roommate that he would never really master English. "I could speak it fluently by Christmas," he would say. Whether the story was true or not, he spoke perfect English, without a French accent, except for a tendency to pronounce "tongue" as "tong," and "swan" as if he were saying "swam." He had the foreigner's Nabokovian love of exhuming dead puns; was tirelessly amused, for instance, by the fact that the Archbishop of Canterbury is officially known as "Primate of all England," and therefore "should be called Chief Chimp."

Tribes and societies interested him because he grew up in a tribe, left it for a society, and belonged to neither. His tribe was French-Algerian: the *pieds noirs*, the European colonists who went to Algeria in the early nineteenth century, and abandoned it en masse at the end of the war for independence in 1962. Like most *pieds noirs*, he never returned, after independence, to the country of his childhood, so that Algeria—and indeed a whole world of Francophone North African experience—could only be experienced in the mind, always practically lost. France, the larger home, was an ambiguous pleasure, as for many of the returning colonists; though his sister settled in Toulon, he never showed much interest in the country, and as a result was refreshingly free of the usual maddening French superiority. Instead, he came to America, where he lived most of his adult life. But he was not an especially eager immigrant, nor a willing democrat; once the early excitements of the Fulbright and graduate school waned, he settled into a familiar European alienation. He lived a lifetime in America, worked here (though for a French company), paid his taxes, read *The New York Review of Books*, bought shirts and underwear at Brooks Brothers, went to new shows at the Metropolitan Museum, but was not an American. Increasingly, American society bewildered and irritated him; the vulgarities and democratic banalities that are merely routinely annoying to educated Americans, or are written off gladly as part of the price of dynamic vitality, gnawed at him. He floated on top of American life, privileged, wounded, unmoored.

I think that the most important book in his study was a huge atlas, wide open on a wooden lectern, the pages turned daily; sometimes we would catch him standing at the lectern, peering down at the dense, abstract grids of some newfound interest. Travel and reading allowed him to collect a frail library of experience. He traveled widely and systematically. Each trip (to Egypt, Greece, Indonesia, Peru, Morocco, Burma, India, Russia) was thoroughly planned out, prepared for with advance reading and orderly itineraries, and then preserved—usually by his wife—in photographs of buildings and cities: pyramids, temples, mosques, streets, columns, ruins. And he read in the same way: he followed interests, like an army moving along a line of supply, and searched out all the available books on a particular subject. John Berryman made fun of Edmund Wilson's relentlessness, because he used to say, when working on an essay, that he was "working my way through the oeuvre" of a given writer. My father-in-law was no Edmund Wilson (to start with, he never wrote anything), and as he got older and busier, he acquired far more books than he could read, but there was a similar intellectual voracity. The acquisition of a book signaled not just the potential acquisition of knowledge but something like the property rights to a piece of ground: the knowledge became a visitable place. His immediate surroundings—his American or Canadian surroundings—were of no great interest to him; I never heard him speak with any excitement about Manhattan, for instance. But the Alhambra in 1492, or the Salonica he remembered from childhood (the great prewar center of Sephardic Jewry, where, he recalled, there were Yiddish newspapers printed in Hebrew characters), or the Constantinople of the late Byzantine Empire, were . . . what? If I say they were "alive" for him (the usual cliché), then I make him sound more scholarly, and perhaps more imaginative, than he actually was. It would be closer to the truth to say that such places were facts for him, in a way that Manhattan and Toronto (and even Paris) were not.

And yet these facts were largely incommunicable. He spent his time among businessmen, not scholars. He rarely invited people to dinner, and he could become emphatic and monologic. He tended to flourish his facts as querulous challenges rather than as invitations to conversation, though this wasn't perhaps his real intention. So there always seemed to be a quality of self-defense about the greedy rate at which he acquired books, as if he were putting on layers of clothing to protect against the drafts of exile.

Libraries are always paradoxical: they are as personal as the collector, and at the same time represent an ideal statement of knowledge that is impersonal, because it is universal, abstract, and so much larger, in sum, than an individual life. Susan Sontag once said to me that her essays were more intelligent than she was, because she worked so hard at them, and expanded into them over several months of writing. I murmured something banal about how the critic conducts his education in public, and she bristled. Gesturing toward her huge library, she said, with certainty, "That isn't what I meant. I've read all these books." I didn't believe her, since no one has read one's entire library; and it seemed strange of her not to comprehend what I intended to say, which was simply that, like her essays, her library was also more intelligent than she was. This was acutely true of my father-in-law's library, which was not, like Sontag's or Wilson's, a working library, but an underemployed collection for a working mind. My father-in-law's will to completion—his need to encompass a subject by buying all the available books and reading them, and then putting them out—represented an ideal, a kind of abstract utopia, a recovered country free of vicissitudes. A long shelf of careful, brilliant books, all devoted to one subject, was the best possible life that subject could enjoy—a golden life for that subject. Here, for instance, is the first foot of a couple of his shelves on Burma: *Kinship and Marriage in Burma*, by Melford E. Spiro; *Political Systems of Highland Burma*, by E. R. Leach; *Forgotten Land: A Rediscovery of Burma*, by Harriet O'Brien; *Burmese Administrative Cycles: Anarchy and Conquest, c. 1580–1760*, by Victor B. Lieberman; *Return to Burma*, by Bernard Fergusson; *Burma and Beyond*, by Sir J. George Scott; *Finding George Orwell in Burma*, by Emma Larkin; *A History of Modern Burma*, by Michael W. Charney. And here are the first entries of two or three shelves devoted to Judaism and Jewry: *A People Apart: The Jews in Europe, 1789–1939*, by David Vital; *Vilna on the Seine: Jewish Intellectuals in France Since 1968*, by Judith Friedlander; *Moments of Crisis in Jewish-Christian Relations*, by Marc Saperstein; *The Russian Jew Under Tsars and Soviets*, by Salo W. Baron; *Le Salut par les juifs*, by Léon Bloy; *Les Juifs d'Espagne: Histoire d'une diaspora, 1492–1992*, by Henry Méchoulan. He had three or four hundred books on aspects of the Byzantine Empire, and probably twice that number on Islamic and Middle Eastern subjects.

I spent the first few days in Canada cataloging the Middle

Eastern books, in the hope that we might be able to keep the collection on Islam and Muslim societies intact, and perhaps give them to an institution—a college, a school, a local library, even a mosque. The librarian in charge of Islamic books at McGill University had kindly agreed to look at such a catalog. It was slow, intricate, engrossing work—fifty-eight books on Egypt alone, from Alfred Butler's *The Arab Conquest of Egypt and the Last Thirty Years of the Roman Dominion*, first published in 1902, to Florence Nightingale's letters from her journey on the Nile, to Taha Hussein's memoir, *An Egyptian Childhood*, originally published in Cairo in 1932. But it soon became apparent that no one really wants hundreds or thousands of old books. Emails sent to the librarians at the local university were unanswered. Someone told us about a public library in a town in Alberta that had burned to the ground. They were going to rebuild, and needed donations. I was ready to ship hundreds. But the website requested only books published in the last two years, which excluded almost everything in my father-in-law's library. Kingston, Ontario, the nearest big town, and the home of Queen's University, had a thriving secondhand book business, so I called one of those shops. Would the owner like to come out to a rural house, about forty minutes from the city, and look over a good library of several thousand volumes? The answer was sympathetic and dismaying. There used to be twelve secondhand bookshops in Kingston, the bookseller told me, and now there are four. "We have the storage space, but no money. The shop along the street has the money to buy books, but no space. This summer at least three big private collections have come onto the market. So I'm afraid it's just not worth it for me to come out to a house and look at four thousand books." It wasn't clear who was supposed to feel sorrier for whom.

We had a couple of breaks. An online bookseller, who deals in rare books and first editions, came and picked through what interested him, and filled his old station wagon with boxes. A few days later, an English bibliophile, who teaches philosophy at Queen's, did the same. I enjoyed their obvious excitement, my enjoyment tempered by the sensation that the library was suffering death by a thousand cuts. For in any private library, the totality of books is meaningful, while each individual volume is relatively meaningless. Or rather, once separated from its family, each individual book becomes relatively meaningless in relation to the original collector, but suddenly newly meaningful as the totality of the author's mind. The lovely book *Mecca: A Literary History of the Muslim Holy Land*, by the great New York University scholar F. E. Peters, says little about my father-in-law, except that he bought it; but it represents a distillation of Professor Peters's lifework. In this strange way, our libraries are like certain paintings that, as you get closer to the canvas, become separate and unreadable blobs and daubs of paint.

And in this way, I began to think, our libraries perhaps say nothing very particular about us at all. Each brick in the wall of a library is a borrowed brick, not one made by the bricklayer: several thousand people, perhaps several hundred thousand, own books by F. E. Peters. If I were led into Edmund Wilson's library in Talcottville, from which all the books written by Wilson had been removed, would I know that it was Edmund Wilson's library, and not Alfred Kazin's or F. W. Dupee's? We tend to venerate libraries once we know whose they are, like admiring a famous philosopher's eyes or a ballet dancer's foot. Pushkin had about a thousand non-Russian books in his library, and the editor of *Pushkin on Literature* helpfully lists all those foreign books, from Balzac and Stendhal to Shakespeare and Voltaire. She confidently announces, "Much can be learnt of a man from his choice of books," and then unwittingly contradicts herself by adding that Pushkin, like many Russians of his class, read mostly in French: "The ancient classics, the Bible, Dante, Machiavelli, Luther, Shakespeare, Leibnitz, Byron . . . all are predominantly in French." This sounds like the library of an extremely well-read Russian gentleman, circa 1830—the kind of reading that Pushkin gave to his standard-issue Russian romantic, Eugene Onegin. But what is especially Pushkinian about the library? What does it tell us about his mind?

Theodor Adorno, in his essay "On Popular Music," pours disdain on the way in which, when we hear a popular hit, we think we are making a personal possession of it ("That's *my* song, the song that was playing when I first kissed X," say), while in fact this "apparently isolated, individual experience of a particular song," is being stupidly shared with millions of other people—so that the listener merely "feels safety in numbers and follows the crowd of all those who have heard the song before and who are supposed to have made its reputation." Adorno, the grand snob, considers this a grave deception. But in a digital age, we surely treat serious classical music in just the same way. And how is a library—in one way of thinking about it, at least—anything but the same kind of self-deception? Isn't a private library simply a universal legacy pretending to be an individual one?

Adorno hated that capitalism, and the branch of it he called the Culture Industry, turned impalpabilities like artworks into things. But there is no escaping that books are most definitely things, and I was struck, working through my father-in-law's books, how quickly I became alienated from their rather stupid materiality. I began to resent his avariciousness, which resembled, in death, any other kind of avariciousness for objects. Again and again, his daughters had begged him to "do something" about his books before he died. Meaning: *we can't take them.* If he knew that, he did nothing about it, and sorting out his library became sadly indistinguishable from sorting out his pictures or his CDs or his shirts. And though my task was very easy compared to my mourning wife's, the experience made me resolve not to leave behind such burdens for my children after my death.

I remember hearing about an accident that befell the scholar and critic Frank Kermode a few years ago. He was moving house and had put all his most precious books (his fiction, his poetry, signed first editions, and the like) in boxes, on the street. The garbage collectors came by and mistakenly took the boxes, leaving Kermode with a great deal of contemporary literary theory. The story once seemed horrifying to me, and now seems almost wonderful. To be abruptly lightened like that, so that one's descendants might not be lingeringly burdened! After all, can I really contend that my own collection of almost unkillable, inert books, ranged on shelves like some bogus declaration of achievement (for surely the philistine is *right* to ask the man of culture, "Have you really read all these?"), tells my children anything more about me than my much smaller collection of postcards and photographs? (W. G. Sebald's work explores this paradox of permanence: a single photograph of a book-filled room might be more redolent of its owner than the very books themselves.)

The more time I spent with my father-in-law's books, the more profoundly they seemed not to be revealing but hiding him, like some word-wreathed, untranslatable mausoleum. His Algerian childhood, his interesting mind, the diversion of that mind into run-of-the-mill business, his isolation and estrangement in America, his confidence and shyness, pugilism and anxiety, the drinking and the anger and the passion and the pressurized responsibility of his daily existence: of course, in some general way, these thousands of volumes—neatly systematic, proudly comprehensive—incarnated the shape of this life, but not the angles of his facets. The books somehow made him smaller, not larger, as if they were whispering: "What a little thing a single human life is, with all its busy, ephemeral, pointless projects." All ruins say this, yet we strangely persist in pretending that books are not ruins, not broken columns.

One of my father-in-law's busy, ephemeral projects fell out of a book about Greek history. A single sheet of paper, with notes written in his careful hand. The date was 2/1/95, and the notes were preparation for a trip to Greece: "History of Ancient Greece. Jean Hatzfeld and Andre Aymard, N.Y., Norton 1966." Under this heading were lines in English:

—Greeks establish themselves during second millennium BC: Greece, Black Sea, Asia Minor, Islands, S.Italy.
—Common language and tradition but very divided. *Hellas* = culture, civiliz. ('Hellenes' does not come until 800 BC. 'Greek' is Roman.)

  —Geographic identity between Greece and Western
Asia Minor: the sea inducted [?] a <u>subsidence</u> which broke
up a continent of recent formation and whose structure was
very complicated—fjords, deep bays, mountains, capes,
islands.

And so on, down the page. Overleaf, he had made a rough drawing of ancient Greece and western Asia Minor (present-day Turkey).
It was his entire world: on one side the Mediterranean, and on the
other the Aegean, west and east. He had marked the most famous
places and circled them: on the Asia Minor side, Aeolia, Lycia, Troy,
Smyrna; and on the Greek side, the honeyed, haunted, lost names:
Illyria, Attica, Argolis, Corinth, Arcadia.

ACKNOWLEDGMENTS

All these essays appeared between 2004 and 2011, in *The New Republic*, *The New Yorker*, and the *London Review of Books*. I am very grateful to the editors and literary editors of these publications, and in particular to Henry Finder and David Remnick at *The New Yorker*, and to Mary-Kay Wilmers at the *London Review of Books*.

The essay on Sebald's *Austerlitz* was first published as an introduction to a new edition of that novel (Random House, 2011); the title essay, on Keith Moon, was also published in *Best Music Writing 2011* (Da Capo, 2011); the essay on George Orwell was also published in *The Best American Essays 2010* (Houghton Mifflin Harcourt, 2010); the essay on Ian McEwan was first delivered as the inaugural Graham Storey Lecture at Cambridge University's Faculty of English. I am grateful to Stefan Collini and Adrian Poole, my hosts.